D1647911

**Donated**
*To The Library by*

MICHAEL BARON

TO CELEBRATE HIS HONORARY

CHAIRMANSHIP OF

NATIONAL LIBRARY WEEK

APRIL 14, 1999

© DEMCO, INC.—Archive Safe

# VIRTUAL ROOTS

# VIRTUAL ROOTS

*A guide to genealogy and local history on the World Wide Web*

## THOMAS JAY KEMP

*Scholarly Resources Inc.*
*Wilmington, Delaware*

© 1997 by Scholarly Resources Inc.
All rights reserved
First published 1997
Printed and bound in the United States of America

Scholarly Resources Inc.
104 Greenhill Avenue
Wilmington, DE  19805-1897

**Library of Congress Cataloging-in-Publication Data**

Kemp, Thomas Jay.
    Virtual roots : a guide to genealogy and local history on the World Wide Web /
Thomas J. Kemp.
        p.    cm.
    ISBN 0-8420-2718-1 (alk. paper). — ISBN 0-8420-2720-3 (pbk. : alk. paper)
    1. Genealogy—computer network resources—Directories.  I. Title.
    CS21.K46    1997
    929'.1'028—dc21                                                           97-18954
                                                                                CIP

*Dedicated to my wife Vi*
*and children Andrew and Sarah*

A Family without a Genealogy Is Like a
Country without a History—Traditional Chinese Saying

# About the Author

THOMAS JAY KEMP is the head of the Special Collections Department of the University of South Florida Library in Tampa. He has served as the chair of the Council of National Library and Information Associations, chair of the History Section of the American Library Association, and president of the American Society of Indexers. He is a member of the Local History Committee of the American Library Association and is the author of numerous books including the *International Vital Records Handbook*, the *Connecticut Researcher's Handbook*, and *The 1995 Genealogy Annual: A Bibliography of Published Sources*.

# Contents

## Family Associations

# Introduction

Virtual Roots is a road map and detailed directory that provides more than one thousand of the best genealogy and local history sites on the Internet. It not only lists websites from around the world but also outlines the important resources and guides found at each site. With more than one million websites or home pages currently on the Internet, *Virtual Roots* allows the user to focus on the best sites, plan research offline, and save time and money when going online. The Internet has made the world much smaller, communication more instantaneous, and the searching of data from the world's archives a practical reality.

The Internet sites listed in *Virtual Roots* are divided into four sections: **General Subjects**, **United States**, **International**, and **Family Associations**. Included with each entry is the e-mail and postal address, along with the telephone and/or fax number, when available, for the reference staff of each website. This information enables the researcher to immediately contact archives, libraries, or societies around the world while still viewing the repository's website on the computer. All of this vital data is brought together in one handy directory, thereby making it the most comprehensive all-in-one guide to collections and website addresses currently available to genealogists.

**General Subjects** includes sites and repositories that focus on a specific category such as church or military records. Entries in the **United States** section include the official state home page, state archives, state library, state genealogical, and state historical society sites, along with other important websites for that state. Sites for national libraries, archives, and record offices, as well as genealogical and historical societies from around the world, are listed in the **International** section. Finally, **Family Associations** provides websites that concentrate on a specific family or surname. Of the more than 1,000 sites described here, 10 are designated Extraordinary Sites and over 120 as Outstanding Sites.

Genealogists and librarians will find many useful sites that they will want to bookmark for easy reference. An online list of some of the more popular sites can be found on the University of South Florida's Genealogy Resources page at [http://www.lib.usf.edu/spccoll/genea.html]. The Family Tree Maker's site can be used to quickly find blank 1790–1920 federal census forms at [http://www.familytreemaker.com/00000061.html], or blank family tree charts on the Ancestors, KBYU/PBS site at [http://www2.kbyu.byu.edu/ancestors/teachersguide/charts-records.html], as well as links for a perpetual calendar by Presstar Printing Corporation at [http://www.presstar.com/w3magic/cgi-bin/homepage.cgi?calendar]. On the German Genealogy Home Page at [http://www.genealogy.com/gene/ghlp/let-pas.html], you will find sample letters for writing to European churches in seven languages. The Social Security Death Index can be found on both the Ancestry, Inc. site at [http://www.ancestry.com/ssdi/] and on the Everton's Genealogical Helper Online site at [http://rro.everton.com/ssmdi.html]. Beginners also can find information on how to start their genealogy research by using the Family History Library guide at [http://www.lds.org/Family_History/How_Do_I_Begin.html], the Everton's Genealogical Helper Online at [http://www.everton.com/], or Ancestry's Family History Academy at [http://www.ancestry.com/home/academy.htm].

The world's archives, libraries, and genealogical societies have begun to use the Internet to present their research guides and holdings, allowing researchers to visit those libraries without leaving home. The Federation of East European Family History Societies at [http://dcn. davis.ca.us/~feefhs/], JewishGen: The Home of Jewish Genealogy at [http://www.jewishgen. org/], and the Australian Family History Compendium at [http://www.cohsoft.com.au/afhc/] are outstanding examples of websites that provide valuable research tips and access that make it easy for genealogists, local historians, and librarians to have instant availability to current information. The California Historical Society at [http://www.calhist.org/] and the Vermont Historical Society at [http://www.cit.state.vt.us:80/vhs/] demonstrate how a lot of information can be easily and logically arranged for the online researcher to obtain basic information quickly and effortlessly.

The Library of Congress at [http://lcweb.loc.gov/] has included many guides and indexes such as those on Afro-American Genealogical Research, Civil War Photographs, and Danish Immigration to America, all of which provide excellent resources and expert advice on a wide range of genealogical topics. The National Archives and Records Administration at [http:// www.nara.gov/] also has added many of its guides to the Internet, including its microfilm catalog guides for Black Studies, Census Records, Genealogical and Biographical Research, Immigrant and Passenger Arrival Records, and Military Service Records. In addition, researchers can obtain current information about important annual genealogical meetings of the National Genealogical Society, the Federation of Genealogical Societies, the GenTech Conference, and the American Library Association.

Several other excellent and important sites serve as mega-listings of genealogical websites. The USGenWeb Project, for instance, at [http://www.usgenweb.com/index.html] has been a strong force in making genealogical resources electronically available by linking volunteers and genealogical societies from around the country. The links on George Archer's NetGuide on the National Genealogical Society site at [http://www.genealogy.org/~ngs/] also provide outstanding sources, as do the Utah State Archives links at [http://www.archives.state.ut.us], the large and growing Cyndi's List of Genealogy Sites on the Internet at [http://www.oz.net/ ~cyndihow/sites.htm], and RootsWeb Genealogical Data Cooperative at [http://www.rootsweb. com/]. An increasing number of online genealogical newsletters are helpful in keeping researchers current. For example, *Eastman's Online Genealogy Newsletter* at [http://www. ancestry.com/home/times.htm] is timely, informative, and can be automatically sent by e-mail, for free, each week to anyone who requests it. Also at that site are *Shaking Your Family Tree* and *DearMYRTLE*. The *Journal of Online Genealogy* at [http://www.onlinegenealogy.com/] provides authoritative and essential reading. The articles in Everton's Genealogical Helper Online at [http://www.everton.com/b1.htm], Family Tree Maker Online at [http://www.family treemaker.com/], and AGLL's *Heritage Quest* at [http://www. agll.com/mag/mag.html] include useful articles as well.

Two impressive sites that demonstrate the potential of the Internet for the genealogist and local historian are The Valley of the Shadow at [http://jefferson.village.Virginia.EDU/vshadow2/contents.html] and Historical Records of Dukes County, Massachusetts, at [http://www.vineyard.net/vineyard/history/]. The first site brings together diaries, photographs, newspaper accounts, family bible records, and a host of other documents that focus on Franklin County, Pennsylvania, and Augusta County, Virginia, just before and during the Civil War. Here the researcher can instantly go from an early diary to see a photograph of its writer, switch to the entry in the Federal Census Records, and then contrast that diary entry with an account from that week's newspaper, all at the click of a button and without leaving home. Similarly, the Historical Records of Dukes County, Massachusetts, site lists indexes to census, military, newspaper, and family records, along with maps and related documents to provide a fairly comprehensive view of the county's genealogical record. One especially convenient feature is that the researcher can easily switch from viewing the census indexes in alphabetical order to the arrangement that the census taker originally used when compiling the census from 1790 to 1910.

It is the author's hope that this guide will assist researchers in promptly finding the answers to their genealogical questions as they communicate with societies, archives, and repositories around the world.

# Glossary of Internet Terms

**e-mail** Electronic mail that can be sent and received from anywhere in the world.

**HTML (HyperText Markup Language)** Language used to give instructions to the computer for mounting images and documents on the Internet.

**HTTP (HyperText Transfer Protocol)** System used to find documents on the World Wide Web.

**Internet, Web, World Wide Web, or WWW** Global network that links computers allowing them to send, post, and receive information. The sites in this book are all part of the Internet.

**Listserv** Program that automatically receives and forwards e-mail messages to a group of subscribers. Often used by family associations to keep in touch with their members.

**Telnet** Service that allows your computer to log on to computers anywhere in the world. Many librarians use Telnet to dial into their online card catalog to find what materials are held in their library.

**URL (Uniform Resource Locator)** Computer address of a website.

**Website** Pages of information prepared by archives, libraries, genealogical societies, or individuals.

# GENERAL SUBJECTS

# AFRICAN AMERICANS

## African American Heritage Preservation Foundation, Inc.
http://www.preservenet.cornell.edu/aahpf/homepage.htm

420 Seventh Street N.W., Suite 501
Washington, DC 20004

E-mail  ReneeI@aol.com.

Franklin Street School (New Jersey)
 [http://www.preservenet.cornell.edu/aahpf/franklin.htm]
John Mercer Langston (Virginia)
 [http://www.preservenet.cornell.edu/aahpf/jml_text.htm]
Stanton Family Cemetery (Virginia)
 [http://www.preservenet.cornell.edu/aahpf/stanton.htm]
Thomas Chapel and Cemetery (Virginia)
 [http://www.preservenet.cornell.edu/aahpf/chapel.htm]

## Afrigeneas
http://www.msstate.edu/Archives/History/afrigen/

Historical Text Archive
Mississippi State University

E-mail  afrigeneas@msstate.edu

African-American Bibliography
 [http://www.msstate.edu/Archives/History/afrigen/bib.txt]
North Carolina Black Craftsmen
 [http://www.msstate.edu/Archives/History/afrigen/craft.html]

## Lest We Forget
http://206.21.13.5:80/people/lwf/

P.O. Box 26148
Trotwood, OH  45426-0148

E-mail  lwf@coax.net

Links, Military
 [http://206.21.13.5:80/people/lwf/portrait.htm]
Links, Organizations
 [http://206.21.13.5:80/people/lwf/organiz.htm]

# ARCHIVES

## ARMA, Association of Records Managers and Administrators, Inc.
http://www.arma.org/hq/

4200 Somerset Drive, Suite 215
Prairie Village, KS 66208

Phone  (913) 341-3808
       (800) 422-2762
Fax    (913) 341-3742
E-mail  76015.3151@COMPUSERVE.COM

Certified Records Manager
 [http://www.arma.org/hq/crminfo.html]
Chapter Directory
 [http://www.arma.org/hq/chappres.html]
Chapter Links
 [http://www.arma.org/index.html]

Other Links
   [http://www.arma.org/hq/links.html]

## International Council on Archives     http://www.archives.ca/ica/english.html

| | |
|---|---|
| Secretariat | Phone   (011) +33 1 40.27.63.06 |
| 60, rue des Francs-Bourgeois | Fax     (011) +33 1 42.72.20.65 |
| 75003 Paris, France | E-mail  100640.54@compuserve.com |

Directory
   [http://www.archives.ca/ica/directory/archive.html]

## Midwest Archives Conference
   http://www.csd.uwm.edu/Dept/Library/arch/mac/mac.htm

| | |
|---|---|
| Marquette University | E-mail  mv9@gml.lib.uwm.edu |
| Archives/Memorial Library | |
| 1415 West Wisconsin Avenue | |
| Milwaukee, WI 53201 | |

Journal of the MAC, Newsletter
   [http://www.csd.uwm.edu/Dept/Library/arch/mac/ai.htm]

## National Association of Government Archives and Records Administrators
   http://www.nagara.org/

| | |
|---|---|
| 48 Howard Street | Phone   (518) 463-8644 |
| Albany, NY 12207 | Fax     (518) 463-8656 |
| | E-mail  nagara@caphill.com |

Institutional Member Internet Sites
   [http://www.nagara.org/websites.html]
Other Links
   [http://www.nagara.org/affiliations.html]

## *Extraordinary Site*

## National Archives and Records Administration     http://www.nara.gov/

**Central Plains Region (Kansas City)**     http://www.nara.gov/nara/regional/06nsgil.html
2312 East Bannister Road     Phone   (816) 926-6272
Kansas City, MO 64131     Fax     (816) 926-6982
E-mail  archives@kansascity.nara.gov

**Mid-Atlantic Region (Philadelphia)**     http://www.nara.gov/nara/regional/03nsgil.html
Ninth and Market Streets     Phone   (215) 597-3000
Philadelphia, PA 19107     Fax     (215) 597-2303
E-mail  archives@philarch.nara.gov

**Northeast Region (Boston)**     http://www.nara.gov/nara/regional/01nsbgil.html
380 Trapelo Road     Phone   (617) 647-8100
Waltham, MA 02154-6399     Fax     (617) 647-8460
E-mail  archives@waltham.nara.gov

**Northeast Region (Pittsfield)**     http://www.nara.gov/nara/regional/01nspgil.html
100 Dan Fox Drive     Phone   (413) 445-6885, x26
Pittsfield, MA 01201-8230     Fax     (413) 445-7599
E-mail  archives@pittsfield.nara.gov

**Northeast Region (New York)**
201 Varick Street
New York, NY 10014

http://www.nara.gov/nara/regional/02nsgil.html
Phone   (212) 337-1300
Fax      (212) 337-1306
E-mail   archives@newyork.nara.gov

**Great Lakes Region (Chicago)**
7358 South Pulaski Road
Chicago, IL 60629

http://www.nara.gov/nara/regional/05nsgil.html
Phone   (312) 581-7816
Fax      (312) 353-1294
E-mail   archives@chicago.nara.gov

**Pacific Region (Laguna Niguel)**
24000 Avila Road
Laguna Niguel, CA 92677

http://www.nara.gov/nara/regional/09nslgil.html
Phone   (714) 360-2641
Fax      (714) 360-2644
E-mail   archives@laguna.nara.gov

**Pacific Region (San Bruno)**
1000 Commodore Drive
San Bruno, CA 94066

http://www.nara.gov/nara/regional/09nssgil.html
Phone   (415) 876-9009
Fax      (415) 876-9233
E-mail   archives@sanbruno.nara.gov

**Pacific Alaska Region (Seattle)**
6125 Sand Point Way N.E.
Seattle, WA  98115

http://www.nara.gov/nara/regional/10nsgil.html
Phone   (206) 526-6507
Fax      (206) 526-4344
E-mail   archives@seattle.nara.gov

**Pacific Alaska Region (Anchorage)**
654 West Third Avenue
Anchorage, AK 99501-2145

http://www.nara.gov/nara/regional/11nsgil.html
Phone   (907) 271-2441
Fax      (907) 271-2442
E-mail   archives@alaska.nara.gov

**Rocky Mountain Region (Denver)**
Denver Federal Center, Building 48
Denver, CO 80225

http://www.nara.gov/nara/regional/08nsgil.html
Phone   (303) 236-0817
Fax      (303) 236-9354
E-mail   archives@denver.nara.gov

**Southeast Region (Atlanta)**
1557 St. Joseph Avenue
East Point, GA 30344-2593

http://www.nara.gov/nara/regional/04nsgil.html
Phone   (404) 763-7477
Fax      (404) 763-7033
E-mail   archives@atlanta.nara.gov

**Southwest Region (Fort Worth)**
501 West Felix Street, Building 1, Dock 1
P.O. Box 62165
Fort Worth, TX 76115

http://www.nara.gov/nara/regional/07nsgil.html
Phone   (817) 334-552
Fax      (817) 334-5621
E-mail   archives@ftworth.nara.gov

Black Studies
    [gopher://clio.nara.gov/11/about/publ/micro/blkstd]
Census, Microfilm Catalogs
    [gopher://clio.nara.gov/11/genealog/holdings/catalogs/census]
Collections
    [http://www.nara.gov/nara/historical.html]
Federal Court Records
    [gopher://clio.nara.gov/11/about/publ/micro/federal]
Federal Records Centers
    [http://www.nara.gov/nara/frc/frchome.html]

Federal Records Guide
    [http://gopher.nara.gov:70/1/inform/guide]
Genealogical and Biographical Research, Microfilm Catalog
    [gopher://clio.nara.gov/11/genealog/holdings/catalogs/research]
Genealogy Holdings
    [http://www.nara.gov/nara/menus/genealog.html]
Government Information Locator Service (GILS)
    [http://www.nara.gov/gils/gils.html]
Immigrant and Passenger Arrivals, Microfilm Catalog
    [http://www.nara.gov/genealog/holdings/catalogs/ipcat/ipcat.html]
Library Resources for Administrative History
    [http://www.nara.gov/nara/naralibrary/govdocs/govinfo0.html]
Military Service Records, Microfilm Catalog
    [http://www.nara.gov/nara/menus/miltoc.html]
Motion Picture, Sound, and Video Research
    [http://www.nara.gov/nara/nn/nns/room.html]
NARA Archival Information Locator, NAIL
    [http://www.nara.gov/nara/nail.html]
National Historical Publications and Records Commission
    [http://www.nara.gov/nara/nhprc/]
NHPRC Newsletter, Annotation
    [http://www.nara.gov/nara/nhprc/annotation/index.html]
Native Americans, Microfilm Catalog
    [gopher://clio.nara.gov/11/about/publ/micro/amind]
Photographs
    [http://www.nara.gov/nara/nn/nns/nnsp.html]
President John F. Kennedy Assassination Files
    [http://www.nara.gov/nara/jfk/jfk_search.html]
Presidential Libraries
    [http://www.nara.gov/nara/president/address.html]
Quarterly, Articles on NARA
    [http://www.nara.gov/nara/naralibrary/journals/qcomp96.html]
Reference at Your Desk
    [http://www.nara.gov/nara/naralibrary/weblinks/yourdesk.html]
Regional Archives
    [http://www.nara.gov/nara/regional/nsrmenu.html]
Table of Contents Service
    [http://www.nara.gov/nara/naralibrary/journals/tctbl.html]

## New England Archivists            http://www.lib.umb.edu/newengarch/

c/o Massachusetts Archives            Phone   (207) 786-6354
Office of the Secretary of State      Fax      (207) 786-6035
220 Morrissey Boulevard               E-mail  cbeam@abacus.bates.edu
Boston, MA 02125

NEA, Newsletter
    [http://www.lib.umb.edu/newengarch/newsletter.html]

## Northwest Archivists              http://www.orst.edu/Dept/archives/misc/nwa.html

1206 S.W. Myrtle Drive                E-mail  kotto@mt.net
Portland, OR 97201

Officers and Board Members
    [http://www.orst.edu/Dept/archives/misc/nwa_officers.html]

## Society of American Archivists          http://www.archivists.org/

600 South Federal, Suite 504              Phone   (312) 922-0140
Chicago, IL 60605                         E-mail  info@archivists.org

Code of Ethics
    [http://www.archivists.org/oldpage/ethics.html]
Donating Family Papers, How to
    [http://www.archivists.org/oldpage/family.html]
Evaluating Archival Institutions
    [http://www.archivists.org/oldpage/evalgui.html]

## Society of Southwest Archivists        http://www.tulane.edu/~lmiller/SSA.html

P.O. Box 569                              E-mail  lmiller@mailhost.tcs.tulane.edu
Liberty TX 77575-0569

Southwestern Archivist, Newsletter
    [http://www.tulane.edu/~lmiller/SWA.html]

# CEMETERIES

## Association for Gravestone Studies      http://www.berkshire.net/ags/

278 Main Street, Suite 207                Phone   (413) 772-0836
Greenfield, MA 01301                      E-mail  ags@berkshire.net

AGS Online Bulletin Board
    [http://apocalypse.berkshire.net/ags/wwwboard/]
Links, Cemetery Related Sites
    [http://www.berkshire.net/ags/links.shtml]
Markers, Journal. Table of Contents
    [http://www.berkshire.net/ags/markers.shtml]
Overview
    [http://www.berkshire.net/ags/ags.shtml]
Publications List
    [http://www.berkshire.net/ags/ags-pub.shtml]
Slide Programs and Video Cassettes
    [http://www.berkshire.net/ags/ags-av.shtml]

# CENSUS RECORDS

*Outstanding Site*

## RootsWeb Genealogical Data Cooperative    http://www.rootsweb.com/

P.O. Box 6798                             E-mail  Webspinner@rootsweb.com
Frazier Park, CA 93222-6798                       rsl@rootsweb.com

Soundex Conversion Program
    [http://searches.rootsweb.com/cgi-bin/Genea/soundex.sh]

## U.S. Census Bureau                    http:www.census.gov

Washington, DC 20233

Age Search Service
   [http://www.census.gov/genealogy/www/agesearch.html]
Frequently Occurring Names
   [http://www.census.gov/genealogy/www/freqnames.html]
Genealogy Guide
   [http://www.census.gov/genealogy/www/]

# CHURCH RECORDS

## *Adventist*

### Adventist Heritage Center
   http://www.andrews.edu/library/collections/departments/ahc.html#Mission

Andrews University                       Phone   (616) 471-3274
James White Library                      Fax     (616) 471-6166
Berrien Springs, MI 49104-1400           E-mail  fordjim@andrews.edu
                                                 CompuServe: 74532,153

Adventist Libraries
   [http://www.andrews.edu/library/collections/departments/sail.html]
Association of Seventh-day Adventist Librarians
   [http://www.andrews.edu/asdal/]
Holdings
   [http://www.andrews.edu/library/collections/departments/ahc.html#General]
Obituary Index
   [http://143.207.5.3:82/search/b]
Seventh-day Adventist Periodical Index
   [http://143.207.5.3:82/screens/opacmenu.html]

### Seventh-day Adventist Church        http://www.adventist.org/

12501 Old Columbia Pike                  Phone   (301) 680-6000
Silver Spring, MD  20904-6600            Fax     (301) 680-6090
                                         E-mail  webmaster@adventist.org

History
   [http://www.adventist.org/history.html]

## *Assembly of God*

### Assemblies of God Archives          http://www.ag.org/

1445 Boonville Avenue                    E-mail  wwarner@missions.ag.org
Springfield, MO 65802-1894

Links, Assembly of God Congregations
   [http://www.ag.org/agchurch.htm]
Links, Assembly of God Sites etc.
   [http://www.ag.org/agsites.htm]

# *Baptist*
## SBCNet
http://www.sbcnet.org/index.htm

Home Mission Board
4200 North Point Parkway
Alpharetta, GA 30202-4176

E-mail  hmb@america.net

Directory, State Conventions
[http://www.sbcnet.org/resource.htm]
Meet Southern Baptists
[http://www.sbcnet.org/all.htm]

# *The Church of Jesus Christ of Latter-day Saints*
## Brigham Young University
http://www.byu.edu/newhome.html

Utah Valley Regional FHC
Harold B. Lee Library, 4th floor
Provo, UT 84601

Phone   (801) 378-6200
E-mail  diane_parkinson@byu.edu

Ancestors, KBYU/PBS Series
[http://www2.kby.byu.edu/ancestors/]
BYU Family History Society
[http://reled.byu.edu/jsblab/society.htm]
Family History Centers Worldwide
[http://www.lib.byu.edu/~uvrfhc/states.html]
Family History Technology Lab
[http://issl.cs.byu.edu/FHiTL/homepage.html]
Utah Valley Regional Family History Center
[http://www.lib.byu.edu/~uvrfhc/]

## *Outstanding Site*

## The Church of Jesus Christ of Latter-day Saints
http://www.lds.org/

35 North West Temple Street
Salt Lake City, UT 84150

Phone   (888) 537-7111
        (800) 346-6044

Family History Library

Phone   (801) 240-2323
Fax     (801) 240-1216

All Family History Centers Listed by State
[http://www.deseretbook.com/famhis/]
All Local Chapels and Meetinghouses
[http://www.deseretbook.com/locate/]
The Family: A Proclamation to the World
[http://www.lds.org/Policy/Family.html]
Family History Library Research Outlines
[file://hipp.etsu.edu/pub/genealogy/LDStext/]
Genealogical Society of Utah
[http://www.fgs.org/~fgs/soc0068.htm]
How Do I Begin?
[http://www.lds.org/Family_History/How_Do_I_Begin.html]

Welcome to the Family History Center™
   [http://www.lds.org/Welcome_to_FamHist/Welcome_to_FamHist.html]
What Is a Family History Center™?
   [http://www.lds.org/Family_History/What_is.html]
Why Family History?
   [http://www.lds.org/Family_History/Why_Family_History.html]
Why Family History? by David Mayfield
   [http://reled.byu.edu/jsblab/why.htm]

## Mormon Pioneer Trail Home Page      http://www.omahafreenet.org/ofn/trails/

E-mail   dbylund@mail.unmc.edu

Links, LDS Heritage Sites
   [http://www.omahafreenet.org/ofn/trails/]

## National Society of the Sons of Utah Pioneers      http://www.uvol.com/sup/

3301 East 2920 South                    E-mail   editor@uvol.com
Salt Lake City, UT 84109-4260

Overview
   [http://www.uvol.com/sup/]

## Tracing Mormon Pioneers      http://www.vii.com/~nelsonb/pioneer.htm

Emigration Card Index
   [http://www.vii.com/~nelsonb/pioneer.htm#europe]
Handcart Companies
   [http://www.vii.com/~nelsonb/handcart.htm]
Mormon Emigrant Ships
   [http://www.vii.com/~nelsonb/pioneer.htm#ships]
Pioneer Companies
   [http://www.vii.com/~nelsonb/company.htm]
Sources for Tracing a Pioneer
   [http://www.vii.com/~nelsonb/pioneer.htm#sources]

## Utah Genealogical Association   http://www.infouga.org/

P.O. Box 1144                       Phone   (888) 463-6842
Salt Lake City, UT 84110-1144       E-mail  perkes@mail.utah.uswest.net

Overview
   [http://www.infouga.org/

# Congregational

*Outstanding Site*

## Congregational Library and Archives      http://www.tiac.net/users/lplato/mainmenu.htm

14 Beacon Street                    Phone   (617) 523-0470
Boston, MA 02108                    Fax     (617) 523-0491
                                    E-mail  blwhfw@aol.com1
                                            lplato@tiac.net

American Congregational Association Records
    [http://www.tiac.net/users/lplato/findaid/aca.htm]
Guide, Associations, Conventions, etc.
    [http://www.tiac.net/users/lplato/assocrec.htm]
Guide, Local Church Records
    [http://www.tiac.net/users/lplato/guidech.htm]
Guide, Missionary, Charitable etc.
    [http://www.tiac.net/users/lplato/organrec.htm]
Guide, Other Records
    [http://www.tiac.net/users/lplato/other.htm]
Guide, Personal Papers
    [http://www.tiac.net/users/lplato/papers.htm]
Women, Collections Relating to
    [http://www.tiac.net/users/lplato/women.htm]

# *Evangelical Covenant*
## Covenant Archives and Historical Library
    http://www.northpark.edu/library/Archives/index.html#anchor66123

| 3225 West Foster Avenue | Phone   (312) 244.6224 |
| Chicago, IL 60625 | Fax     (312) 267.2362 |
| | E-mail  tjohnso1@gumby.npcts.edu |

Guide
    [http://www.northpark.edu/library/Covenant_Archives/churchis.html]

# *Greek Orthodox*
## Greek Orthodox Archdiocese of America     http://www.goarch.org/

8 East 79th Street         E-mail  archdiocese@goarch.org
New York, NY 10022

Archives
    [HTTP://WWW.GOARCH.ORG/goa/departments/]
Links, Diocese
    [HTTP://WWW.GOARCH.ORG/goa/]
Links, Other Orthodox Related Sites
    [HTTP://WWW.GOARCH.ORG/goa/relatedpages]
Orthodox Observer, Journal
    [HTTP://WWW.GOARCH.ORG/goa/observer/]

# *Jewish*
## American Jewish Archives     http://members.gnn.com/apeck3101/index.htm

| 3101 Clifton Avenue | Phone   (513) 221-7444 Ext. 403 |
| Cincinnati, OH 45220-2488 | Fax     (513) 221-7812 |
| | E-mail  abraham.peck@uc.edu |

Archives
    [http://members.gnn.com/apeck3101/collect.htm#top]
Cincinnati Jewry
    [http://members.gnn.com/apeck3101/cinti.htm]

## American Jewish Historical Society

http://www.ajhs.org/

2 Thornton Road
Waltham, MA 02154

Phone   (617) 891-8110
Fax      (617) 899-9208
E-mail  dbear@ajhs.org

Archival Collections
    [http://www.ajhs.org/collect.htm]
Genealogical Reference Service
    [http://www.ajhs.org/genealog.htm]
Genealogical Resources
    [http://www.jewishgen.org/boston/ajhs.html]
Jewish Genealogical Societies
    [http://www.jewishgen.org/ajgs/ajgs-jgss.html]
Jewish Historical Societies
    [http://www.ajhs.org/jhs.htm]
Library and Archives
    [http://www.ajhs.org/libarch.htm]
Links in American Jewish History
    [http://www.ajhs.org/other.htm]
Publications
    [http://www.ajhs.org/publica.htm]
Universities Teaching American Jewish History
    [http://www.ajhs.org/depart.htm]

### *Outstanding Site*

## Avotaynu

http://www.avotaynu.com/

P.O. Box 900
Teaneck, NJ 07666

Phone   (201) 387-7200
Fax      (201) 387-2855
E-mail  webmasters@avotaynu.com

Avotaynu Consolidated Jewish Surname Index
    [http://www.avotaynu.com/csi/csi-home.html]
Avotaynu, Journal. Index
    [http://www.avotaynu.com/SUBINDEX/indexsum.html]

## Leo Baeck Institute

http://www.users.interport.net/~lbi1/

129 East 73rd Street
New York, NY 10021

Phone   (212) 744-6400
Fax      (212) 988-1305
E-mail  lbi1@interport.net
         baeck1@metgate.metro.org

LBI Newsletter
    [http://www.users.interport.net/~lbi1/]
Stammbaum, Genealogical Journal
    [http://www.jewishgen.org/stammbaum/]

### *Outstanding Site*

## JewishGen: The Home of Jewish Genealogy

http://www.jewishgen.org/

Association of Jewish Genealogical Societies
P.O. Box 50245
Palo Alto, CA 94303

E-mail  support@jewishgen.org
Phone   (415) 424-1622
E-mail  RWeissJGS@aol.com

Association of Jewish Genealogical Societies
[http://www.jewishgen.org/ajgs/index.html]
International Jewish Cemetery Project
[http://www.jewishgen.org/cemetery/index.html]
List of Jewish Genealogical Societies
[http://www.jewishgen.org/ajgs/ajgs-jgss.html]

## Jewish Genealogical Society of Greater Boston     http://www.jewishgen.org/boston/

| | |
|---|---|
| P.O. Box 610366 | Phone (617) 283-8003 |
| Newton, MA 02161-0366 | E-mail fdavis@tiac.net |

Jewish Sources, Boston
[http://www.jewishgen.org/boston/bostres.html]

## Jewish Theological Seminary of America     http://www.jtsa.edu/

| | |
|---|---|
| Library | Phone (212) 678-8075 |
| 3080 Broadway | E-mail library@jtsa.edu |
| New York, NY 10027 | |

Between the Lines, Newsletter
[http://www.jtsa.edu/library/libhtm/news.html]
JST Library
[http://www.jtsa.edu/library/index.html]
Links
[http://www.jtsa.edu/affiliat/jewish.html]
Masoret Magazine
[http://www.jtsa.edu/masoret/index.html]
Online Catalog
[http://www.jtsa.edu/library/libhtm/catalog.html]
Seminary Update, Newsletter
[http://www.jtsa.edu/pubs/index.html]
Special Collections
[http://www.jtsa.edu/library/libhtm/special.html]

## World Zionist Organization     http://www.wzo.org.il/index.htm

| | |
|---|---|
| Central Zionist Archives | Phone (011) +972 02 6526 155 |
| P.O. Box 92 | Fax (011) +972 02 6527 029 |
| Zalman Shazar 4 | E-mail cza@wzo.org.il |
| Jerusalem 91920 Israel | |

Central Zionist Archives
[http://www.wzo.org.il/cza/]
Collection Guide
[http://www.wzo.org.il/cza/record.htm]

## Yad Vashem—Holocaust Martyrs' and Heroes' Remembrance Authority
http://www.yad-vashem.org.il/AA_INDEX.HTM

| | |
|---|---|
| P.O. Box 3477 | Phone (011) +972-2-6751-611 |
| Jerusalem 91034, Israel | Fax (011) +972-2-6433-511 |
| | E-mail archive@yad-vashem.org.il Archives |
| | library@yad-vashem.org.il Library |
| | names@yad-vashem.org.il Hall of Names |

Archives
[http://www.yad-vashem.org.il/ARCHIVE.HTM]
Hall of Names
[http://www.yad-vashem.org.il/HALL_O_N.HTM]
Library
[http://www.yad-vashem.org.il/LIBRARY.HTM]

## Yivo Institute
http://spanky.osc.cuny.edu/~rich/yivo/

1048 Fifth Avenue
New York, NY 10028

Phone   (212) 535-6700

Genealogy Resources
[http://spanky.osc.cuny.edu/~rich/yivo/Genealogy.html]
Holocaust Resources
[http://spanky.osc.cuny.edu/~rich/yivo/Holocaust.html]
Library
[http://spanky.osc.cuny.edu/~rich/yivo/Library_Fact_Sheet.html]
Photograph Collections
[http://spanky.osc.cuny.edu/~rich/yivo/Photo_Collection.html]

# *Lutheran*

## Evangelical Lutheran Church in America
http://www.elca.org/os/archives/intro.html

8765 West Higgins Road
Chicago, IL 60631

Phone   (312) 380-2818
Fax      (312) 380-2977
E-mail  archives@elca.org

Genealogy Help
[http://www.elca.org/os/archives/geneal.html]
Guide for ELCA Congregation Archives
[http://www.elca.org/os/archives/guide.html]
History of the ELCA
[http://www.elca.org/co/roots.html]
Maintaining the Parish Register
[http://www.elca.org/os/parishre.html]
Oral History Collections
[http://www.elca.org/os/archives/oralhist.html]
Published Guides
[http://www.elca.org/os/archives/publist.html]
Regional/Synodical Archives
[http://www.elca.org/os/archives/regsyn.html]

## Lutheran Church Missouri Synod
http://www.lcms.org/

1333 South Kirkwood Road
St. Louis, MO 63122

E-mail  ic_hoopslc@lcms.org

Concordia Historical Institute
[gopher://gopher.cuis.edu:70/11gopher_root2:[chi]
Directory of Congregations
[HTTP://WWW.LCMS.ORG/WWW/LCMS/CHURCHES/LCMS.HTM]

## Pacific Lutheran University    http://www.plu.edu/

Mortvedt Library                    Phone    (206) 535-7586
Tacoma, WA 98447                    E-mail  RINGDAK@plu.edu

Archives and Special Collections
    [http://www.plu.edu/libr/archives]
Auxilium, Library Newsletter
    [http://www.plu.edu/libr/newsletter.html]
Library
    [http://www.plu.edu/libr/library.html]
Links
    [http://www.plu.edu/home/beyond.html]
Scandinavian Immigrant Experience Collection
    [http://www.plu.edu/libr/siec.html]

# *Mennonite*

## Center for Mennonite Brethren Studies    http://www.fresno.edu/cmhs/home.htm

California Mennonite Historical Society    Phone    (209) 453-2225
4824 East Butler Street                    Fax      (209) 452-1757
Fresno, CA 93727-5097                      E-mail  kennsrem@fresno.edu

Archival Collections
    [http://www.fresno.edu/cmbs/archives.htm]
California Mennonite Historical Society Bulletin
    [http://www.fresno.edu/cmhs/bulletin.htm]
Genealogical Resources
    [http://www.fresno.edu/cmbs/geneal.htm]
GRANDMA (Genealogical Registry and Database of Mennonite Ancestry)
    [http://www.fresno.edu/cmhs/gpc/home.htm]
Historical Commission, Mennonite Brethren Churches
    [http://www.fresno.edu/hc/home.htm]
Mennonite Brethren Archives
    [http://www.fresno.edu/cmbs/archives/mbsystem.htm]

## General Conference of Mennonite Brethren Churches
    http://www.fresno.edu/hc/home.htm

Historical Commission                Phone    (209) 453-2225
4824 East Butler Street              Fax      (209) 452-1757
Fresno, CA 93727-5097                E-mail  kennsrem@fresno.edu

Bibliography
    [http://www.fresno.edu/hc/biblio.htm]
Genealogical Resources
    [http://www.fresno.edu/cmbs/geneal.htm]
Network of Mennonite Brethren Archival Centers
    [http://www.fresno.edu/cmbs/archives/mbsystem.htm]

## Mennonite Historical Society    http://www.pond.com/~mennhist/welcome.html

565 Yoder Road                       Phone    (215) 256-3020
P.O. Box 82                          E-mail  mennhist@pond.com
Harleysville, PA 19438

Genealogical Resources
    [http://www.pond.com/~mennhist/Library.html#Genealogical]
Library
    [http://www.pond.com/~mennhist/Library.html]

## Mennonite Library and Archives          http://www.bethelks.edu/services/mla/

Bethel College                              Phone   (316) 284-5304
300 East 27th Street                        Fax     (316) 284-5286
North Newton, KS 67117                      E-mail  mla@bethelks.edu

Congregational Records
    [http://www.bethelks.edu/services/mla/holdings/cong-records.html]
General Conference Records
    [http://www.bethelks.edu/services/mla/holdings/gcmc.html]
Manuscripts
    [http://www.bethelks.edu/services/mla/holdings/manuscript-1.html]
Mennonite Organizations
    [http://www.bethelks.edu/services/mla/holdings/men-rel-org.html]
Oral Histories
    [http://www.bethelks.edu/services/mla/holdings/oral-history.html]
Photograph Collection
    [http://www.bethelks.edu/services/mla/holdings/voth/voth-1.html]

# *Methodist*

## Central Methodist College             http://cmc2.cmc.edu/index.html

Smiley Library                              Phone   (816) 248-3391, ext 271
Fayette, MO 65248                           Fax     (816) 248-1148
                                            E-mail  MUMA@CMC2.CMC.Edu

Missouri Methodist Historical Society
    [http://cmc2.cmc.edu/soc.html]
Missouri United Methodist Archives
    [http://cmc2.cmc.edu/arc.html]

## Methodist Church History              http://www.umc.org/umhist.html

The Archives and History Center of the United Methodist Church
P.O. Box 127                                Phone   (201) 408-3189
Madison, NJ  07940                          Fax     (201) 408-3909
                                            E-mail  dpatters@drew.edu

Directories
    [http://www.umc.org/umoffice.html]
Guide
    [http://www.umc.org/archives/]
Links to Local Churches
    [http://www.umc.org/churches/index.html]
Links to Other Sites
    [http://www.umc.org/othersit.html]

## Millsaps College                      http://www.millsaps.edu/

J.B. Cain Archives of Mississippi Methodism  Phone   (601) 974-1070
Wilson Library                               Fax     (601) 974-1082
Jackson, MS 39210-0001                       E-mail  MCINTDW@okra.millsaps.edu

Archives, Mississippi Methodism
 [http://www.millsaps.edu/www/library/archives/cain.html]
Millsaps-Wilson Library
 [http://www.millsaps.edu/www/library/index.html]

## Mississippi Conference of the Methodist Church  http://www.mississippi-umc.org/

| | |
|---|---|
| 321 Mississippi Street | Phone  (601) 948-4561 |
| P.O. Box 931 | Fax  (601) 948-5981 |
| Jackson, MS 39205 | E-mail  msumconf@internetpro.com |
| | |
| Commission on History and Archives | Phone  (800) 888-6772 |
| | E-mail  jenkins@datasync.com |

Commission on History and Archives
 [http://www.waidsoft.com/methodist.html]
First United Methodist Church, Picayune, MS
 [http://www.waidsoft.com/methpic.html]
John Ford House
 [http://www.waidsoft.com/methford.html]
Links, Methodists, MS
 [http://www.mississippi-umc.org/msmeth.htm]

## United Methodist Information  http://www.umc.org

| | |
|---|---|
| 475 Riverside Drive | E-mail  websysop@gbgm-umc.org |
| New York, NY 10115 | |

Directory, Local Churches
 [http://gbgm-umc.org/connections/umlocal.html]
Links, Methodist Publications
 [http://www.umc.org/publications.html]
The Wesleys and Their Times
 [http://gbgm-umc.org/Umhistory/Wesley/index.html]

# *Pentecostal*

## Institute for the Study of American Evangelicals
 http://www.wheaton.edu/bgc/isae/index.html

| | |
|---|---|
| Wheaton College | E-mail  isae@wheaton.edu |
| Wheaton, IL 60187-5593 | |

Evangelical Studies Bulletin
 [http://www.wheaton.edu/bgc/isae/esbpage.html]
Links, Related Sites
 [http://www.wheaton.edu/bgc/isae/wwwsite.html]

## International Pentecostal Holiness Church  http://www.iphc.org/

| | |
|---|---|
| IPH Church Archives | Phone  (405) 787-7110 |
| P.O. Box 12609 | Fax  (405) 789-3945 |
| Oklahoma City, OK 73157 | E-mail  archives@iphc.org |

Cyberjournal for Pentecostal Research, Fulltext
 [http://web2010.com/pctii/cyber/index.html]

History of the IPHC
    [http://www.iphc.org/docs/iphchist.html]
International Pentecostal Holiness Church Archives
    [http://www.pctii.org/archives.html]
Legacy, Newsletter, Fulltext
    [http://www.pctii.org/legacy.htm]
Links to Repositories
    [http://www.pctii.org/research.html]

# *Presbyterian*

## Orthodox Presbyterian Church          http://opc.org/

| | |
|---|---|
| 607 North Easton Road, Building E | Phone   (215) 830-0900 |
| Box P | Fax     (215) 830-0350 |
| Willow Grove, PA 19090-0920 | E-mail  webmaster@opc.org. |

Directory, Local Congregations
    [http://opc.org/Directories/Congregations.html]

## Presbyterian Church, USA          http://www.pcusa.org/

| | |
|---|---|
| 100 Witherspoon Street | Phone   (502) 569-5000 |
| Louisville, KY 40202 | Fax     (502) 569-5018 |
| | E-mail  presbytel@pcusa.org |

| | |
|---|---|
| Department of History | Phone  (215) 627-1825 |
| Presbyterian Historical Society | E-mail  Dept.of.History.Phil@pcusa.org |
| 425 Lombard Street | |
| Philadelphia, PA 19147 | |

Links, Presbyterian
    [http://www.pcusa.org/pcnet/pcother.html]
Links, Synods and Presbyteries
    [http://www.cyberspace.com/~hackett/allsynod.html]
Presbyterian Historical Society
    [http://libertynet.org/~iha/_phs.html]

## Unofficial Presbyterian Church in America (PCA) HomePage
    http://www.nol.net/~wqent/pca/index.html

| | |
|---|---|
| 1852 Century Place, Suite 190 | Phone   (404) 320-3366 |
| Atlanta, GA 30345 | E-mail  info@ac.pca-atl.org |

| | |
|---|---|
| Historical Center | Phone   (314) 469-9077 |
| 12330 Conway Road | |
| St. Louis, MO 63141 | |

Church Archives
    [http://library.wustl.edu/~spec/archives/aslaa/presbyterian.html]
Links, Local Congregations
    [http://www.nol.net/~wqent/pca/pca_churches_ab.html]
Links, Presbyteries
    [http://www.nol.net/~wqent/pca/presbyteries.htm]

# Reformed

## Reformed Church in the United States
http://www.geocities.com/Heartland/1136/rcus.html

E-mail  rcuswalk@lightspeed.net

Directory of Local Congregations
[http://www.geocities.com/Heartland/1136/dirrcus.html]

# Religious Society of Friends

## Religious Society of Friends     http://www.quaker.org/

E-mail  nelson@quaker.org

Links
[http://www.quaker.org/]
Quaker Meetings, Directory
[http://www.quaker.org/meetings.html]

## Religious Society of Friends     http://www.rootsweb.com/~quakers/index.htm

The Quaker Corner                   E-mail  jrabun@ix.netcom.com
Kindred Keepsakes
P.O. Box 41552
Eugene, OR 97404-0369

Links
[http://www.rootsweb.com/~quakers/index.htm]
Quaker Roots Discussion Group
[http://www.rootsweb.com/~quakers/quaker-r.htm]
Research Resources
[http://www.rootsweb.com/~quakers/resource.htm]

# Roman Catholic

## Outstanding Site

## Catholic Resources on the Net     http://www.cs.cmu.edu/People/spok/catholic.html

Catholic Encyclopedia, 1913
[http://www.knight.org/advent/cathen/cathen.htm]
Links, Dioceses Worldwide
[http://www.cs.cmu.edu/People/spok/catholic/dioceses.html]
Links, Media Directory
[http://www.nd.edu/~theo/RCD/Directory5.html]
Links, Parishes
[http://www.catholic-church.org/dioceses/]
Links, Religious Orders
[http://www.cs.cmu.edu/People/spok/catholic/organizations.html#orders]

## U.S. Catholic Historical Society     http://www.catholic.org/uschs/index.html

The Catholic Center                 Phone   (800) 225-7999
1011 First Avenue                   E-mail  UPTA57A@prodigy.com
New York, NY 10022

U.S. Catholic Historian
[http://www.catholic.org/uschs/history.html]

## *Salvation Army*

Salvation Army                    http://www.christcom.net/salvation/home.htm

National Headquarters            Phone    (703) 684-5500
615 Slaters Lane                 Fax      (703) 684-3478
Alexandria, VA 22313

Links, Salvation Army, Worldwide
    [http://www.salvationarmy.org/where.htm]

# EMBASSIES

Embassy Page                     http://www.embpage.org/

                                 E-mail   info@globescope.com
Embassies, Directory, Worldwide
    [http://www.xs4all.nl/~airen/countries.html]
Foreign Consular Offices in the US
    [http://www.state.gov/www/travel/consular_offices/fco_index.html]
Links to Foreign Embassies in the US
    [http://www.embpage.org/]
Links, US Embassies Worldwide
    [http://travel.state.gov/links.html]
Links, USIA Offices, Missions Worldwide
    [http://www.usia.gov/regional/posts/posts.htm]

# FOREIGN EXCHANGE RATES

Foreign Exchange Resources     http://dylee.keel.econ.ship.edu/intntl/intfin/ex-rate.htm

Constants, Current and Historical Exchange Rates
    [http://www.best.com/~ftmexpat/html/taxsites/currency.html]
Cross Exchange Rates Between Major Currencies
    [http://www.dna.lth.se/cgi-bin/kurt/rates]
Olsen & Associates 164 Currencies Converter
    [http://www.olsen.ch/cgi-bin/exmenu]

# GENEALOGY

Ancestors, PBS Series            http://www2.kbyu.byu.edu/ancestors/

Brigham Young University             E-mail   ancestors@byu.edu
Provo, UT 84601

Charts and Forms
    [http://www.pbs.org/kbyu/ancestors/teachersguide/charts-records.html]
Links
    [http://www.pbs.org/kbyu/ancestors/links.html]
Series Overview
    [http://www.pbs.org/kbyu/ancestors/ancseries.html]
Teacher's Guide, by Episode
    [http://www.pbs.org/kbyu/ancestors/teachersguide/]
Viewer's Guide, by Episode
    [http://www.pbs.org/kbyu/ancestors/viewersguide/]

## *Outstanding Site*

## Ancestry, Inc.    http://www.ancestry.com/

P.O. Box 476    Phone   (801) 375-2227
Salt Lake City, UT 84110-0476    E-mail   Webmaster@infobases.com

American Biographical Library
  [http://www.ancestry.com/abl/]
American Marriages
  [http://www.ancestry.com/marriage/]
Early American Immigrants
  [http://www.ancestry.com/il/]
GENNAM-L Archive
  [http://www.ancestry.com/gennam-l/]
Links
  [http://ssdi2.ancestry.com/ssdi/travel_bureau/links.htm]
Newsletters, DearMYRTLE, Eastman's Online Genealogy Newsletter and
  Shaking Your Family Tree
  [http://www.ancestry.com/home/times.htm]
ROOTS-L Archive
  [http://www.ancestry.com/roots-l/]
Social Security Death Index
  [http://www.ancestry.com/ssdi/]

## Association of One-Name Studies    http://www.mediasoft.net/ScottC/aons.htm

2509 Placid Place
Virginia Beach, VA 23456

Membership Directory
  [http://www.mediasoft.net/ScottC/aons.htm]

## Association of Professional Genealogists    http://www.apgen.org/~apg/

3421 M Street N.W., Suite 236    E-mail   apg-admin@apgen.org
Washington, DC 20007-3552

Overview
  [http://www.apgen.org/~apg/]

## *Outstanding Site*

## Cyndi's List of Genealogy Sites on the Internet
  http://www.oz.net/~cyndihow/sites.htm

E-mail   cyndihow@oz.net

Links, Links, Links (Arranged by Topic)
  [http://www.oz.net/~cyndihow/sites.htm]

## Digital Librarian a Librarian's Choice of the Best of the Web
  http://www.servtech.com/public/mvail/genealogy.html

E-mail   mvail@servtech.com

Genealogy Links
  [http://www.servtech.com/public/mvail/genealogy.html]

## *Outstanding Site*

# Eastman's Online Genealogy Newsletter
http://www.ancestry.com/home/times.htm

E-mail   roots@cis.compuserve.com
            subscribe@rootscomputing.com

Current Online Newsletter
[http://www.ancestry.com/home/times.htm]

## *Outstanding Site*

# Everton's Genealogical Helper Online       http://www.everton.com/index.html

Logan, UT 84323-0368                    Phone   (800) 443-6325
                                        Fax     (801) 752-0425

Everton's Genealogical Helper Online (Full Text)
[http://www.everton.com/b1.htm]

## *Outstanding Site*

# Family Tree Maker Online       http://www.familytreemaker.com/

39500 Stevenson Place, Suite 204        Phone   (800) 474-8696
Fremont, CA 94539                       Fax     (510) 794-9152

African American Genealogy
[http://www.familytreemaker.com/issue12.html]
Biography Assistant
[http://www.familytreemaker.com/bio/index.html]
Census Records
[http://www.familytreemaker.com/issue13.html]
Church Records
[http://www.familytreemaker.com/issue5.html]
Civil War Research
[http://www.familytreemaker.com/issue7.html]
Family Finder Index
[http://www.familytreemaker.com/ffitop.html]
Genealogy How To Guide
[http://www.familytreemaker.com/mainmenu.html]
Immigration and Passenger Lists
[http://www.familytreemaker.com/issue8.html]
Irish Research
[http://www.familytreemaker.com/issue4.html]

## *Outstanding Site*

# Federation of East European Family History Societies
http://dcn.davis.ca.us/~feefhs/

P.O. Box 51089
Salt Lake City, UT  84151-0898

FEEFHS Membership Directory and Links
[http://dcn.davis.ca.us/~feefhs/]

FEEFHS Membership by Location
[http://dcn.davis.ca.us/~feefhs/location.html]

## *Outstanding Site*

### Federation of Genealogical Societies    http://www.fgs.org/~fgs/

P.O. Box 830220
Richardson, TX 75083-0220

Phone    (972) 907-9727
Fax       (972) 907-9727
E-mail   fgs-office@fgs.org

Links, Links, Links
[http://www.fgs.org/~fgs/]

## *Outstanding Site*

### Genealogical Society of Utah    http://www.fgs.org/~fgs/soc0068.htm

Family History Library
35 North West Temple Street
Salt Lake City, UT 84150

Phone    (801) 240-2323
          (800) 346-6044
Fax       (801) 240-1216

All Family History Centers Listed by State
[http://www.deseretbook.com/famhis/]
All Local Chapels and Meetinghouses
[http://www.deseretbook.com/locate/]
The Family: A Proclamation to the World
[http://www.lds.org/Policy/Family.html]
Family History Centers Worldwide
[http://www.lib.byu.edu/~uvrfhc/states.html]
Family History Library Research Outlines
[file://hipp.etsu.edu/pub/genealogy/LDStext/]
How Do I Begin?
[http://www.lds.org/Family_History/How_Do_I_Begin.html]
Welcome to the Family History Center™
[http://www.lds.org/Welcome_to_FamHist/Welcome_to_FamHist.html]
What Is a Family History Center™?
[http://www.lds.org/Family_History/What_is.html]
Why Family History?
[http://www.lds.org/Family_History/Why_Family_History.html]
Why Family History? by David Mayfield
[http://reled.byu.edu/jsblab/why.htm]

## Genealogy Forum on CompuServe®
   http://ourworld.compuserve.com/homepages/roots/

E-mail   roots@compuserve.com

Genealogy Forum
[http://ourworld.compuserve.com:80/homepages/roots/goroots.htm]
Genealogy Vendors Support Forum
[http://ourworld.compuserve.com:80/homepages/roots/gogensup.htm]
Links, Genealogy
[http://www.rootscomputing.com/register.htm]
RootsComputing
[http://www.rootscomputing.com/]

## *Outstanding Site*

## Genealogy Home Page

http://www.genhomepage.com/

E-mail genhome@genhomepage.com.

Links, Links, Links (Arranged by Topic)
[http://www.genhomepage.com/]

## *Outstanding Site*

## Genealogy Resources on the Internet

http://users.aol.com/johnf14246/gen_mail.html

E-mail johnf14246@aol.com

E-mail Sites
[http://users.aol.com/johnf14246/gen_email.html]
Usenet Newsgroups
[http://users.aol.com/johnf14246/gen_use.html]
Websites
[http://www-personal.umich.edu/~cgaunt/gen_web.html]

## *Outstanding Site*

## Genealogy Toolbox

http://genealogy.tbox.com/genealogy.html

Links, Links, Links (Arranged by Topic)
[http://genealogy.tbox.com/genealogy.html]

## GENTECH, Inc.

http://gentech.org/~gentech/

P.O. Box 28021
Dallas, TX 75228-0021

Phone (972) 495-1569
Fax (972) 495-1569
E-mail jwylie@metronet.com

Overview of the Annual Gentech Conference
[http://gentech.org/~gentech/]

## *Outstanding Site*

## Horus' Web Links to History Resources

http://www.ucr.edu/h-gig/

Department of History
University of California, Riverside
Riverside, CA 92521

E-mail horus@h-gig.ucr.edu

Census and Public Records
[http://www.ucr.edu/h-gig/hist-publications/censu.html]
H-GIG, Genealogical Links for Historians
[http://www.ucr.edu/h-gig/hist-preservation/genea.html]
Links, Links, Links
[http://www.ucr.edu/h-gig/hist-preservation/genea.html]

## *Outstanding Site*

## Internet Business Connection, Genealogy, Searchable Sites
http://www.isleuth.com/gene.html

8 Sea Watch Terrace
Ormond Beach, FL 32176

Phone (904) 441-1648

Albright Surname
[http://genealogy.org/~smcgee/genweb/other_db.html#albright]

Ancestry's American Marriages
    [http://www.ancestry.com/marriage/]
Ancestry's Early American Immigrants
    [http://www.ancestry.com/il/]
Ancestry's Social Security Death Index
    [http://www.ancestry.com/SSDI/Main.htm]
Barrington Surname
    [http://www.ced.tuns.ca/~parkerb/Barrington/gedx.html]
Cunniff Surname
    [http://genealogy.org/~smcgee/genweb/other_db.html#cunniff]
Harrington Surname
    [http://genealogy.org/~smcgee/genweb/genweb.html#harrington]
Hayden Surname
    [http://genealogy.org/~smcgee/genweb/other_db.html#hayden]
Ezekiel Johnson, (b. 1750) Database
    [http://genealogy.org/~smcgee/genweb/genweb.html#ej1750]
Ezekiel Johnson (b. 1754) Database
    [http://genealogy.org/~smcgee/genweb/genweb.html#ej1754]
Illinois Ancestor Exchange
    [http://www.outfitters.com/illinois/history/family/IAE/search.html]
Illinois Databases
    [gopher://gopher.uic.edu/11/library/libdb/landsale]
Kentucky Vital Records
    [gopher://gopher.uky.edu/1menu%20vitalrec%21191/vital.info]
Law Surname
    [http://boreal.med.umich.edu/cgi-bin/gedsrch/n=Law]
Links, Searchable Databases Worldwide
    [http://www.isleuth.com/gene.html]
McGee Surname
    [http://genealogy.org/~smcgee/genweb/genweb.html#mcgee]
Magee Surname
    [http://genealogy.org/~smcgee/genweb/other_db.html#magee]
Murphy Surname
    [http://genealogy.org/~smcgee/genweb/other_db.html#jmurphy]
Reilly Surname
    [http://genealogy.org/~smcgee/genweb/other_db.html#reilly]
Royal Families
    [http://www.dcs.hull.ac.uk/public/genealogy/royal/catalog.html]
Royal, Queen Elizabeth
    [http://genealogy.org/~smcgee/genweb/other_db.html#royal92]
Rutan Surname
    [http://genealogy.org/~smcgee/genweb/other_db.html#rutan]
Scahill Surname
    [http://genealogy.org/~smcgee/genweb/other_db.html#scahill]
Simmons Surname
    [http://genealogy.org/~smcgee/genweb/other_db.html#simmons]

## *Outstanding Site*

# Journal of Online Genealogy

http://www.onlinegenealogy.com/

Toolbox Internet Marketing Services, Inc.
506 Wesley Avenue
Savoy, IL 61874

Phone   (217) 352-1309
E-mail   editor@onlinegenealogy.com

Issues
  [http://www.onlinegenealogy.com/]

## *Extraordinary Site*

### National Genealogical Society          http://www.genealogy.org/~ngs/

| 4527 17th Street, North | Phone | (703) 525-0050 - Office |
| Arlington, VA 22207-2399 | | (703) 841-9065 - Library |
| | Fax | (703) 525-0052 |
| | E-mail | 76702.2417@compuserve.com |
| | | ngslibe@wizard.net Library |

Archer's NetGuide (Important Guide to Links Worldwide)
  [http://www.genealogy.org/~ngs/netguide/welcome.html]
Links, Genealogy Sites
  [http://www.genealogy.org/~gwsc/]
NGS Quarterly
  [http://www.genealogy.org/~ngs/ngsqtoc.html]
PAF Review
  [http://www.genealogy.org/~paf/]

## *Outstanding Site*

### RootsWeb Genealogical Data Cooperative
  http://www.rootsweb.com/rootsweb/searches/rslsearch.html

| P.O. Box 6798 | E-mail | Webspinner@rootsweb.com |
| Frazier Park, CA 93222-6798 | | rsl@rootsweb.com |

Arkansas Databases
  [http://www.rootsweb.com/rootsweb/searches/#ar]
California Databases
  [http://www.rootsweb.com/rootsweb/searches/#ca]
Roots Surname List
  [http://www.rootsweb.com/rootsweb/searches/#rsl]
Soundex Conversion Program
  [http://searches.rootsweb.com/cgi-bin/Genea/soundex.sh]
South Carolina Databases
  [http://www.rootsweb.com/rootsweb/searches/#sc]
South Dakota Databases
  [http://www.rootsweb.com/rootsweb/searches/#sd]
Tennessee Databases
  [http://www.rootsweb.com/rootsweb/searches/#tn]
Usenet Newsgroups Archives
  [http://www.rootsweb.com/rootsweb/searches/#usenet]
Vermont Databases
  [http://www.rootsweb.com/rootsweb/searches/#vt]
Wisconsin Databases
  [http://www.rootsweb.com/rootsweb/searches/#wi]

### Shaking Family Trees          http://www.ancestry.com/home/times.htm

| | E-mail | myra_gormley@prodigy.net |

Missing Links, Online Newsletter
  [http://www.ancestry.com/home/times.htm]

## *Extraordinary Site*

USGenWeb Project http://www.usgenweb.com/index.html

E-mail admin@usgenweb.com

Links, by State of Genealogical Data, Queries, and Groups
[http://www.usgenweb.com/index.html]
Links, by State. Subsitute 2 Digit State Code for xx
[http://www.usgenweb.com/xx]

## *Extraordinary Site*

Utah State Archives http://www.archives.state.ut.us

State Capitol, Archives Building Phone (801) 538-3013
Salt Lake City, UT 84114-1021 Fax (801) 538-3354
E-mail esearch@email.state.ut.us

Guide to Archives and Manuscript Collections in Selected Utah Repositories
[http://www.ce.ex.state.ut.us/history/utahguid.htm]
Links, Links, Links (Well Organized and Easy to Use)
[http://www.archives.state.ut.us/referenc/world.htm]
Links, Archives
[http://www.archives.state.ut.us/referenc/archive.htm]
Links, Genealogy
[http://www.archives.state.ut.us/referenc/genealo.htm]
Links, History
[http://www.archives.state.ut.us/referenc/history.htm]
Links, Legal and Government
[http://www.archives.state.ut.us/referenc/legal.htm]
Links, Library Catalogs
[http://www.archives.state.ut.us/referenc/cats.htm]
Links, Utah
[http://www.archives.state.ut.us/referenc/utah.htm]
Reference Services
[http://www.archives.state.ut.us/referenc/referen.htm]

## *Outstanding Site*

Yahoo. Genealogy™
http://www.yahoo.com/Arts/Humanities/History/Genealogy/

Links to Genealogy Sites on the Web
[http://www.yahoo.com/Arts/Humanities/History/Genealogy/]

# HERALDRY

## *Outstanding Site*

François Velde's Heraldry Site http://128.220.1.164/heraldry/intro.htm

E-mail f.velde@jhu.edu

Bibliography
[http://128.220.1.164/heraldry/biblio/index.htm]

Bibliography, Library of Congress
[gopher://marvel.loc.gov:70/00/research/reading.rooms/genealogy/bibs.guides/herald]
Coats of Arms of Famous Americans
[http://128.220.1.164/heraldry/topics/usa/usfamous.htm]
Heraldic Glossaries
[http://128.220.1.164/heraldry/topics/glossary/]
Jewish Heraldry
[http://128.220.1.164/heraldry/TOPICS/Jewish.htm]
Links
[http://128.220.1.164/heraldry/intro.htm#elsewhere]
Right to Bear Arms
[http://128.220.1.164/heraldry/topics/right.htm]

# HISTORY

## American Association of State and Local History
http://www.Nashville.Net/~aaslh/

| | |
|---|---|
| 530 Church Street | Phone (615) 255-2971 |
| Nashville, TN 37219-2325 | Fax (615) 255-2979 |
| | E-mail aaslh@nashville.net |

Overview
[http://www.Nashville.Net/~aaslh/]

## American Historical Association
http://web.gmu.edu/chnm/aha/

| | |
|---|---|
| 400 A Street, S.E. | Phone (202) 544-2422 |
| Washington, DC 20003 | Fax (202) 544-8307 |
| | E-mail aha@gmu.edu |

Affiliated Societies
[http://web.gmu.edu/chnm/aha/pubs/afil.html]
Calendar
[http://web.gmu.edu/chnm/aha/calendar/]

## Association for History and Computing
http://grid.let.rug.nl/ahc/welcome

| | |
|---|---|
| Dept of History, 614 | Phone (612) 290 2904 |
| Social Sciences | Fax (612) 624 7096 |
| University of Minnesota | E-mail gunnarth@isv.uit.no |
| Minneapolis, MN 55455 | |

| | |
|---|---|
| History and Computing, Journal | E-mail s.baskerville@tees.ac.uk |
| Steven W. Baskerville | |
| Director of the School of Law | |
| Humanities and International Studies | |
| University of Teeside | |
| Middlesborough, TSI, 3BA, UK | |

History and Computing, Journal
[http://grid.let.rug.nl/ahc/journal.html]
Listserv
[http://grid.let.rug.nl/ahc/intern/ahc_book.html#internet]

# College and University History Department Home Pages Worldwide
http://www.gmu.edu/departments/history/depts/
http://grid.let.rug.nl/ahc/history.html

E-mail  amcmicha@gmu.edu
E-mail  welling@let.rug.nl

George Mason University Site
[http://www.gmu.edu/departments/history/depts/]
Netherlands Site
[http://grid.let.rug.nl/ahc/history.html]
Links, Worldwide
[http://www.gmu.edu/departments/history/depts/]
Links, Worldwide
[http://grid.let.rug.nl/ahc/history.html]

## *Extraordinary Site*

## H-Net                                    http://h-net2.msu.edu/

301 Morrill Hall                         Phone   (517) 355-9300
Michigan State University                Fax     (517) 355-8363
East Lansing, MI 48824                   E-mail  H_NET_DIR@APSU01.APSU.EDU

Directory of the 50+ Discussion Lists
[http://h-net2.msu.edu/lists/]
H-California
[http://h-net2.msu.edu/~cal/about/intro.html]
H-Local
[http://h-net2.msu.edu/~local/]
Local History Links
[http://h-net2.msu.edu/~local/links/links.html#localhist]
State Humanities Councils
[http://h-net2.msu.edu/~local/emails.html]

## History Computerization Project          http://www.directnet.com/history/

24851 Piuma Road                         E-mail  history@history.la.ca.us
Malibu, CA 90265-3036

Overview
[http://www.directnet.com/history/]

## *Outstanding Site*

## Horus' Web Links to History Resources        http://www.ucr.edu/h-gig/

Department of History                    E-mail  horus@h-gig.ucr.edu
University of California, Riverside
Riverside, CA 92521

Census and Public Records
[http://www.ucr.edu/h-gig/hist-publications/censu.html]
H-GIG, Genealogical Links for Historians
[http://www.ucr.edu/h-gig/hist-preservation/genea.html]
Links, Links, Links
[http://www.ucr.edu/h-gig/hist-preservation/genea.html]

## *Extraordinary Site*

## Making of America                    http://www.umdl.umich.edu/moa/index.html

E-mail  moa-feedback@umich.edu

Fulltext, 5,000 books on American History Published in the 19th Century
   [http://www.umdl.umich.edu/moa/about.html]

## National Council on Public History     http://www.iupui.edu/it/ncph/ncph.html

327 Cavanaugh Hall                      Phone   (317) 274-2716
IUPUI                                   Fax     (317) 274-2347
425 University Boulevard                E-mail  ncph@iupui.edu
Indianapolis, IN 46202-5140

Consultants' Directory
   [http://www.iupui.edu/it/ncph/con.html]
Public Historian, Contents
   [http://library.berkeley.edu:8080/ucalpress/journals/tph/tocs.html]
Public Historian, Index.
   [http://library.berkeley.edu:8080/ucalpress/journals/tph/authors.html]

## Oral History Association              http://www.Baylor.edu/~OHA/

Baylor University                       Phone   (817) 755-2764
P.O. Box 97234                          Fax     (817) 755-1571
Waco, TX 76798-7234                     E-mail  OHA_Support@baylor.edu

Links, Oral History Related Sites
   [http://www.Baylor.edu/~OHA/Othersites.html]
Publications
   [http://www.Baylor.edu/~OHA/Publications.html]

## Organization of American Historians    http://www.indiana.edu/~oah/index.html

112 Bryan Street                        Phone   (812) 855-7311
Bloomington, IN 47408                   Fax     (812) 855-0696
                                        E-mail  oah@oah.indiana.edu
Links, History
   [http://www.indiana.edu/~oah/links.html]
OAH Publications
   [http://www.indiana.edu/~oah/pubs.html]

## *Outstanding Site*

## Yahoo. History™                       http://www.yahoo.com/Arts/Humanities/History/

Links to History Sites on the Web
   [http://www.yahoo.com/Arts/Humanities/History/]

# LIBRARIES

## American Library Association          http://www.ala.org/

50 East Huron Street                    Phone   (800) 545-2433
Chicago, IL 60606                       E-mail  ala@ala.org

Genealogical Publishing Co. Award
   [http://weber.u.washington.edu/~mudrock/HIST/awa.html]
Genealogy and Local History Discussion Group
   [http://weber.u.washington.edu/~mudrock/HIST/disc1.html]
Genealogy Committee
   [http://weber.u.washington.edu/~mudrock/HIST/gen.html]
History in Libraries Discussion Group
   [http://weber.u.washington.edu/~mudrock/HIST/disc2.html]
History Section
   [http://weber.u.washington.edu/~mudrock/HIST/]
Local History Committee
   [http://weber.u.washington.edu/~mudrock/HIST/loc.html]
Reference and User Services Association
   [http://www.ala.org/rusa/]

## Association of Research Libraries    http://arl.cni.org/

21 Dupont Circle, Suite 800              Phone   (202) 296-2296
Washington, DC 20036                     Fax     (202) 872-0884
                                         E-mail  ARLHQ@cni.org

Directory of ARL Member Libraries
   [http://arl.cni.org/members.html]
Directory of Electronic Journals and Newsletters
   [http://arl.cni.org/scomm/edir/index.html]

## Commission on Preservation and Access
   http://www-cpa.stanford.edu/cpa/index.shtml

1400 16th Street N.W., Suite 715         Phone   (202) 939-3400
Washington, DC 20036                     Fax     (202) 939-3407
                                         E-mail  dmarcum@cpa.org

Overview
   [http://www-cpa.stanford.edu/cpa/index.shtml]

## Council on East Asian Libraries   http://darkwing.uoregon.edu/~felsing/cea/welcome.html

c/o East Asian Library                   Phone   (312) 702-8436
1100 East 57th Street                    Fax     (312) 702-6623
Chicago, IL 60637-1502                   E-mail  felsing@oregon.uoregon.edu

CEAL Bulletin
   [http://darkwing.uoregon.edu/~felsing/ceal/reports.html]
Links, China-Hong Kong
   [http://darkwing.uoregon.edu/~felsing/hkstuff/hkshelf.html]
Links, China-Macau
   [http://darkwing.uoregon.edu/~felsing/macstuff/macshelf.html]
Links, China-PRC
   [http://darkwing.uoregon.edu/~felsing/cstuff/cshelf.html]
Links, China-PRC Libraries
   [http://darkwing.uoregon.edu/~felsing/cstuff/clib.html]
Links, China-Taiwan
   [http://darkwing.uoregon.edu/~felsing/rocstuff/rocshelf.html]
Links, China-Taiwan Libraries
   [http://darkwing.uoregon.edu/~felsing/rocstuff/lib.html]

Links, East Asian Institutes and Programs
    [http://darkwing.uoregon.edu/~felsing/ceal/caps.html]
Links, Japan
    [http://darkwing.uoregon.edu/~felsing/jstuff/jshelf.html]
Links, Japan Libraries
    [http://darkwing.uoregon.edu/~felsing/jstuff/lib.html]
Links, Korea
    [http://darkwing.uoregon.edu/~felsing/kstuff/kshelf.html]
Links, Korea Libraries
    [http://darkwing.uoregon.edu/~felsing/kstuff/lib.html]
Member Libraries, Online Library Catalogs
    [http://darkwing.uoregon.edu/~felsing/ceal/ceallibs.html]

## *Outstanding Site*

### Family History Library                http://www.fgs.org/~fgs/soc0068.htm

Genealogical Society of Utah          Phone   (801) 240-2323
35 North West Temple Street            Fax     (801) 240-1216
Salt Lake City, UT 84150

All Family History Centers Listed by State
    [http://www.deseretbook.com/famhis/]
All Local Chapels and Meetinghouses
    [http://www.deseretbook.com/locate/]
The Family: A Proclamation to the World
    [http://www.lds.org/Policy/Family.html]
Family History Centers Worldwide
    [http://www.lib.byu.edu/~uvrfhc/states.html]
Family History Library Research Outlines
    [file://hipp.etsu.edu/pub/genealogy/LDStext/]
How Do I Begin?
    [http://www.lds.org/Family_History/How_Do_I_Begin.html]
Welcome to the Family History Center™
    [http://www.lds.org/Welcome_to_FamHist/Welcome_to_FamHist.html]
What Is a Family History Center™?
    [http://www.lds.org/Family_History/What_is.html]
Why Family History?
    [http://www.lds.org/Family_History/Why_Family_History.html]
Why Family History? by David Mayfield
    [http://reled.byu.edu/jsblab/why.htm]

### Librarians Serving Genealogists     http://www.cas.usf.edu/lis/genealib/

                                       E-mail  dsmith@luna.cas.usf.edu
Links
    [http://www.cas.usf.edu/lis/genealib/]

## *Extraordinary Site*

### Library of Congress                   http://lcweb.loc.gov/

                                       Phone   (202) 707-5510
                                       Fax     (202) 707-2076
                                       E-mail  lcweb@loc.gov

**American Folklife Center**
Jefferson Building, Room LJ G17
Washington, DC 20540

Phone    (202) 707-5537

**Local History and Genealogy Reading Room**
Jefferson Building, Room LJ G20
Washington, DC 20540

Phone    (202) 707-8419
Fax      (202) 707-7161

**NUCMC Team**
101 Independence Avenue, S.E.
Washington, DC 20540-4375

E-mail   nucmc@mail.loc.gov

Afro-American Genealogical Research
    [gopher://marvel.loc.gov/00/research/reading.rooms/genealogy/bibs.guides/afro]
American Folklife Center
    [http://lcweb.loc.gov/folklife/afc.html]
American Memory Project
    [http://lcweb2.loc.gov/ammem/ammemhome.html]
Center for the Book
    [http://lcweb.loc.gov/loc/cfbook/]
Civil War Photographs
    [http://lcweb2.loc.gov/ammem/cwphome.html]
Collections, by State
    [http://lcweb.loc.gov/folklife/states.html]
County Studies, Area Handbooks
    [http://lcweb2.loc.gov/frd/cs/cshome.html]
Daguerreotype Collection
    [http://lcweb2.loc.gov/ammem/daghtml/daghome.html]
Danish Immigration to America
    [gopher://marvel.loc.gov/00/research/reading.rooms/genealogy/bibs.guides/danish]
Encoded Archival Description (EAD) and SGML
    [http://lcweb.loc.gov/coll/nucmc/ead.html]
English Genealogy
    [gopher://marvel.loc.gov/00/research/reading.rooms/genealogy/bibs.guides/england]
Genealogical Periodicals in the Local History and Genealogy Reading Room
    [gopher://marvel.loc.gov/00/research/reading.rooms/genealogy/bibs.guides/genperio]
Guides to Genealogical Research
    [gopher://marvel.loc.gov/00/research/reading.rooms/genealogy/bibs.guides/guideres]
HALS, Handbook on Latin American Studies
    [http://lcweb2.loc.gov/hlas/]
Handbooks for Foreign Genealogical Research
    [gopher://marvel.loc.gov/00/research/reading.rooms/genealogy/bibs.guides/foreign]
Heraldry
    [gopher://marvel.loc.gov/00/research/reading.rooms/genealogy/bibs.guides/herald]
Hispanic Reading Room
    [http://lcweb.loc.gov/rr/hispanic/]
Immigrant Arrivals
    [gopher://marvel.loc.gov/00/research/reading.rooms/genealogy/bibs.guides/immigrant]
Irish Genealogy
    [gopher://marvel.loc.gov/00/research/reading.rooms/genealogy/bibs.guides/ireland]
Links, Book Organizations
    [http://lcweb.loc.gov/loc/cfbook/cob4.html]
Links, Manuscripts and Archives
    [http://lcweb.loc.gov/rr/mss/other.html#arch]

Links, State and Local Government
   [http://lcweb.loc.gov/global/state/stategov.html]
Links, State Libraries
   [http://lcweb.loc.gov/global/library/statelib.html]
Local History and Genealogy Room
   [http://lcweb.loc.gov/rr/genealogy/]
Local History and Genealogy Room, Collections
   [http://lcweb.loc.gov/rr/genealogy/lhgcoll.html#top]
LOCIS, Online Catalog
   [gopher://lcweb.loc.gov/00/locis/overview]
Manuscripts Reading Room
   [http://lcweb.loc.gov/rr/mss/]
MARVEL, Online Catalog
   [gopher://marvel.loc.gov/11/about]
National Union Catalog of Manuscript Collections, NUCMC
   [http://lcweb.loc.gov/coll/nucmc/nucmc.html]
National Union Catalog of Manuscript Collections, NUCMC, Cataloging
   [http://lcweb.loc.gov/coll/nucmc/nucmccat.html]
National Union Catalog of Manuscript Collections, NUCMC, Online Catalog
   [http://lcweb.loc.gov/z3950/rlinamc.html]
Norwegian-American Immigration
   [gopher://marvel.loc.gov/00/research/reading.rooms/genealogy/bibs.guides/norway]
Newspaper and Periodical Reading Room
   [http://lcweb.loc.gov/global/ncp/ncp.html]
Newspapers, Links U.S. and Worldwide
   [http://lcweb.loc.gov/global/ncp/extnewsp.html]
Preservation
   [http://lcweb.loc.gov/preserv/preserve.html]
Prints and Photographs Reading Room
   [http://lcweb.loc.gov/rr/print/]
Russian Task Force
   [http://lcweb2.loc.gov/frd/tfrquery.html]
Scottish Genealogy
   [gopher://marvel.loc.gov/00/research/reading.rooms/genealogy/bibs.guides/scotland]
Special Collections Department, Index
   [http://lcweb.loc.gov/spcoll/spclhome.html]
Surnames
   [gopher://marvel.loc.gov/00/research/reading.rooms/genealogy/bibs.guides/surnames]
Telephone and City Directories
   [gopher://marvel.loc.gov/00/research/reading.rooms/genealogy/bibs.guides/telephon]
Today in History
   [http://lcweb2.loc.gov/ammem/today/today.html]
Vietnam POW/MIA Index
   [http://lcweb2.loc.gov/pow/powhome.html]
Welsh Genealogy
   [gopher://marvel.loc.gov/00/research/reading.rooms/genealogy/bibs.guides/wales]
WPA, Life History Manuscripts
   [http://lcweb2.loc.gov/ammem/wpaintro/wpahome.html]

## *Extraordinary Site*

| Libweb | http://sunsite.Berkeley.EDU/Libweb/ |

E-mail  tdowling@ohiolink.edu

Africa, Asia, Australia, and New Zealand, Libraries
    [http://sunsite.Berkeley.EDU/Libweb/asia-aus.html]
Canada, Libraries
    [http://sunsite.Berkeley.EDU/Libweb/canada.html]
Europe, Libraries
    [http://sunsite.Berkeley.EDU/Libweb/europe.html]
Library Online Catalogs, Gateways
    [http://www.lib.ncsu.edu/staff/morgan/alcuin/wwwed-catalogs.html]
Library Schools
    [http://www.shef.ac.uk/uni/academic/I-M/is/lecturer/tom2a.html]
Library-Related Companies
    [http://sunsite.Berkeley.EDU/Libweb/comp.html]
Mexico, the Caribbean, Central America, and South America, Libraries
    [http://sunsite.Berkeley.EDU/Libweb/mex.html]
Nordic Library Webservers
    [http://www.ub2.lu.se/resbyloc/Nordic_lib.html]
Submission Form for New or Revised Entries
    [http://sunsite.Berkeley.EDU/Libweb/submission.html]
United States, Academic Libraries
    [http://sunsite.Berkeley.EDU/Libweb/usa-acad.html]
United States, National Libraries and Library Organizations
    [http://sunsite.Berkeley.EDU/Libweb/usa-org.html]
United States, Public Libraries
    [http://sunsite.Berkeley.EDU/Libweb/usa-pub.html]
United States, Regional Consortia
    [http://sunsite.Berkeley.EDU/Libweb/usa-consortia.html]
United States, Special and School Libraries
    [http://sunsite.Berkeley.EDU/Libweb/usa-special.html]
United States, State Libraries
    [http://sunsite.Berkeley.EDU/Libweb/usa-state.html]

## Research Libraries Group, Inc.  http://www.rlg.org/welcome.html

| | |
|---|---|
| 1200 Villa Street | Phone   (415) 691-2294 |
| Mountain View, CA 94041-1100 | (800) 537-7546 |
| | Fax     (415) 964.9751 |
| | E-mail  bl.sal@rlg.org |

English Short Title Catalogue (ESTC)
    [http://www.rlg.org/eurestc.html]
Eureka on the Web, Online Catalog
    [http://www.rlg.org/eurekaweb.html]
Preserving Digital Information: Final Report
    [http://www.rlg.org/ArchTF/]
RLG Databases
    [http://www.rlg.org/databases.html]
RLG News, Magazine
    [http://www.rlg.org/rlgnews/rlgnews.html]
RLIN Focus is a bimonthly newsletter
    [http://www.rlg.org/r-focus.html]

## Special Libraries Association  http://www.sla.org/

| | |
|---|---|
| 1700 Eighteenth Street, N.W. | Phone   (202) 234-4700 |
| Washington, DC 20009-2514 | Fax     (202) 265-9317 |
| | E-mail  sla@sla.org |

Bibliographies
   [http://www.sla.org/membership/irc/irc1.html#topics]
Links, Listserv etc.
   [http://www.sla.org/other.html]


# MAPS

## *Outstanding Site*

### Avis                                   http://www.avis.com/maps/

U.S. Cities, Street Maps
900 Old Country Road
Garden City, NY 11530


## *Outstanding Site*

### Lycos RoadMaps                 http://www.proximus.com/lycos/index.html

500 Old Connecticut Path,  2nd Floor       Phone   (508) 424-0400
Framingham, MA 01701-9378                  E-mail   editorial@lycos.com

Road Maps, U.S.
   [http://www.proximus.com/lycos/index.html]


### Tiger Map Service                     http://tiger.census.gov/

U.S. Census Bureau                         Phone   (301) 457-2822
Washington, DC 20233                       E-mail   TMS@Census.GOV

Geographic Names Information System
   [http://www-nmd.usgs.gov/www/gnis/gnisform.html]
Resizing Maps
   [http://tiger.census.gov/cgi-bin/mapbrowser]


### U.S. Geological Survey                http://www.usgs.gov/

523 National Center                        Phone   (703) 648-4544
Reston, VA 20192                                    (800) 872-6277
                                           E-mail   gnis_manager@usgs.gov
Foreign Gazetteers
   [http://www-nmd.usgs.gov/www/gnis/foreigninstr.html]
Geographic Names Information System
   [http://www-nmd.usgs.gov/www/gnis/]
Mapping Information Service
   [http://www-nmd.usgs.gov/www/html/nmp_prog.html]
National Gazetteer
   [http://www-nmd.usgs.gov/www/gnis/gnisgaz.html]
Regional Mapping Centers
   [http://www-nmd.usgs.gov/www/html/1nmdsite.html]
Topographic Mapping
   [http://www-nmd.usgs.gov/misc/evolution.html]

# MAYFLOWER

## *Outstanding Site*

## Caleb Johnson's Mayflower Web Page
http://members.aol.com/calebj/mayflower.html

E-mail  CalebJ@aol.com.

Hypocricie Unmasked, 1646
[http://members.aol.com/calebj/hypocricie.html]
Mayflower Compact
[http://members.aol.com/calebj/compact.html]
Mayflower Passenger List
[http://members.aol.com/calebj/alphabet.html]
Mayflower, Ship
[http://members.aol.com/calebj/ship.html]
Revolutionary War Veterans
[http://members.aol.com/calebj/revolutionary_war.html]
Thomas Prince's Register
[http://members.aol.com/calebj/prince.html]
U.S. Presidents, Mayflower Descendants
[http://members.aol.com/calebj/presidents.html]

## General Society of Mayflower Descendants
http://members.aol.com/calebj/GSMD.html

P.O. Box 3297
Plymouth, MA 02361

Florida State Chapter Online
[http://gator.naples.net/~dnpope/]
Overview
[http://members.aol.com/calebj/GSMD.html]

## Mayflower 2000 Project
http://www.demon.co.uk/history/mayflower/mayflower.html

2 Beaulieu Close                    Phone    (011) +44 (0)171 733 7868
London SE5 8BA                   E-mail   101607.771@compuserve.com

Links, Mayflower Sites
[http://www.demon.co.uk/history/mayflower/links.html]
Mayflower History
[http://www.demon.co.uk/history/mayflower/history.html]
Project Voyage
[http://www.demon.co.uk/history/mayflower/voyage.html]

## Pilgrim Society                    http://media3.com/pilgrimhall/

75 Court Street                     Phone    (508) 746-1620
Plymouth, MA 02360

Pilgrim Hall Museum
[http://media3.com/pilgrimhall/]

## Plimoth Plantation                    http://media3.com/plymouth/plant.htm

P.O. Box 1620                             Phone   (508) 746-1622
Plymouth, MA 02362                        Fax     (508) 830-6022

Virtual Tour of Plimoth Plantation
    [http://pilgrims.net/plimothplantation/vtour/index.htm]

# MILITARY RECORDS

## American Civil War Home Page
    http://funnelweb.utcc.utk.edu/~hoemann/warweb.html

The University of Tennessee              E-mail  hoemann@utk.edu
Knoxville, TN 37996

Civil War Roundtables
    [http://funnelweb.utcc.utk.edu/~hoemann/warweb.html#roundtable]
Links, Civil War Sites
    [http://funnelweb.utcc.utk.edu/~hoemann/warweb.html]
Rosters
    [http://funnelweb.utcc.utk.edu/~hoemann/warweb.html#rosters]

## Descendants of Mexican War Veterans
    http://member.aol.com/dmwv/home.htm

P.O. Box 830482                           E-mail  DMWV@aol.com
Richardson, TX 75083-0482

Mexican War Journal
    [http://member.aol.com/dmwv/mwj.htm]

## French and Indian War                 http://web.syr.edu/~laroux/

                                         E-mail  lroux@ix.netcom.com
Bibliography
    [http://web.syr.edu/~laroux/reference/refer.html]
French Soldiers List
    [http://web.syr.edu/~laroux/lists/alpha.html]
Links
    [http://web.syr.edu/~laroux/links/links.html]

## Grand Army of the Republic            http://pages.prodigy.com/CGBD86A/garhp.htm

                                         E-mail  cgbd86a@prodigy.com
Links
    [http://pages.prodigy.com/CGBD86A/pg7link.htm]
Tracing a Veteran in GAR Records
    [http://pages.prodigy.com/CGBD86A/pg6rec.htm]

*Outstanding Site*

## National Park Service                  http://www.nps.gov/

Washington, DC 20013-7127                Phone   (202) 208-4747
                                         Fax     (202) 501-8920

African-Americans in the Civil War
[http://www.itd.nps.gov/cwss/africanh.html]
Battlefield Update, Newsletter. Fulltext
[http://www.nps.gov/crweb1/abpp/latest.htm]
Civil War Soldiers and Sailors System
[http://www.itd.nps.gov/cwss/usct.html]
Federal, State, Private Grants
[http://www.nps.gov/crweb1/helpyou.htm]
Historic American Buildings Survey
[http://www.nps.gov/crweb1/habshaer/collectn.htm]
Links, NPS Civil War Site
[http://www.itd.nps.gov/cwss/sites.html]
National Register of Historic Places
[http://www.nps.gov/crweb1/nr/nrhome.html]
U.S. Colored Troops (USCT) Database
[http://www.itd.nps.gov/cwss/usct.html]

## Outstanding Site

| National Personnel Records Center | http://gopher.nara.gov/nara/frc/nprc.html |
|---|---|

| | |
|---|---|
| Military Records Facility<br>9700 Page Avenue<br>St. Louis, MO 63132-5100 | Phone  (314) 538-4243 Air Force<br>(314) 538-4261 Army<br>(314) 538-4141 Navy, Marine Corps, Coast Guard<br>Fax  (314) 538-4175<br>E-mail  center@stlouis.nara.gov |
| Civilian Records Facility<br>111 Winnebago Street<br>St. Louis, MO 63118-4199 | Phone  (314) 425-5761<br>Fax  (314) 425-5719<br>E-mail  center@cpr.nara.gov |

**Civilian Records Facility**
Clinical, Medical Records
[http://gopher.nara.gov/nara/frc/cclinref.html]
Record Access Policies
[http://gopher.nara.gov/nara/frc/cpubref.html]
Records, Federal Employees
[http://gopher.nara.gov/nara/frc/cpershld.html]

**Military Records Facility**
Alternate Record Sources
[http://gopher.nara.gov/nara/frc/mpralts.html]
Fire, 1973
[http://gopher.nara.gov/nara/frc/mprfire.html]
Hospital Inpatient Records
[http://gopher.nara.gov/nara/frc/mprcli.html]
Links
[http://gopher.nara.gov/nara/frc/mprhelp.html]
Medical Records, Dependents etc.
[http://gopher.nara.gov/nara/frc/mprmtr.html]
Personnel and Medical Record Collections
[http://gopher.nara.gov/nara/frc/mpromp.html]
Pearl Harbor Casualty List
[http://www.mit.edu:8001/afs/athena/activity/a/afrotc/www/names]

Record Collections
   [http://gopher.nara.gov/nara/frc/mprmpm.html]
Records NOT at the NPRC
   [http://gopher.nara.gov/nara/frc/mprfrr.html]
Service/Social Security Numbers
   [http://gopher.nara.gov/nara/frc/mprssn.html]
Vietnam POW/MIA Database
   [http://lcweb2.loc.gov/pow/powhome.html]

## Sons of Union Veterans of the Civil War          http://suvcw.org/

GAR, Grand Army of the Republic
   [http://suvcw.org/gar.htm]
Overview
   [http://suvcw.org/]

## *Outstanding Site*

## U.S. Air Force                         http://www.dtic.mil/airforcelink/

Air Force Historical Research Agency     Fax     (334) 953-7428
HQ AFHRA/RSA                             E-mail  AFHRANEWS1%RS%AFHRA@MAX
600 Chennault Circle                             1.au.af.mil
Maxwell AFB, AL 36112-6424

USAF Museum                              Phone   (937) 255-3284
1100 Spaatz Street
Wright-Patterson AFB, OH 45433-7102

Active Duty Personnel, Emergency Contact Service
   [http://www.nacec.org/]
Aircraft Index
   [http://www.wpafb.af.mil/museum/ind/ind.htm]
Biographical Sources
   [http://www.dtic.mil/airforcelink/lib/bio/index.html]
Guide to Air Force Heraldry
   [http://www.au.af.mil/au/athra/heraldry.zip]
Historical Gallery
   [http://www.wpafb.af.mil/museum/history/history.htm]
Library
   [http://www.dtic.mil/airforcelink/lib/]
Links
   [http://www.dtic.mil/airforcelink/sites/]
   [http://www.wpafb.af.mil/museum/related.htm]
Personal Papers in the AFHRA
   [http://www.au.af.mil/au/afhra/pp2.htm]
Personnel Information
   [http://www.au.af.mil/au/afhra/seeking.htm]
Personnel Locator, Active
   [http://136.149.4.192/afwwloc.htm]
Photographs
   [http://www.dtic.mil/airforcelink/photos/]
Units
   [http://www.dtic.mil/airforcelink/pa/indexpages/fs_index.html#ORGANIZATIONS]

USAF Historical Studies
[http://www.au.af.mil/au/afhra/hisstud2.htm]
WWII Bombardiers
[http://www.wpafb.af.mil/museum/history/wwii/bomb.htm]

## *Outstanding Site*

| U.S. Army | http://www.army.mil/ |
|---|---|

| | |
|---|---|
| Center of Military History<br>Historical Resources Branch<br>U.S. Army Center of Military History<br>1099 14th Street N.W.<br>Washington, DC 20005-3402 | http://www.army.mil/cmh-pg<br>Phone (202) 761-5416 |
| Military History Institute<br>Carlisle Barracks<br>Carlisle, PA 17013 | http://carlisle-www.army.mil/usamhi/<br>Phone (717) 245-3601<br>E-mail MHI-HR@carlisle-emh2.army.mil<br>Archives MHI-AR@carlisle-emh2.army.mil<br>Photos MHI-SC@carlisle-emh2.army.mil |
| West Point, U.S. Military Academy | http://www.usma.edu/ |

**Center of Military History**
Army Alumni Organizations
[http://www.army.mil/vetinfo/vetloc.htm]
Campaigns
[http://www.army.mil/cmh-pg/campaign.htm]
Gulf War Bibliography
[http://www.army.mil/cmh-pg/reference/gulfbib.htm]
Manuscripts
[http://www.army.mil/cmh-pg/ocmh1st.htm]
Master Index of Army Record Groups
[http://www.army.mil/cmh-pg/records.htm]
Medal of Honor Recipients
[http://www.army.mil/cmh-pg/moh1.htm]
U.S. Army Museums
[http://www.army.mil/cmh-pg/musdir.htm]
Unit Lineages
[http://www.army.mil/cmh-pg/lineage/revwar.htm]

**Military History Institute**
Army Alumni Organizations
[http://www.army.mil/vetinfo/vetloc.htm]
Civil War Biographical Bibliography
[http://carlisle-www.army.mil/usamhi/ACWBiogs.html]
Civil War Unit Bibliographies
[http://carlisle-www.army.mil/usamhi/ACWUnits.html]
Collection Index (RefBibs)
[http://carlisle-www.army.mil/usamhi/RefBibs.html]
Manuscripts Index
[http://carlisle-www.army.mil/usamhi/ArchivesDB.html]
Normandy Photo
[http://carlisle-www.army.mil/usamhi/Normandy/NormandyPhotos.html]

Photograph Collection Index
    [http://carlisle-www.army.mil/usamhi/PhotoDB.html]

**West Point, U.S. Military Academy**
E-mail Addresses
    [http://cgi.usma.edu/cgi-bin/Whois]
E-mail Addresses, Graduates
    [http://www.aog.usma.edu/contact/mmia.HTM]
Museum
    [http://www.usma.edu/Museum/]

## U.S. Civil War Center                    http://www.cwc.lsu.edu/index.htm

Agnes Morris House                    Phone    (504) 388-3151
Louisiana State University            Fax      (504) 388-4876
Baton Rouge, LA 70803                 E-mail   hammer@cwc.lsu.edu

Civil War Sesquicentennial News
    [http://www.cwc.lsu.edu/projects/sesqui.htm]

## *Outstanding Site*

## U.S. Coast Guard                          http://www.dot.gov/dotinfo/uscg/

Bibliographies
    [http://www.dot.gov/dotinfo/uscg/h_biblio/h_bibidx.html]
Women
    [http://www.dot.gov/dotinfo/uscg/hq/g-cp/history/h_womn.html]
WWII
    [http://www.dot.gov/dotinfo/uscg/hq/g-cp/history/h_cgnvy.html]
WWII, Atlantic
    [http://www.dot.gov/dotinfo/uscg/hq/g-cp/history/h_AtlWar.html]
WWII, Normandy
    [http://www.dot.gov/dotinfo/uscg/hq/g-cp/history/h_norman.html]
WWII, Pacific
    [http://www.dot.gov/dotinfo/uscg/hq/g-cp/history/h_pacwar.html]

## *Outstanding Site*

## U.S. Navy                                 http://www.navy.mil/

Naval Historical Center            http://www.history.navy.mil/index.html
Washington Navy Yard               Phone    (202) 433-4132
901 M Street S.E.                  Fax      (202) 433-9553
Washington, DC 20374-5060          E-mail   dlriley@hop-uky.campus.mci.net

Marine Corps Historical Center     Phone    (202) 433-3483
Washington Navy Yard, Building 58  E-Mail   Washington, DC 20374-0580
Washington, DC 20374-0580                   homepage.usmc@notes-smtp.hqi.usmc.mil

Active Duty Personnel, Emergency Contact Service
    [http://www.nacec.org/]
Active Duty Personnel, Marines
    [http://www.usmc.mil/usmcfaq/20fa.htm]
Active Duty Personnel, Navy
    [http://www.ncts.navy.mil/homepages/bupers/locator.html]

Active Duty Personnel, Navy E-mail
[http://www.ncts.navy.mil/homepages/bupers/email.html]
Art Collection Branch
[http://www.history.navy.mil/branches/nhcorg6.htm]
Aviation History Branch
[http://www.history.navy.mil/branches/nhcorg4.htm]
Aviation Unit Lineages
[http://www.history.navy.mil/faqs/faq6-1.htm]
Bibliography
[http://www.history.navy.mil/biblio/biblio1/biblio1.htm]
Biographical Sources
[http://www.history.navy.mil/biblio/biblio1/bibli1ar.htm]
BUPERS, Navy Personnel
[http://www.ncts.navy.mil/homepages/bupers/]
Contemporary History Branch, 1945- .
[http://www.history.navy.mil/branches/nhcorg1.htm]
Early History Branch, Revolution-WWI
[http://www.history.navy.mil/branches/nhcorg3.htm]
History, Navy Re-establishment
[http://www.history.navy.mil/biblio/biblio4/biblio4.htm]
Korean War Project, KIA/MIA
[http://www.onramp.net/~hbarker/]
Links
[http://www.history.navy.mil/nhc9.htm]
Manuscripts, Guide
[http://www.history.navy.mil/biblio/biblio1/biblio1.htm]
Manuscripts, Name Index
[http://www.history.navy.mil/branches/org10-4.htm]
Marine Corps History
[http://www.usmc.mil/wwwmain/hist.htm]
Marine E-mail Addresses
[http://www.usmc.mil/usmcfaq/212e.htm]
Marine Link, Index
[http://www.usmc.mil/opages/index.htm]
Naval Aviation News
[http://www.history.navy.mil/branches/nhcorg5.htm]
Navy Department Library
[http://www.history.navy.mil/branches/nhcorg7.htm]
Navy Museum
[http://www.history.navy.mil/branches/nhcorg8.htm]
Operational Archives Branch
[http://www.history.navy.mil/branches/nhcorg10.htm]
Photograph Collections
[http://www.history.navy.mil/faqs/faq22-1.htm]
Photograph Collections, Marine
[http://www.usmc.mil/usmcfaq/2116.htm]
Photograph Guidelines
[http://www.history.navy.mil/branches/nhcorg11.htm]
Service and Medical Records
[http://www.history.navy.mil/faqs/faq19-1.htm]
Service Records, Marine
[http://www.usmc.mil/usmcfaq/2112.htm]

Ships History Branch
    [http://www.history.navy.mil/branches/nhcorg9.htm]
U.S. Naval Academy Alumni Information
    [http://www.nadn.navy.mil/alumni.html]
Women in the Navy
    [http://www.history.navy.mil/faqs/faq48-1.htm]
WWII, Navy and Marine Casualties
    [http://www.history.navy.mil/faqs/faq11-1.htm]
WWII, Navy Cruise Books
    [http://www.history.navy.mil/biblio/biblio2/biblio2.htm]
WWII, Navy POWs
    [http://www.history.navy.mil/faqs/faq41-1.htm]

## *Extraordinary Site*

# Valley of the Shadow: The Civil War as Seen by Franklin County, Pennsylvania and Augusta County, Virginia
    http://jefferson.village.Virginia.EDU/vshadow2/contents.html

| | |
|---|---|
| University of Virginia | Phone   (804) 924-7834 |
| Alderman Library, Room 553 | Fax     (804) 982-2363 |
| Charlottesville, VA 22903 | E-mail  will@jefferson.village.virginia.edu |

Church Records
    [http://jefferson.village.Virginia.EDU/vshadow2/church.html]
Letter and Diaries
    [http://jefferson.village.Virginia.EDU/vshadow2/letters.html]
Maps and Images
    [http://jefferson.village.Virginia.EDU/vshadow2/maps.html]
Military Records
    [http://jefferson.village.Virginia.EDU/vshadow2/military.html]
Newspaper Reading Room
    [http://jefferson.village.Virginia.EDU/vshadow2/newspapers.html]
Public Records
    [http://jefferson.village.Virginia.EDU/vshadow2/public.html]
Reception Area
    [http://jefferson.village.Virginia.EDU/vshadow2/reception.html]
Reference Center
    [http://jefferson.village.Virginia.EDU/vshadow2/reference.html]

## *Outstanding Site*

# VietNam Casualty Search Page            http://www.sersoft.com/vietnam/

| | |
|---|---|
| Friends of the Vietnam Veterans Memorial | Phone   (703) 525-1107 |
| 2030 Clarendon Boulevard, Suite 412 | E-mail  71035.3126@Compuserve.com |
| Arlington, VA 22201 | Corky6@earthlink.net |

Friends of the VietNam Veterans Memorial (FVVM)
    [http://www.sersoft.com/vietwall/]
    [http://www.vietvet.org/friends.htm]
VietNam War Casualty Search Page
    [http://www.sersoft.com/vietnam/]
VietNam Veterans HomePage
    [http://www.vietvet.org/index.htm]

Vietnam Veterans Organizations and Support Groups
    [http://www.vietvet.org/vetorgs.htm]
The Wall on the Web
    [http://www.vietvet.org/thewall/thewallm.html]

# NATIVE AMERICANS

## Chickasaw People and Their Historic Homeland
    http://www.usit.net/tngenweb/chicksaw/

Chickasaw Cessions—1816 and 1818
    [http://www.usit.net/tngenweb/chicksaw/1816-18.htm]
Chickasaw in Mississippi and Oklahoma
    [http://www.usit.net/tngenweb/chicksaw/missokla.htm]

# NEWSPAPERS

## History Buff's Homepage
    http://www.serve.com/ephemera/historybuff.html

                                        E-mail  ephemera@mail.serve.com
Calendar, Universal. 1000AD-1997
    [http://www.serve.com/ephemera/cgi-bin/calendar.cgi]
Links, History
    [http://www.serve.com/ephemera/history/journalismlinks.html]
Newspaper Collectors Society of America
    [http://www.serve.com/ephemera/about.html]
Old Newspaper Price Guide
    [http://www.serve.com/ephemera/prices.html]
Primer on Collecting Old Newspapers
    [http://www.serve.com/ephemera/primer.html]

## Newspaper Association of America          http://www.naa.org/

1921 Gallows Road, Suite 600              Phone  (703) 902-1600
Vienna, VA 22182                         Fax    (703) 917-0636
                                         E-mail  tayld@naa.org
Links, Newspapers by State
    [http://www.naa.org/hot/index.html]
Links, Press Associations by State
    [http://www.naa.org/hot/spa.html]

## Reporter's Network          http://www.reporters.net/

                                        E-mail  membership@reporters.net
Links, Newspapers and More
    [http://www.reporters.net/jlinks/resource.htm]

## U.S. Newspaper Program          http://www.loc.gov/global/ncp/usnp.html

Library of Congress              Phone  (202) 707-5874
Washington, DC 20540-5590

Links to State Newspaper Projects
    [http://www.libs.uga.edu/darchive/newspape/usnp.html]
National Repository Projects
    [http://www.loc.gov/global/ncp/usnp.html#repos]
U.S. Newspaper Program Participants
    [http://www.loc.gov/global/ncp/usnp.html#forn]]

## *Outstanding Site*

## Yahoo—Regional/State Newspapers
    http://www.yahoo.com/News_and_Media/Newspapers/Regional/U_S__States/

Links, Newspapers for all 50 States
    [http://www.yahoo.com/News_and_Media/Newspapers/Regional/U_S__States/]

# OBITUARIES

## Dead People Server                     http://www.scarletfire.com/dps/

                                          E-mail   dead@scarletfire.com
Listing of Celebrities, Dates of Death etc.
    [http://www.scarletfire.com/dps/]

# PALATINES

## Palatines to America                   http://genealogy.org/~palam/

Membership Registrar                      Phone   (614) 236-8281
Capital University, Box 101               E-mail  mccrea@epix.net
Columbus, OH 43209-2394

Just what is a "Palatine"?
    [http://genealogy.org/~palam/palatine.htm]
On-line Immigrant Ancestor Register Index
    [http://genealogy.org/~palam/ia_index.htm]

# PHOTOGRAPHS

## Daguerreian Society                    http://java.austinc.edu/dag/

3045 West Liberty Avenue, Suite Seven     Phone   (412) 343-5525
Pittsburgh, PA 15216-2460                 Fax     (412) 563-5972
                                          E-mail  dagsocpgh@aol.com
DagNews, Newsletter
    [http://java.austinc.edu/dag/resource/dagnews/dagnews.html]
Daguerreotype Bibliography
    [http://java.austinc.edu/dag/resource/biblio/biblio.html]
Daguerreotype, 19th C. Guides, Full Text
    [http://java.austinc.edu/dag/resource/texts.html]
Links, Daguerreotypes
    [http://java.austinc.edu/dag/resource/links.html]

Links, Photo History
[http://java.austinc.edu/dag/resource/links2.html]

## Federal Emergency Management Agency—FEMA
http://www.fema.gov/

| P.O. Box 129 | Phone | (800) 879-6076 |
| Berryville, VA 22611 | Fax | (703) 542-2484 |

Saving Photographs after the Flood
[http://www.fema.gov/DIZAS/photos.htm]

# SCHOOL RECORDS

*Outstanding Site*

## College and University Home Pages
http://www.mit.edu:8001/people/cdemello/univ.html

E-mail  cdemello@athena.mit.edu

College and University Home Pages
[http://www.mit.edu:8001/people/cdemello/univ.html]

## Yahoo-Education-Universities    http://www.yahoo.com/Education/Universities

Links, Universities
http://www.yahoo.com/Education/Universities

# SOCIAL SECURITY RECORDS

## Ancestry, Inc.    http://www.ancestry.com

| P.O. Box 476 | Phone | (801) 375-2227 |
| Salt Lake City, UT 84110-0476 | E-mail | Webmaster@infobases.com |

Social Security Death Index
[http://www.ancestry.com/ssdi/]

## Everton's Genealogical Helper Online    http://www.everton.com

| Logan, UT 84323-0368 | Phone | (800) 443-6325 |
| | Fax | (801) 752-0425 |

Social Security Death Index
[http://rro.everton.com/ssmdi.html]

# SURNAMES

## Surnames. What's in a Name?    http://clanhuston.com/name/name.htm

| 4413 West Oakland | E-mail | hoefling@ix.netcom.com |
| Broken Arrow, OK 74012-9123 | | |

Surname Origins
[http://clanhuston.com/name/name.htm]

## U.S. Surname Distribution Map           http://www.hamrick.com/names/

Surname Distribution Maps
   [http://www.hamrick.com/names/]

# TELEPHONE DIRECTORIES
*Outstanding Site*

## International Telephone Directories
   http://www.infobel.be/infobel/infobelworld.html

Kapitol                          Phone  (011) +32-2-344 42 42
31 Rue E. Gossart                Fax    (011) +32-2-344 22 96
B-1180 Brussels - Belgium        E-mail  kapitol@infobel.be

Argentina Telephone Books
   [http://www.telecom.com.ar/guia/index.html]
Australia Telephone Books
   [http://www.whitepages.com.au/]
Belgium Telephone Books
   [http://www.infobel.be/]
Canada Telephone Books
   [http://canada411.sympatico.ca/]
France Telephone Books
   [http://epita.fr:5000/11/english.html]
Germany Telephone Books
   [http://www.etv.de/]
International. Fax, Yellow Pages, etc.
   [http://www.infobel.be/infobel/infobelworld.html]
Japan Telephone Books
   [http://www.pearnet.org/jtd/]
Luxembourg Telephone Books
   [http://www.editus.lu/html/ws.html]
Malaysia Telephone Books
   [http://www.tpsb.com.my/cgi-bin/wp]
Netherlands Telephone Books
   [http://www.telefoongids.ptt-telecom.nl/index2.html]
New Zealand Telephone Books
   [http://tdl.tols.co.nz/]
Slovakia Telephone Books
   [http://tis.telekom.si/] and [http://www.telekom.si/]

*Outstanding Site*

## Switchboard.com™           http://www.switchboard.com/

Telephone Numbers and Address, U.S.
   [http://www.switchboard.com/]

*Outstanding Site*

## Yahoo People Search™           http://www.yahoo.com/search/people/

Telephone Number, Address, E-mail, HomePage
   [http://www.yahoo.com/search/people/]

# VITAL RECORDS

## Ancestry's American Marriage Records          http://www.ancestry.com

P.O. Box 476
Salt Lake City, UT 84110-0476

Phone   (801) 375-2227
E-mail  Webmaster@infobases.com

American Marriage Records Index
[http://www.ancestry.com/marriage/]

## Funeral Net          http://www.funeralnet.com

Phone   (800) 721-8166
E-mail  info@funeralnet.com

Funeral Homes, U.S.
[http://www.funeralnet.com/search.html]

## Vital Records State Index          http://www.inlink.com/~nomi/vitalrec/staterec.html

E-mail  orsay@inquest.net

Links, by State
[http://www.inlink.com/~nomi/vitalrec/staterec.html]

## VitalChek Network          http://www.vitalchek.com/

4512 Central Pike
Hermitage, TN  36976

Phone   (800) 255-2414
E-mail  info@vitalchek.com

State Agencies, Telephone List
[http://www.vitalchek.com/statephn.html]

# WOMEN'S HISTORY

*Outstanding Site*

## Women's History          http://frank.mtsu.edu/~kmiddlet/history/women.html

Todd Library
Middle Tennessee State University
Murfreesboro, TN 37132

Phone   (615) 898-2549
E-mail  kmiddlet@frank.mtsu.edu

Bibliographies
[http://frank.mtsu.edu/~kmiddlet/history/women/wom-bibl.html]
Biographical Sources
[http://frank.mtsu.edu/~kmiddlet/history/women/wombio-todd.html]
Guide to Sources, by State
[http://frank.mtsu.edu/~kmiddlet/history/women/wh-state.html]
Listserv's
[http://frank.mtsu.edu/~kmiddlet/history/women/network.html]

# UNITED STATES

# ALABAMA

## State Home Page

Alabama State HomePage            http://alaweb.asc.edu/govern.html

Links, Alabama
    [http://alaweb.asc.edu/govern.html]

## State Archives

### Alabama Department of Archives and History
http://www.asc.edu/archives/agis.html

624 Washington Avenue               Phone    (334) 242-4363, ext. 274
Montgomery, AL 36130-0024           Fax      (334) 240-3433
                                    E-mail   archref@dsmd.dsmd.state.al.us

African American Records
    [http://www.asc.edu/archives/referenc/rec.html]
Alabama History On-line
    [http://www.asc.edu/archives/aho.html]
Alabama Historical Quarterly, Table of Contents
    [http://www.lib.auburn.edu/special/docs/ahistqtr.html]
Census Records
    [http://www.asc.edu/archives/referenc/census.html]
City Directories
    [http://www.asc.edu/archives/referenc/micro.html]
County Records
    [http://www.asc.edu/archives/referenc/procount.html]
Files and Indexes, Subject Headings
    [http://www.asc.edu/archives/referenc/vertical.html]
Government Records News
    [http://www.asc.edu/archives/gov_rec.html]
Legal Admissibility of Public Records
    [http://www.asc.edu/archives/leg_adm.html]
Links, Alabama History
    [http://www.asc.edu/archives/related.html#Historical]
Links, Alabama Websites
    [http://www.asc.edu/archives/related.html]
Manuscripts
    [http://www.asc.edu/archives/referenc/sources.html]
Online Research Request Form
    [http://www.asc.edu/archives/referenc/request.html]
Public Records, Responsibilities
    [http://www.asc.edu/archives/pub_off.html]
Records Not at the ADAH
    [http://www.asc.edu/archives/referenc/notat.html]
Vital Records
    [http://www.asc.edu/archives/referenc/vital.html]
Women, Bibliography
    [http://www.asc.edu/archives/referenc/wbooks.html]
Women, State Records
    [http://www.asc.edu/archives/referenc/wrec.html]
Women, Subject Files
    [http://www.asc.edu/archives/referenc/wvert.html]

Women, Unprocessed Records
   [http://www.asc.edu/archives/referenc/wpriv.html]

# Other State Sites

## Auburn University                    http://www.auburn.edu/

| | |
|---|---|
| Special Collections Department | Phone   (334) 844-1700 |
| Draughon Library | E-mail  fostecd@lib.auburn.edu |
| 231 Mell Street | |
| Auburn University, AL 36849 | |

Alabama Authors
   [http://www.lib.auburn.edu/madd/docs/ala_authors/contents.html]
Alabama Collection, Accessions List
   [http://www.lib.auburn.edu/special/docs/alaindex.html]
Alabama Heritage. Table of Contents
   [http://www.lib.auburn.edu/special/docs/alaheritage.html]
Alabama Review - Table of Contents
   [http://www.lib.auburn.edu/special/docs/alarevu.html]
Gulf Coast Historical Rev. Table of Contents
   [http://www.lib.auburn.edu/special/docs/gchr.html]
Library
   [http://www.lib.auburn.edu/index.html]
Links, Alabama
   [http://www.eng.auburn.edu/alabama/resource.html]
Online Catalog
   [http://www.lib.auburn.edu/remote.html]
Special Collections Department
   [http://www.lib.auburn.edu/special/docs/collections.html]

## Birmingham Public Library        http://www.bham.lib.al.us/

| | |
|---|---|
| 2100 Park Place | Phone   (205) 226-3665 |
| Birmingham, AL 35203 | E-mail  rtorbert@bham.lib.al.us |

Archives and Manuscripts
   [http://www.bham.lib.al.us/archives.html]
Bibliography, Birmingham and Alabama, Articles
   [http://www.bham.lib.al.us/articles.htm]
Bibliography, Birmingham and Alabama, Books
   [http://www.bham.lib.al.us/books.htm]
Bibliography, Birmingham and Alabama, Dissertations
   [http://www.bham.lib.al.us/theses.htm]
Genealogy Resources, Tutwiler Collection
   [http://www.bham.lib.al.us/gene.htm]
Linn-Henley Research Library
   [http://www.bham.lib.al.us/linn.htm]
Southern History Department
   [http://www.bham.lib.al.us/south.html]

## Blount County Historical Society    http://members.aol.com/egun/Blhome.html

| | |
|---|---|
| P.O. Box 45 | Phone   (205) 274-7641 |
| Oneonta, AL 35121 | E-mail  BlountAL@aol.com |

Biography Index
    [http://members.aol.com/egun/bio.html]
Census, 1900 Index
    [http://members.aol.com/Blountal/1900Con.html]
County Courthouse Records
    [http://members.aol.com/egun/Records.html]

## *Outstanding Site*

| Tracking Your Roots ® | http://members.aol.com/genweblisa/genealog.htm |
|---|---|
| | E-mail  GenWebLisa@aol.com |

Links to Alabama Genealogical Sites
    [http://members.aol.com/genweblisa/genealog.htm]

| University of Alabama | http://www.ua.edu/ |
|---|---|
| Hoole Special Collections Library<br>P.O. Box 870266<br>Tuscaloosa, AL 35487-0266 | Phone  (205) 348-0500<br>E-mail  awatson@ua1vm.ua.edu |
| Alabama Heritage<br>P.O. Box 870342<br>Tuscaloosa, AL 35487-0342 | Phone  (205) 348-7467<br>E-mail  Heritage@ua1vm.ua.edu |

African American Resources
    [http://www.lib.ua.edu/genepath.htm]
Alabama Heritage, Journal
    [http://www.as.ua.edu/heritage/]
C.S.S. Alabama Collection, Virtual Tour
    [http://www.slis.ua.edu/tgtest/cssala/back2.htm]
Genealogy Resources
    [http://www.lib.ua.edu/genepath.htm]
Hoole Special Collections Library
    [http://www.lib.ua.edu/hoole.htm]
Post Card Collection
    [http://www.slis.ua.edu/projects/pcards/pcard.htm]
Southern Surgical Association
    [http://www.lhl.uab.edu:80/reynolds/ssa.html]

# ALASKA

## State Home Page

| Alaska State Government | http://www.state.ak.us |
|---|---|
| P.O. Box 110001<br>Juneau, AK 99811 | Phone  (907) 465-3500<br>Fax      (907) 465-3532<br>E-mail  Office_of_the_Governor@gov.state.ak.us |

Alaska Court System
    [http://www.alaska.net/~akctlib/homepage.htm]

Bureau of Vital Statistics
[http://health.hss.state.ak.us/htmlstuf/dph/vitals/vitalst.hTM]

# State Archives

| Alaska State Archives | http://ccl.alaska.edu/local/archives/table.html |
|---|---|

| 141 Willoughby Avenue<br>Juneau, AK 99801-1720 | Phone (907) 465-2270<br>Fax (907) 465-2465<br>E-mail archives@muskox.alaska.edu<br>johns@muskox.alaska.edu |

General overview of the State Archives
[http://ccl.alaska.edu/local/archives/table.html]

# State Library

| Alaska State Library | http://www.educ.state.ak.us/lam/library.html |
|---|---|

| P.O. Box 110571<br>Juneau, AK 99811-0571 | Phone (907) 465-2925<br>Fax (907) 465-2990<br>E-mail asl@muskox.alaska.edu<br>gladik@muskox.alaska.edu |

Alaska Historical Collections
[http://www.educ.state.ak.us/lam/library/hist/hist.html]
Alaska Library Directory
[http://ccl.alaska.edu/local/library/new/librarydirectory.html]
Alaska Newspaper Project
[http://www.educ.state.ak.us/lam/library/hist/newspaper.html]
Alaska State Publications Program
[http://www.educ.state.ak.us/lam/library/asp/asp.html]
Books About Alaska
[http://www.educ.state.ak.us/lam/library/hist/somebooks/some95.html]
SLED, Statewide Library Electronic Doorway
[http://sled.alaska.edu/Library.html]

# Other State Sites

| Fairbanks Genealogical Society | http://www.polarnet.com/users/fgs/ |
|---|---|

P.O. Box 60534
Fairbanks, AK 99706-0534

FGS Database
[http://www.polarnet.com/users/fgs/research/database.html]
Links
[http://www.polarnet.com/users/fgs/research/roots.html]

## *Outstanding Site*

| Ghosts of the Klondike Gold Rush | http://gold-rush.org |
|---|---|

Pan for Gold Database
[http://gold-rush.org/ghost-07.htm]

# ARIZONA

## State Home Page

State of Arizona WWW Page | http://www.state.az.us/

Links to Arizona Local and County Government
[http://www.state.az.us/pages/other.html]

## State Library and Archives

Arizona Department of Library, Archives and Public Records
http://www.lib.az.us/

State Capitol, Suite 442
1700 West Washington
Phoenix, AZ 85007

Phone (602) 542-4159
Fax (602) 542-4402
E-mail archive@dlapr.lib.az.us

State Board on Geographic and Historic Names

E-mail aznames@dlapr.lib.az.us

Arizona Libraries NewsWeek
[http://www.lib.az.us/newslttr/nov29.html]
Arizona Newspaper Project
[http://www.lib.az.us/research/newspapr.html]
Guide to Public Records
[http://www.lib.az.us/archives/guideto.html]
Links to other Arizona Libraries
[http://www.lib.az.us/dlapr/url.html]
Resources by County
[http://www.lib.az.us/archives/resource.html]
Where to Find Arizona Public Records
[http://www.lib.az.us/records/findrecs.html]

## Other State Sites

Arizona State University Library | http://www.lib.asu.edu/

Department of Archives and Manuscripts
Charles Trumbull Hayden Library, 4th Level
Tempe, AZ 85287

Phone (602) 965-4932
Fax (602) 965-0776
E-mail archives@asuvm.inre.asu.edu

Archives and Manuscripts Department
[http://www.lib.asu.edu/archives/dampage.htm]
Arizona Collection
[http://www.lib.asu.edu/archives/arizona.htm]
Arizona Historical Foundation
[http://www.public.asu.edu/~wabbit/ahf.htm]
Hayden Arizona Pioneer Biographies Collection
[http://www.lib.asu.edu/webdev/bios.html]
Labriola National American Indian Data Center
[http://www.lib.asu.edu/archives/labriola.htm]
Manuscript Collections
[http://www.lib.asu.edu/archives/msscoll.htm]

Family History Society of Arizona      http://www.getnet.com/charity/fhs/

P.O. Box 63094                                    E-mail   jeannie@getnet.com
Phoenix, AZ 85082-3094

Joint AGCIG and FHS Surname Project
    [http://surnames.com/agcig/topnames.htm]
Arizona Genealogical Societies List
    [http://www.getnet.com/charity/fhs/society.html]

# ARKANSAS

## State Home Page

State of Arkansas HomePage        http://www.state.ar.us:80/home.html

Arkansas Department of Health Services
    [http://health.state.ar.us/htm/serveidx.htm]
Arkansas Judiciary Home Page
    [http://www.state.ar.us:80/supremecourt/home.html]
Division of Vital Records Services
    [http://health.state.ar.us/htm/vr_faq.htm]
Links to Arkansas Sites
    [http://www.aristotle.net/arkansas/arklink.html]

## State Archives

Arkansas History Commission and State Archives
    http://www.state.ar.us:80/ahc/index.htm

One Capitol Mall                          Phone   (501) 682-6900
Little Rock, AR 72201

Overview of Resources
    [http://www.state.ar.us:80/ahc/resource.htm]

## State Library

Arkansas State Library            http://www.state.ar.us/html/ark_library.html

One Capitol Mall                          Phone   (501) 682-1527
Little Rock, AR 72201-1081

Overview
    [http://www.state.ar.us/html/ark_library.html]

## Other State Sites

Arkansas Department of Heritage Services
    http://wwwheritage.state.ar.us/dahhome.html

1500 Tower Building                       Phone   (501) 324-9150
Little Rock, AR 72201                     Fax     (501) 324-9154
                                          E-mail  INFO@DAH.STATE.AR.US

Delta Cultural Center
[http://wwwheritage.state.ar.us:80./her_dcc.html]

## Arkansas GenWeb Project          http://bl-12.rootsweb.com/~argenweb/

Ancestors of President Bill Clinton
[http://www.dsenter.com/arkansas/charts/ch1.htm]
Arkansas Query System
[http://bl-12.rootsweb.com/~argenweb/index.html#query]
Biography Index
[http://bl-12.rootsweb.com/~argenweb/index.html#biographies]
Guide to Genealogy Research in AR
[http://www.dsenter.com/arkansas/arreschk.htm]
Links
[http://bl-12.rootsweb.com/~argenweb/links.htm]
Surnames and Databases Online
[http://www.cswnet.com/~michael/connect.htm#top]

## Arkansas Internet Project          http://www.compnetar.com/~billc/

County Resources List
[http://www.compnetar.com/~billc/#ABOUT]
Links
[http://www.compnetar.com/~billc/]

## Arkansas Municipal League
http://www.aiea.ualr.edu/dina/mleague/publications/publications.html

| P.O. Box 38 | Phone | (501) 374-3484 |
| North Little Rock, AR 72115 | Fax | (501) 374-0541 |
| | E-mail | hhamner@aristotle.net |

Arkansas Cities
[http://www.aiea.ualr.edu/dina/cities.html]
City and Town Magazine
[http://www.aiea.ualr.edu/dina/mleague/publications/citytown/citytown.html]
Other Links
[http://www.aiea.ualr.edu/dina/commlinks/links.html]

## University of Arkansas Library Home Page
http://www.uark.edu/campus-resources/libinfo/

| Fayetteville, AR 72701-1201 | Phone | (501) 575-5577 |
| | Fax | (501) 575-6656 |
| | Telnet | tn library.uark.edu (login: infolink) |

Arkansas Links
[http://www.uark.edu/libinfo/arkres/index.html]
Biography and Genealogy
[http://cavern.uark.edu/libinfo/speccoll/shortguides/genealogy.html]
Index to the Vertical File
[http://cavern.uark.edu/libinfo/speccoll/vertfil1.html]
Japanese-American Internment
[http://cavern.uark.edu/libinfo/speccoll/shortguides/japanese.html]
Manuscripts, Civil War
htttp://cavern.uark.edu/libinfo/speccoll/civilwar.html]

Manuscripts, Women's Studies
    [http://cavern.uark.edu/libinfo/speccoll/specwom.html]
Special Collections Division
    [http://cavern.uark.edu/libinfo/speccoll/index.html]

# CALIFORNIA

## State Home Page

| California State Home Page | http://www.state.ca.us/ |
|---|---|

California History
    [http://library.ca.gov/california/cahhisto.html]

## State Archives

| California State Archives | http://www.ss.ca.gov/archives/archives_home.htm |
|---|---|

1020 "O" Street                          Phone   (916) 653-2246
Sacramento, CA 95814-5704                Fax      (916) 653-7363
                                         E-mail  ArchivesWeb@SS.CA.GOV

Collections
    [http://www.ss.ca.gov/archives/archives_home.htm#collections]

## State Library

| California State Library | http://library.ca.gov/california/State_Library/ |
|---|---|

P.O. Box 942837                          Phone   (916) 654-0174
Sacramento, CA 94237-0001                        (916) 654-0176 CA History Room

Library and Courts Building I            E-mail  csl-adm@library.ca.gov
914 Capitol Mall, Room 220
Sacramento, CA 95814

Sutro Library                            Phone   (415) 731-4477
480 Winston Drive
San Francisco, CA 94132-1777

California Library Directory, 1996
    [http://www.lib.berkeley.edu:8000/STLIB/index.html]
    [http://library.ca.gov/california/State_Library/publibs.html]
Online Catalog
    [http://library.ca.gov/california/State_Library/pubser/pubser03.html]
Sutro Library
    [http://sfpl.lib.ca.us/gencoll/gencolsu.htm]

## State Genealogical Society

| California Genealogical Society | http://pw2.netcom.com/~dwilma/cgs.html |
|---|---|

300 Brannan Street, Suite 409            Phone   (415) 777-9936
P.O. Box 77105
San Francisco, CA 94107-0105

California GenWeb Project
    [http://www.compuology.com/cagenweb/]

Library
[http://pw2.netcom.com/~dwilma/cgs.html#Library]

# State Historical Society

## California Historical Society        http://www.calhist.org/

678 Mission Street                    Phone   (415) 357-1848
San Francisco, CA 94105-4014          Fax     (415) 357-1850
                                      E-mail  info@calhist.org

California City Directories
[http://www.calhist.org/Support_Info/Collections/Library-Misc/CalifCityDir.html]
California Historical Agencies by County
[http://www.calhist.org/Support_Info/CHAs.htmld/]
California History (Journal). Index.
[http://www.calhist.org/Pub.html]
Guide to California County Histories
[http://www.calhist.org/Support_Info/Collections/Library-Misc/CACountyHistoriesGuide.htmld/]
Manuscript Collection, Descriptive Guides
[http://www.calhist.org/Support_Info/Collections/Manuscripts/MSDescriptiveGuides.htmld/]
Photograph Collection Guides and Indexes
[http://www.calhist.org/Photo.html]
San Francisco Manuscript Collections. Preliminary Listing
[http://www.calhist.org/Support_Info/Collections/Manuscripts/MSS-SF-Guide/MS-SFColl1-Intro.html]

# Other State Sites

## California State University, Chico       http://www.csuchico.edu/

Meriam Library, Room 305a, zip 295    Phone   (916) 898-6342
Chico, CA 95929-0295                  E-mail  nhoward@ecst.csuchico.edu
                                              mgillis@oavax.csuchico.edu

Association for Northern California Records and Research
P.O. Box 3024
Chico, CA 95927

Association for Northern California Records and Research
[http://www.csuchico.edu/ancrr/hist.html]
Library
[http://www.csuchico.edu/lbib/]
Manuscript Collections
[http://www.csuchico.edu/lbib/spc/msstitl.htm]
Northeastern California Photo Collection
[http://www.csuchico.edu/lbib/spc/fotocoll.html]
Special Collections Department
[http://www.csuchico.edu/lbib/spc/spbrochr.html]

## California State University, Fresno      http://duchess.lib.csufresno.edu/

Special Collections Department         E-mail  specialc@listserv.csufresno.edu
Henry Madden Library
Fresno, CA 93740

June English (Local History and Genealogy) Collection
    [http://duchess.lib.csufresno.edu/SpecialCollections/EnglishCollection.html]
Special Collections Department
    [http://duchess.lib.csufresno.edu/SpecialCollections/Welcome.html]

## California State University, Northridge       http://www.csun.edu/

Special Collections Department                  Phone   (818) 677-2832
Oviatt Library, Room 4                          E-mail  tgardner@csun.edu
Northridge, CA 91330-1600

California Studies Collection
    [http://www.csun.edu/~spcoll/hpsclist.html#calif]
Guide to Collections on Los Angeles
    [http://www.csun.edu/~spcoll/laguide.html]
Index of Research Topics
    [http://www.csun.edu/~spcoll/urban_archives/hbrestop.html]
Japanese-American Internment, 1942-1945
    [http://www.csun.edu/~spcoll/fdgds6.html#heart]
Special Collections Department
    [http://www.csun.edu/~vfoao0cq/hbspcoll.html]

## California Views                       http://www.caviews.com/

Pat Hathaway Collection of Historical Photos    Phone   (408) 373-3811
469 Pacific Street                              E-mail  hathaway@mbay.net
Monterey, CA 93940-2702

Guide to California Historical Photographs
    [http://www.caviews.com/]

## Chinese Historical Society of Southern California       http://www.chssc.org/

P.O. Box 862647                         E-mail  chssc@chssc.org
Los Angeles, CA 90086-2647

Overview
    [http://www.chssc.org/]

## H-California                        http://h-net2.msu.edu/~cal/

California Online History Network
    [http://h-net2.msu.edu/~cal/about/intro.html]

## Japanese American History Archives
    http://www.e-media.com/fillmore/museum/jt/jaha/jaha.html

1840 Sutter Street                      Phone   (415) 776-0661
San Francisco, CA 94115

Photograph Archives
    [http://www.e-media.com/fillmore/museum/jt/jaha/jaha3.html]

## Outstanding Site

### Museum of the City of San Francisco
http://www.sfmuseum.org

2801 Leavenworth Street
San Francisco, CA 94133-1117

Phone   (415) 928-0289
E-mail  curator@sfmuseum.org

Data and Links about San Francisco History
    [http://www.sfmuseum.org/hist1/subjects.html]
San Francisco History By Subject
    [http://www.sfmuseum.org/hist1/index0.html]
San Francisco History By Year
    [http://www.sfmuseum.org/hist1/index.html]
San Francisco History Index
    [http://www.sfmuseum.org/hist1/subjects.html]

### San Diego Historical Society
http://edweb.sdsu.edu/SDHS/histsoc.html

Casa de Balboa, Lower Level
1649 El Prado, Balboa Park
P.O. Box 81825
San Diego, CA 92138-1825

Phone   (619) 232-6203

Overview
    [http://edweb.sdsu.edu/SDHS/histsoc.html]

### San Francisco History
http://www.zpub.com/sf/history/

Extensive site with data, articles and related links
    [http://www.zpub.com/sf/history/]
Notes on San Francisco Genealogy
    [http://www.sfo.com/~timandpamwolf/sfrancty.htm]
Selected Annotated Bibliography
    [http://rs6.loc.gov/papr/sfbib.html]

### San Francisco Public Library
http://sfpl.lib.ca.us/

Civic Center
San Francisco, CA 94102

Phone   (415) 557-4400
E-mail  ennism@sfpl.lib.ca.us

Genealogy Page
    [http://sfpl.lib.ca.us/gencoll/gencolgn.htm]
History and Biography
    [http://sfpl.lib.ca.us/gencoll/gencol09.htm]

### San Francisco State University
http://www.sfsu.edu

Library
480 Winston Drive
San Francisco, CA 94132-1719

Phone  (415) 564-4010
Fax     (415) 564-3606
E-mail  larc@sfsu.edu

Labor Archives and Research Center
    [http://www.sfsu.edu/~library/ServColl/larc.html]
Library
    [http://www.sfsu.edu/~library]

Listing of Collections
   [http://www.sfsu.edu/~library/ServColl/holdings.html]

## Sonoma State University          http://www.sonoma.edu

Library                         Phone   (707) 664-2861
1801 East Cotati Avenue         E-mail  Lisa Strawter @sonoma.edu
Rohnert Park, CA 94928-3609             Sandra Walton@Sonoma.edu

Finley McFarling Genealogy Collection
   [http://www.sonoma.edu/library/special/Finley.html]
Indo-Chinese Collection
   [http://www.sonoma.edu/library/special/indo.html]
John Schackelford Taylor Papers
   [http://www.sonoma.edu/library/special/taylor.html]
Library
   [http://www.sonoma.edu/library/]
NorthBay Ethnic Archive
   [http://www.sonoma.edu/library/special/North.html]
Northwestern Pacific Railroad Historical Society, Inc.
   [http://www.sonoma.edu/library/special/NWPHShomepage.html]
Special Collections Department
   [http://www.sonoma.edu/library/special/]

## Southern California Chapter Association of Professional Genealogists
   http://www.compuology.com/sccapg/

P.O. Box 9486                   E-mail  Tkashuba@aol.com
Brea, CA 92822-9486                     BarbZR@msn.com

Overview of the Chapter and Area Events
   [http://www.compuology.com/sccapg/]

## University of California, Berkeley    http://www.berkeley.edu/

The Bancroft Library            Phone   (510) 642-6481
Berkeley, CA 94720-6000

Bancroft Library
   [http://www.lib.berkeley.edu/BANC/]
California Heritage Collection Digital Image Access Project
   [http://sunsite.berkeley.edu/CalHeritage/]
California Newspaper and Periodical Indexes
   [http://library.berkeley.edu/BANC/banccoll/newsindexes.html]
Collection Guides
   [http://www.lib.berkeley.edu/BANC/#collect]
Finding Aids for Archival Collections
   [http://sunsite.berkeley.edu/FindingAids/]
Friends of the Bancroft Library
   [http://www.lib.berkeley.edu/BANC/Friends/]
Latin Americana
   [http://library.berkeley.edu/BANC/banccoll/latin.html]
Online Catalogs
   [http://infolib.berkeley.edu/Catalogs/]

Pictorial Collections
   [http://library.berkeley.edu/BANC/pictorial.html]
Regional Oral History Office
   [http://www.lib.berkeley.edu/BANC/ROHO/]
Sanborn and Other Fire Insurance Maps
   [http://www.lib.berkeley.edu/EART/sanborn.html]
UC Berkeley Libraries
   [http://www.lib.berkeley.edu/]

## University of California, Davis   http://www.lib.ucdavis.edu/speccoll/

| | |
|---|---|
| Department of Special Collections | Phone   (916) 752-1621 |
| General Library | Fax      (916) 752-3148 |
| Davis, CA 95616-5292 | E-mail  jlskarstad@ucdavis.edu |

California History Collection
   [http://www.lib.ucdavis.edu/speccoll/html/ca_hist.html]
Guide to Manuscripts
   [http://www.lib.ucdavis.edu/speccoll/html/manu_idx.html#Jabber]

# COLORADO

## State Home Page

## Colorado State Homepage   http://www.state.co.us/

Links, Colorado Cities
   [http://www.state.co.us/communities_dir/communitiesmenu.html]
Links, Colorado Government
   [http://www.state.co.us/gov_dir/govmenu.html]
Links, Colorado Groups and Organizations
   [http://www.state.co.us/org_dir/orgmenu.html]
Links, Colorado Newspapers
   [http://www.state.co.us/today_dir/todaymenu.html]
Vital Records
   [http://www.state.co.us/gov_dir/cdphe_dir/hs/cshom.html#Birth Certificate]

## State Archives

## Colorado State Archives   http://www.state.co.us/gov_dir/gss/archives/index.html

| | |
|---|---|
| 1313 Sherman Street, Room 1B-20 | Phone   (303) 866-2358 |
| Denver, CO 80203 | (800) 305-3442 |
| | Fax      (303) 866-2257 |

Colorado Civil War Casualties
   [http://www.state.co.us/gov_dir/gss/archives/ciwardea.html]
Colorado History, Biography etc.
   [http://www.state.co.us/gov_dir/gss/archives/arc_colr.html]
Court Records
   [http://www.state.co.us/gov_dir/gss/archives/court.html]
Marriage and Divorce Records
   [http://www.state.co.us/gov_dir/gss/archives/marr1.html]
Military Records
   [http://www.state.co.us/gov_dir/gss/archives/military.html]

Naturalization Records
  [http://www.state.co.us/gov_dir/gss/archives/natural.html]
Prison Records
  [http://www.state.co.us/gov_dir/gss/archives/prison.html]
Spanish American War Volunteers
  [http://www.state.co.us/gov_dir/gss/archives/spamwar.html]
School Records
  [http://www.state.co.us/gov_dir/gss/archives/school.html]

# State Library

## Office of Library and Adult Services        http://www.aclin.org/

| Colorado Department of Education | Phone | (303) 866-6900 |
| 201 East Colfax Avenue | Fax | (303) 830-0793 |
| Denver, CO 80203 | | |

Access Colorado Library and Information Network
  [http://www.aclin.org/about.html]
Access Colorado Library and Information Network, News
  [http://www.aclin.org/news/aclin/]
Links, Colorado Libraries
  [http://www.aclin.org/libraries/coweb.html]

# State Genealogical Society

## Colorado Genealogical Society        http://www.cogensoc.org/cgs/cgs-home.htm

| P.O. Box 9218 | Phone | (303) 571-1535 |
| Denver, CO 80209-0218 | E-mail | genealogist@cogensoc.org |

Colorado Genealogical Societies
  [http://www.cogensoc.org/cgs/cgs-soc.htm]

# Other State Sites

## Auraria Library        http://www.cudenver.edu/public/library/

| Lawrence at 11th Street | Phone | (303) 556-8373 |
| Denver, CO 80204 | Fax | (303) 556-3528 |
| | E-mail | ftapp@carbon.cudenver.edu |

Archives and Special Collections
  [http://www.cudenver.edu/public/library/archives/archives.html]
Manuscript Collections
  [http://www.cudenver.edu/public/library/archives/archives.html]

## Colorado College
  http://www.cc.colorado.edu/Library/SpecialCollections/Special.html

| Special Collections and Archives | Phone | (719) 389-6668 |
| Tutt Library | Fax | (719) 389-6859 |
| 1021 North Cascade Avenue | E-mail | VKIEFER@cc.Colorado.edu |
| Colorado Springs, CO 80903 | | |

Archives and Records Survey Project Manual
  [http://www.cc.colorado.edu/Library/SpecialCollections/ArchiveProject/TOC.html]

Colorado Photograph Index
[gopher://academic.cc.colorado.edu:70/11%5B_library._data._SPEC_COLL._
PHOTO_FILE%5D]
Colorado and Pikes Peak Region Collection
[http://www.cc.colorado.edu/Library/SpecialCollections/Colo.html]
Colorado Prospector Index
[gopher://academic.cc.colorado.edu:70/0%5B_library._data._SPEC_COLL._
PPRAMI%5D_COLO_PROS.LIS]
Colorado Subject File
[gopher://academic.cc.colorado.edu:70/0%5B_library._data._SPEC_COLL._
PPRAMI%5D_COLO_INFO.LIS]
Diaries
[gopher://academic.cc.colorado.edu:70/0%5B_library._data._SPEC_COLL._
PPRAMI%5D_DIAR_SUMM.LIS]
Manuscript Collections Index
[gopher://academic.cc.colorado.edu:70/11%5B_library._data._SPEC_COLL._MAN_COLL%5D]

## Colorado Health Statistics and Vital Records Division
http://www.state.co.us/gov_dir/cdphe_dir/hs/cshom.html

| | |
|---|---|
| Colorado Department of<br>    Public Health and Environment<br>4300 Cherry Creek Drive South<br>Denver, CO 80222-1530 | Phone   (303) 782-5576<br>Fax       (303) 756-4464<br>E-mail  linda.eisnach@state.co.us |

Application forms for Birth and Death Certificates
[http://www.state.co.us/gov_dir/cdphe_dir/hs/cshom.html]

## Denver Public Library
http://www.denver.lib.co.us/

| | |
|---|---|
| 10 West 14th Avenue Parkway<br>Denver, CO 80204 | Phone   (303) 640-6200 |

Genealogy Resources
[gopher://dpl20.denver.lib.co.us:70/11/reference/Genealogy]

## University of Northern Colorado
http://www.univnorthco.edu

| | |
|---|---|
| James A. Michener Library<br>Greeley, CO 80639 | Phone   (970) 351-2854<br>Fax       (970) 351-2540<br>E-mail  mlinscom@mail.UnivNorthCo.edu |

Archives and Special Collections
[http://www.univnorthco.edu/library/archives.htm]
Finding Aids Index
[http://www.univnorthco.edu/library/arc_a-b.htm]
Library
[http://www.univnorthco.edu/library]

# CONNECTICUT
## State Home Page

## Connecticut State Home Page
http://www.state.ct.us/index.html

Connecticut Judicial System
[http://www.cslnet.ctstateu.edu/judicial/direct.htm]

Links, Connecticut Cities and Towns
      [http://www.state.ct.us/MUNIC/town.htm]
Links to Connecticut Libraries
      [http://spirit.lib.uconn.edu/ConnState/Libraries.html]
Motor Vehicle Department Registration Data
      [http://www.cslnet.ctstateu.edu/dmv/copypg.htm]
Vital Records
      [http://www.ctstateu.edu/~dph/vr-birth.html]

# State Library and Archives
## *Outstanding Site*

| Connecticut State Library | http://www.www.cslnet.ctstateu.edu/ |
| --- | --- |

| 231 Capitol Avenue<br>Hartford, CT 06106 | Phone   (860) 566-4301<br>Fax      (860) 566-8940<br>E-mail  rakeroyd@csunet.ctstateu.edu |
| Connecticut Newspaper Project | Phone   (860) 566-3557<br>Fax      (860) 566-8940<br>E-mail  janec@cslnet.ststateu.edu |
| History and Genealogy Section | Phone   (860) 566-3692<br>Fax      (860) 566-2133<br>E-mail  richardr@cslnet.ctstateu.edu |
| Museum of Connecticut History | Phone   (860) 566-3056<br>Fax      (860) 566-2133<br>E-mail  deann@cslnet.ctstateu.edu |
| Public Records Examiner | Phone   (860) 566-5088<br>Fax      (860) 566-2133<br>E-mail  euniced@cslnet.ctstateu.edu |
| State Archives | Phone   (860) 566-5650<br>Fax      (860) 566-2133<br>E-mail  markj@cslnet.ctstateu.edu |

Bible Records
      [http://www.cslnet.ctstateu.edu/bible.htm]
Bibliography
      [http://www.cslnet.ctstateu.edu/history.htm]
Cemetery Index
      [http://www.cslnet.ctstateu.edu/halecol2.htm#halecem]
Census, Military Preparedness, 1917
      [http://www.cslnet.ctstateu.edu/miltrec.htm]
Census Records
      [http://www.cslnet.ctstateu.edu/cenintro.htm]
Church Records
      [http://www.cslnet.ctstateu.edu/church.htm]
Connecticut Charter of 1662
      [http://www.ctstateu.edu/state/historical/colony.html]
Connecticut Constitution
      [http://www.ctstateu.edu/state/historical/ct_const.html]

Connecticut Newspaper Project
    [http://www.cslnet.ctstateu.edu/cnp.htm]
Connecticut State Historical Records Advisory Board
    [http://www.cslnet.ctstateu.edu/cshrab.htm]
Digital Library Resources
    [http://www.cslnet.ctstateu.edu/diglib.htm]
Fundamental Orders (First Constitution)
    [http://www.ctstateu.edu/state/historical/first.html]
Genealogical Sources
    [http://www.cslnet.ctstateu.edu/basic.htm]
German-Americans
    [http://www.cslnet.ctstateu.edu/germans.htm]
History and Genealogy Section
    [http://www.cslnet.ctstateu.edu/handg.htm]
Irish Genealogy Resources
    [http://www.cslnet.ctstateu.edu/irish.htm]
Italian Genealogy Resources
    [http://www.cslnet.ctstateu.edu/italians.htm]
Land Records
    [http://www.cslnet.ctstateu.edu/landrec.htm]
Laws, Public Acts
    [http://www.cslnet.ctstateu.edu/pa/index.htm]
Laws, Special Acts
    [http://www.cslnet.ctstateu.edu/sa/index.htm]
LDS Family History Centers
    [http://www.cslnet.ctstateu.edu/ldsmicro.htm]
Military Records
    [http://www.cslnet.ctstateu.edu/miltrec.htm]
Native American Resources
    [http://www.cslnet.ctstateu.edu/indians.htm]
Naturalization Records
    [http://www.cslnet.ctstateu.edu/natural.htm]
Newspaper Abstracts
    [http://www.cslnet.ctstateu.edu/halecol2.htm#abstract]
Newspaper, Marriages and Deaths Index
    [http://www.cslnet.ctstateu.edu/halecol2.htm#mardeth]
Newspapers, History of in Connecticut
    [http://www.cslnet.ctstateu.edu/cnp_np.htm]
Newspapers, Links to Connecticut Online
    [http://www.cslnet.ctstateu.edu/cnp_hp.htm]
Passenger Lists
    [http://www.cslnet.ctstateu.edu/passlist.htm]
Polish American Genealogical Resources
    [http://www.cslnet.ctstateu.edu/polish.htm]
Probate Records
    [http://www.cslnet.ctstateu.edu/probintr.htm]
Public Records Administrator
    [http://www.cslnet.ctstateu.edu/opra.htm]
Rules and Procedures
    [http://www.cslnet.ctstateu.edu/arcrules.htm]
State Archives
    [http://www.cslnet.ctstateu.edu/archives.htm]

Towns, Dates of Founding etc.
    [http://www.cslnet.ctstateu.edu/cttowns.htm]
Towns, Links
    [http://www.state.ct.us/MUNIC/munic.htm]
Veteran's Death Indexes
    [http://www.cslnet.ctstateu.edu/halecol2.htm#vet]
Vital Records
    [http://www.cslnet.ctstateu.edu/vitals.htm]
Vital Records, Barbour Collection
    [http://www.cslnet.ctstateu.edu/barbour.htm]
Vital Records, Divorce Records
    [http://www.cslnet.ctstateu.edu/divorce.htm]
Vital Records, Law. Public Act 96-258.
    [http://www.cslnet.ctstateu.edu/pa/pa000252.htm]
Vital Records, Private Sources
    [http://www.cslnet.ctstateu.edu/private.htm]
Women's Archival Resources
    [http://www.cslnet.ctstateu.edu/women.htm]

# State Genealogical Society

## Connecticut Society of Genealogists, Inc.          http://www.fgs.org/~fgs/soc0034.htm

P.O. Box 435                          Phone    (860) 569-0002
Glastonbury, CT 06033-0435

Overview
    [http://www.fgs.org/~fgs/soc0034.htm]

# State Historical Society

## Connecticut Historical Society          http://www.hartnet.org/chs/main.htm

1 Elizabeth Street                    Phone    (860) 236-5621
Hartford, CT 06105                    Fax      (860) 236-2664
                                      E-mail  ewilkie@ix.netcom.com
Library
    [http://www.hartnet.org/chs/library.htm]

# Other State Sites

## Essex Historical Society          http://www.essexct.com/#Top

P.O. Box 261                          Phone    (860) 767-8269
Essex, CT 06426                       E-mail  EssexCT@aol.com

A Brief History of Essex by Donald Malcarne
    [http://www.essexct.com/History/]
Directions, Including Maps and Links to nearby Towns
    [http://www.essexct.com/Directions/]

## Middlesex Genealogical Society          http://www.darien.lib.ct.us/mgs/default.htm

P. O. Box 1111                        Phone    (203) 655-2734
Darien, CT 06820-1111                 E-mail  sfpr48a@prodigy.com
                                              dbowley@concentric.net

Links
    [http://www.darien.lib.ct.us/mgs/default.htm]

## Mystic Seaport      http://www.mystic.org/welcome.html

| G. W. Blunt White Library | Phone | (860) 572-5367 |
| P.O. Box 6000 | Fax | (860) 572-5394 |
| Mystic, CT 06355 | TDD | (860) 572-5319 |

Collections
    [http://www.mystic.org/public/collections/collections.html]
David Gelston Papers
    [http://www.mystic.org/public/collections/manuscripts/coll.inventories/coll170br.html]
Library
    [http://www.mystic.org/public/collections/blunt.library.html]
Manuscripts
    [http://www.mystic.org/public/collections/manuscripts.html]
Oral History
    [http://www.mystic.org/public/collections/manuscripts/coll.inventories/coll170br.html]
Rosenfeld Photograph  Collection
    [http://www.mystic.org/public/collections/rosenfeld.html]
Ship Plans
    [http://www.mystic.org/public/collections/ships.plans.html]

## Stamford Historical Society      http://www.cslnet.ctstateu.edu/stamford/index.htm

| 1508 High Ridge Road | Phone | (203) 329-1183 |
| Stamford, CT 06903 | Fax | (203) 322-1607 |

Bibliography by Ronald Marcus
    [http://www.cslnet.ctstateu.edu/stamford/biblio.htm]
Grand Lists, 1641-1821
    [http://www.cslnet.ctstateu.edu/stamford/granlist.htm]
Historic Postcards Tour
    [http://www.cslnet.ctstateu.edu/stamford/photo.htm]
History of Stamford
    [http://www.cslnet.ctstateu.edu/stamford/history.htm]

## Trumbull Bicentennial Page      http://trumbull.ct.us/history/

    E-mail  auria@worldnet.att.net

History of the Town of Trumbull. By Helen Plumb
    [http://trumbull.ct.us/history/thistory.htm]

## Trumbull Historical Society      http://pages.prodigy.com/sakal/ths.htm

| 1856 Huntington Turnpike | Phone | (203) 377-6620 |
| P.O. Box 312 | | |
| Trumbull, CT 06611 | | |

Overview of the Society
    [http://pages.prodigy.com/sakal/ths.htm]

# DELAWARE

## State Home Page

| State of Delaware HomePage | http://www.state.de.us |
|---|---|

Links, Delaware
[http://www.state.de.us/www/intro.htm]

## State Archives

| Delaware Public Archives | http://del-aware.lib.de.us/archives/ |
|---|---|

Hall of Records
Dover, DE 19901

Phone    (302) 739-5318
Fax       (302) 739-2578
E-mail  archives@state.de.us

Census Records
[http://del-aware.lib.de.us/archives/census.htm]
Civil War Records
[http://del-aware.lib.de.us/archives/civilwar.htm]
Delaware Historical Records Advisory Board
[http://del-aware.lib.de.us/archives/dhrab.htm]
Directory of Historical Records in DE Repositories
[http://www.magpage.com/~tdoherty/dehisrec.html]
Friends of the Delaware Archives
[http://del-aware.lib.de.us/archives/foda.htm]
Guide to Holdings
[http://del-aware.lib.de.us/archives/guide.htm]
Kent County Probate Index
[http://del-aware.lib.de.us/archives/kc.htm]
Other Delaware Repositories
[http://del-aware.lib.de.us/archives/list.htm]
Overview
[http://del-aware.lib.de.us/archives/general.htm]
Vital Records
[http://del-aware.lib.de.us/archives/vital.htm]

## State Library

| Delaware State Library | http://www.lib.de.us/ |
|---|---|

43 South DuPont Highway
Dover, DE 19901-7430

Phone    (302) 739-4748
Fax       (302) 739-6948
E-mail  webmaster@lib.de.us

Delaware On-line Library Catalogs
[http://www.lib.de.us/about/index.html#Del-AWARE]
Links, Delaware Libraries
[http://www.lib.de.us/de-libs.html]

## State Genealogical Society

| Delaware Genealogical Society | http://www.magpage.com/~tdoherty/ |
|---|---|

505 Market Street Mall
Wilmington, DE 19801-3091

E-mail  tdoherty@magpage.com

Delaware Counties, Hundreds, Towns, Places
[http://www.magpage.com/~tdoherty/delhund.html]
Delaware Families Project
[http://www.magpage.com/~tdoherty/delfam.html]
Delaware Genealogical Research Guide
[http://www.magpage.com/~tdoherty/dgsguide.html]
Delaware Genealogical Society Journal. Table of Contents.1980- .
[http://www.magpage.com/~tdoherty/dgsj.html]
Historical Records in Delaware
[http://www.magpage.com/~tdoherty/dehisrec.html]
Queries and Index
[http://www.magpage.com/~tdoherty/dgsmemq.html]

## State Historical Society

| Historical Society of Delaware | http://www.hsd.org/ |
|---|---|
| 505 North Market Street<br>Wilmington, DE 19801-3091 | Phone (302) 655-7161<br>Fax (302) 655-7844<br>E-mail hsd@dca.net |

Overview
[http://www.hsd.org/]

## Other State Sites

| Delaware GenWeb Project | http://www.geocities.com/Heartland/8074/state_de.htm |
|---|---|
| | E-mail crossd@cyberia.com |

Links to County Sites
[http://www.geocities.com/Heartland/8074/state_de.htm]
New Castle County Data
http://www.geocities.com/Heartland/8074/newcastle_lookups.html]
Sussex County Lookups
[http://www.geocities.com/Heartland/8074/sussex_lookups.html]

| University of Delaware | http://www.lib.udel.edu/ |
|---|---|
| Special Collections Department<br>Library<br>Newark, DE 19717-5267 | Phone (302) 831-6952<br>Fax (302) 831-1046<br>E-mail timothy.murray@mvs.udel.edu<br>lrjm@udel.edu |

Delaware in Wartime
[http://www.lib.udel.edu/ud/spec/exhibits/wartime.html]
Finding Aids
[http://www.lib.udel.edu/ud/spec/sc_mss.html]
Special Collections Department
[http://www.lib.udel.edu/ud/spec/]

# FLORIDA

## State Home Page

| Florida Home Page | http://www.state.fl.us/ |
|---|---|

Links, Florida
[http://fcn.state.fl.us/fcn/3/index.phtml]

# State Archives

## Bureau of Archives and Records Management
http://www.dos.state.fl.us/dlis/archives.html

R. A. Gray Building                Phone   (904) 487-2073
500 South Bronough Street          Fax     (904) 488-4894
Tallahassee, FL   32399-0250       E-mail  barm@mail.dos.state.fl.us

Archives Catalog
   [http://www.dos.state.fl.us/dlis/barm/aiims/aiims1.htm]
Collections
   [http://www.dos.state.fl.us/dlis/barm/fsa.html#coll]
Florida Records Storage Center
   [http://www.dos.state.fl.us/dlis/barm/fsrc.html]
Florida State Archives
   [http://www.dos.state.fl.us/dlis/barm/fsa.html]
Photograph Collection
   [http://www.dos.state.fl.us/fpc/]
Records Schedules
   [http://www.dos.state.fl.us/dlis/barm/gensched.htm]
Technical Bulletin, Newsletter Fulltext
   [http://www.dos.state.fl.us/dlis/barm/techbull/techindx.htm]

# State Library

## State Library of Florida          http://www.dos.state.fl.us/sos/divisions/dlis/dlis.html

R. A. Gray Building, Second Floor    Phone   (904) 487-2651
Tallahassee, FL 32399-0250           Fax     (904) 488-2746

City Directories
   [http://www.dos.state.fl.us/dlis/citydir.html]
New Book List
   [http://www.dos.state.fl.us/dlis/blns/newbooks/booksmay.htm]
Orange Seed, Technical Bulletin, Fulltext
   [http://www.dos.state.fl.us/dlis/Orange/index.htm]

# State Genealogical Society

## Florida State Genealogical Society       http://www.fgs.org/~fgs/soc0275.htm

P.O. Box 10249
Tallahassee, FL 32302

Overview
   [http://www.fgs.org/~fgs/soc0275.htm]

# State Historical Society

## Florida Historical Society          http://www.lib.usf.edu/spccoll/fhs/fhs.html

1320 Highland Avenue                 Phone   (407) 259-0947
Melbourne, FL 32935

Overview
   [http://www.lib.usf.edu/spccoll/fhs/fhs.html]

# Other State Sites

## Historical Museum of Southern Florida
http://www.historical-museum.org/index.htm

101 West Flagler Street
Miami, FL 33130

Phone   (305) 375-1492
E-mail  hasf@ix.netcom.com

Collection Guide
    [http://www.historical-museum.org/collect/guide/guide.htm]
Ethnic Groups
    [http://www.historical-museum.org/folklife/groups.htm]
History, Articles, Fulltext
    [http://www.historical-museum.org/history/history.htm]

## Orlando Public Library
http://www.ocls.lib.fl.us/index.htm

101 East Central Boulevard
Orlando, FL 32801

Phone   (407) 425-4694

Genealogy Department Guide
    [http://www.ocls.lib.fl.us/infodge.htm]

## Seminole Tribe of Florida
http://www.gate.net/~semtribe

E-mail  semtribe@gate.net.

Library
    [http://www.gate.net/~semtribe/library/library.html]

## Society of Florida Archivists
http://mailer.fsu.edu/~baltman/sfa.html

Historical Association of Southern Florida
14220 Leaning Pine Drive
Miami Lakes, FL 33014

E-mail  baltman@mailer.fsu.edu

Overview
    [http://mailer.fsu.edu/~baltman/sfa.html]

## University of Florida
http://www.ufl.edu/

P. K. Yonge Library of Florida History
208 Smathers Library
Gainesville, FL 32611

Phone   (352) 392-0319
E-mail  jeingr@nervm.nerdc.ufl.edu

Biographical Materials
    [http://caroline.eastlib.ufl.edu/spec/pkyonge/biogpkt.html]
Church Records
    [http://caroline.eastlib.ufl.edu/spec/pkyonge/religion.html]
Collections, Chronological Guide
    [http://caroline.eastlib.ufl.edu/spec/pkyonge/chronol0.html]
Collections, Spanish Borderlands
    [http://caroline.eastlib.ufl.edu/spec/pkyonge/brdrland.html]
Historical Society Newsletters
    [http://caroline.eastlib.ufl.edu/spec/pkyonge/histsoc.html]

Libraries
    [http://caroline.eastlib.ufl.edu/]
Manuscripts
    [http://caroline.eastlib.ufl.edu/spec/pkyonge/manuscrp.html]
Maps
    [http://caroline.eastlib.ufl.edu/spec/pkyonge/fhmaps.html]
Newspapers
    [http://caroline.eastlib.ufl.edu/spec/pkyonge/newspap.html]
P. K. Yonge Library
    [http://caroline.eastlib.ufl.edu/spec/pkyonge/]

# University of Miami                    http://www.miami.edu/

| | |
|---|---|
| Archives and Special Collections Department<br>Richter Library<br>Coral Gables, FL 33124 | Phone         (305) 284-3247<br>Fax     (305) 665-7352<br>E-mail   wbrown@miami.ir.miami.edu |

Archives and Special Collections Department
    [http://www.library.miami.edu/archives/intro.html]
Collections
    [http://www.library.miami.edu/archives/cuban.html]
Cuban Collection
    [http://www.library.miami.edu/archives/cuban.html]
New Acquisitions
    [http://www.library.miami.edu/archives/intro.html]
Richter Library
    [http://www.library.miami.edu/]

## *Outstanding Site*

# University of South Florida          http://www.usf.edu

| | |
|---|---|
| Special Collections Department<br>USF Library, LIB 407<br>4202 East Fowler Avenue<br>Tampa, FL 33620-5400 | Phone   (813) 974-2731<br>Fax     (813) 974-5153<br>E-mail  tomkemp@lib.usf.edu |

Biography Index
    [http://www.lib.usf.edu/spccoll/guide/b/biograph/guide.html]
Census Records
    [http://www.lib.usf.edu/spccoll/guide/contain/f11con.html]
City Directories
    [http://www.lib.usf.edu/spccoll/city.html]
Genealogy Resources, Including Links to the Best Sites
    [http://www.lib.usf.edu/spccoll/genea.html]
Hillsborough County Marriage Records, Original Documents
    [http://www.lib.usf.edu/spccoll/marriage.html]
Librarians Serving Genealogists
    http://www.cas.usf.edu/lis/genealib/
Links, Florida
    [http://www.lib.usf.edu/spccoll/flweb.html]
Photograph Collections
    [http://www.lib.usf.edu/spccoll/photo.html]

"Psssstt....Want to See the Future of Online Genealogy?" by Mark Howells. Journal of Online
    Genealogy, December 1996.
    [http://www.tbox.com/jog/dec96/newsites.htm]
Special Collections Department
    [http://www.lib.usf.edu/spccoll/]

## *Outstanding Site*

## WebLUIS!

Florida Center for Library Automation     E-mail  fclmmd@nervm.nerdc.ufl.edu

Links, State University Libraries, SUS
    [http://www.fcla.edu/SUSstuff/suslibs.html]
WebLUIS, Statewide Online Library Catalog
    [http://www.fcla.edu/cgi-bin/cgiwrap/~fclwptl/webportal]

# GEORGIA

## State Home Page

Georgia Online Network     http://www.state.ga.us/

Links, Georgia Cities and Counties
    [http://www.state.ga.us/gacities.html]

## State Archives

Georgia Department of Archives and History
    http://www.State.Ga.US/SOS/Archives/

| | |
|---|---|
| 330 Capitol Avenue, S.E. | Phone  (404) 656-2393 |
| Atlanta, Georgia 30334 |           (404) 656-2350 |
| | Fax    (404) 657-8427 |

Civil War Unit Histories
    [http://www.State.Ga.US/SOS/Archives/tracingc.htm]
Genealogical Resources
    [http://www.State.Ga.US/SOS/Archives/resource.htm]
Georgia Historical Records Advisory Board
    [http://www.State.Ga.US/SOS/Archives/ghrab1.htm]
Vital Records
    [http://www.State.Ga.US/SOS/Archives/birth.htm]

## State Library

Georgia Division of Public Library Services
    http://galileo.gsu.edu/Homepage.cgi

156 Trinity Avenue, S.W.     Phone  (404) 656-2461
Atlanta, GA 30303-3652

Links, Georgia Libraries
    [http://www.peachnet.edu/galileo/libraries.html]

# State Genealogical Society

| Georgia Genealogy Society | http://members.gnn.com/georgiagen/index.htm |
|---|---|
| P.O. Box 54575<br>Atlanta, GA 30308-0575 | Phone  (404) 475-4404<br>E-mail  Georgiagen@gnn.com |

Book Reviews
   [http://members.gnn.com/georgiagen/book.htm]
Genealogy Links
   [http://members.gnn.com/georgiagen/links.htm]

# State Historical Society

| Georgia Historical Society | http://www.savga.com/ghs/ |
|---|---|
| 501 Whitaker Street<br>Savannah, GA 31401-4889 | Phone  (912) 651-2128<br>Fax    (912) 651-2831 |

Library and Archives
   [http://www.savga.com/orgs/ghs/collections.htm]

# Other State Sites

| Archdiocese of Atlanta | http://www.archatl.com |
|---|---|
| Archives<br>The Catholic Center<br>680 West Peachtree Street, N.W.<br>Atlanta, GA 30308 | Phone  (404) 888-7802<br>Fax    (404) 885-7494 |

Archives
   [http://www.archatl.com/archatl.htm]
Catholic Church In Georgia
   [http://www.archatl.com/aa-hist.htm]
Parish Profiles
   [http://www.archatl.com/profiles.htm]

| Atlanta History Center | http://www.atlhist.org/ |
|---|---|
| 130 West Paces Ferry Road, N.W.<br>Atlanta, GA 30305-1366 | Phone  (404) 814-4040<br>E-mail  webmaster@atlhist.org |

Atlanta History Museum Virtual Tours
   [http://www.atlhist.org/html/exhibit.htm]
Civil War Manuscript Collections
   [http://www.atlhist.org/html/civilgu.htm]

| Georgia College and State University | http://Peacock.GAC.PeachNet.EDU/ |
|---|---|
| Ina Dillard Russell Library<br>Milledgeville, GA 31061-0490 | Phone  (912) 454-0988<br>Fax    (912) 453-6847<br>E-mail  scinfo@mail.gac.peachnet.edu |

Links to Other Georgia Sites
  [http://library.gac.peachnet.edu/~sga/repos.html]
Local History Resources at GC and SU
  [http://Peacock.GAC.PeachNet.EDU/~sc/lochis.html]
Special Collections Department
  [http://Peacock.GAC.PeachNet.EDU/~sc/]

## Society of Georgia Archivists          http://library.gac.peachnet.edu/~sga/index.html

P.O. Box 80631
Athens, GA 30608-0631

Georgia Archives Institute
  [http://library.gac.peachnet.edu/~sga/gai.html]
Links to Georgia Sites
  [http://library.gac.peachnet.edu/~sga/repos.html]

## University of Georgia          http://www.uga.edu/

Hargrett Library                     Phone   (706) 542-0626
University of Georgia Libraries              (706) 542-7123
Athens, GA 30602-1641                E-mail  web_editor@mail.libs.uga.edu

Confederate Constitution
  [http://www.libs.uga.edu/darchive/hargrett/const/const.html]
Digital Archive
  [http://www.libs.uga.edu/darchive/darchive.html]
GALIN On-line Catalog
  [http://www.libs.uga.edu/galincon.html]
Georgia Newspaper Project
  [http://www.libs.uga.edu/darchive/aboutgnp.html]
Georgia Newspapers
  [http://www.libs.uga.edu/darchive/newspape/masthds.html]
Libraries
  [http://www.libs.uga.edu/index.html]
Special Collections Department
  [http://www.libs.uga.edu/darchive/hargrett.html]

# HAWAII

## State Home Page

## Hawaii State Government HomePage          http://www.hawaii.gov/

Birth and Death Certificates
  [http://www.hawaii.gov/health/vr_b_d.htm]
Hawaii State Courts at a Glance
  [http://www.hawaii.gov/jud/PG2.HTM]
Marriage and Divorce Certificates
  [http://www.hawaii.gov/health/vr_m_d.htm]
Vital Records
  [http://www.hawaii.gov/health/vr_howto.htm]

# State Archives

## Hawaii State Archives | http://www.htdc.org/~hsa/

| Department of Accounting and General Services | Phone | (808) 586-0329 |
| Kekauluohi Building | | (808) 586-0316 |
| Iolani Palace Grounds | | (800) 486-4644 In Hawaii Only |
| Honolulu, HI 96813 | Fax | (808) 586-0330 |

Collections
  [http://www.htdc.org/~hsa/describe.html]

# State Library

## Hawaii State Public Library System | http://www.hcc.hawaii.edu/hspls/

| Hawaii State Library | Phone | (808) 586-3535 |
| 478 South King Street | | |
| Honolulu, HI 96813-2901 | | |

Directory of HSPLS Libraries
  [http://www.hcc.hawaii.edu/hspls/dirlibs.html]
Local and State Officials
  [http://www.hawaii.gov/lrb/dir/dirtble.html#topd]
Online Hawaii Links
  [http://www.hcc.hawaii.edu/hspls/onlhaw.html]

# State Historical Society

## Hawaiian Historical Society | http://www.aloha.com/~mem/hhshome.html

| 560 Kawaiahao Street | Phone | (808) 537-6271 |
| Honolulu, HI 96813 | Fax | (808) 537-6271 |
| | E-mail | edunn@lava.net |

Hawaiian Journal of History. Back Issues
  [http://www.aloha.com/~mem/hjhlist.html]
Hawaiian Journal of History. Current Issue
  [http://www.aloha.com/~mem/hjhmain.html]
Historical Records Repositories in Hawaii
  [http://www.aloha.com/~mem/hrr.html]
Library Services
  [http://www.aloha.com/~mem/rschcoll.html]

# Other State Sites

## Hawaii Library Association | http://nic2.hawaii.net/hla/

P.O. Box 4441
Honolulu, HI 96813

Hawaii Library Association Journal Index
  [http://nic2.hawaii.net/hla/indexs.html]

## University of Hawaii at Manoa | http://www.hawaii.edu/

| Special Collections Department | Phone | (808) 956-8264 |
| Hamilton Library, 5th Floor | Fax | (808) 956-5968 |
| 2550 The Mall | E-mail | speccoll@hawaii.edu |
| Honolulu, HI 96822 | | jimc@hawaii.edu |

Hawaii War Records Depository
    [http://www2.hawaii.edu/~speccoll/hwrd/]
Hawaiian Collection
    [http://nic2.hawaii.net/~speccoll/h.html]
Local Identity in Hawaii
    [http://nic2.hawaii.net/~speccoll/hlocal.html]
Pacific Collection
    [http://nic2.hawaii.net/~speccoll/pabout.html#panchor1]
Special Collections Department
    [http://nic2.hawaii.net/~speccoll/welcome.html]
Trust Territory, Pacific Archives
    [http://nic2.hawaii.net/~speccoll/pabout.html#panchor1]
UH Press
    [http://www2.hawaii.edu/uhpress/UHPHome.html]

# IDAHO

## State Home Page

| Idaho Home Page | http://www.state.id.us/ |
|---|---|

Idaho Court System
    [http://www.idwr.state.id.us/judicial/judicial.html]
Links, Idaho
    [http://www.state.id.us/orgs.html]
Links, Idaho Cities
    [http://www.state.id.us/city.html]
Links, Idaho Counties
    [http://www.state.id.us/county.html]

## State Library

| Idaho State Library | http://www.state.id.us/isl/hp.htm |
|---|---|

325 West State Street
Boise, ID 83702

Phone   (208) 334-2150
Fax     (208) 334-4016
E-mail  Webteam@isl.state.id.us

Overview
    [http://www.state.id.us/isl/ls.htm]

## State Genealogical Society

| Idaho Genealogical Library | http://www.rmci.net/idaho/genidaho/index.htm |
|---|---|

9846 Westview Drive
Boise, ID 83704

E-mail  dyingst@rmci.net

City, County and Regional Directories
    [http://www.rmci.net/idaho/genidaho/director.htm]
Family Data in Idaho Carey Act Records
    [http://www.rmci.net/idaho/genidaho/careyact.htm]
Federal Land Records
    [http://www.rmci.net/idaho/genidaho/fedland.htm]

Genealogy Idaho, Journal
    [http://www.rmci.net/idaho/genidaho/contents.htm]
Idaho Vital and County Records
    [http://www.rmci.net/idaho/genidaho/vit_cnty.htm]
Links to Idaho Sites
    [http://www.rmci.net/idaho/genidaho/index.htm]
Newspapers
    [http://www.rmci.net/idaho/genidaho/newsppr.htm]

## Other State Sites

| University of Idaho | http://www.uidaho.edu/ |
| --- | --- |

| University Library<br>Moscow, ID 83844-2351 | Phone  (208) 885-7951<br>Fax     (208) 885-6817<br>E-mail  tabraham@uidaho.edu |
| --- | --- |

Genealogy, Idaho
    [http://www.lib.uidaho.edu/special-collections/genealgl.htm]
Manuscripts
    [http://www.lib.uidaho.edu/special-collections/Manuscripts/]
Special Collections and Archives
    [http://www.lib.uidaho.edu/special-collections/]

# ILLINOIS

## State Home Page

| State of Illinois Home Page | http://www.state.il.us/ |
| --- | --- |

Links, Illinois Libraries & Museums
    [http://www.state.il.us/cms/hp0030.htm]

## State Archives

| Illinois State Archives | http://www.sos.state.il.us/depts/archives/arc_home.html |
| --- | --- |

| Margaret Cross Norton Building<br>Capitol Complex<br>Springfield, IL 62756 | Phone  (217) 782-3492<br>Fax     (217) 524-3930 |
| --- | --- |

Chicago City Council, 1833-1871
    [http://www.sos.state.il.us/depts/archives/data_chi.html]
Local Governmental Records
    [http://www.sos.state.il.us/depts/archives/data_loc.html]
Public Domain Land Sale Records
    [http://www.sos.state.il.us/depts/archives/data_lan.html]
State Governmental Records
    [http://www.sos.state.il.us/depts/archives/data_sta.html]

## State Library

| Illinois State Library | http://www.sos.state.il.us/depts/library/isl_home.html |
| --- | --- |

| 300 South Second Street<br>Springfield, IL 62701-1796 | Phone  (217) 785-5600<br>         (800) 665-5576 In Illinois Only<br>TDD    (217) 524-1137 |
| --- | --- |

Collections
   [http://www.sos.state.il.us/depts/library/collect/collect.html]

# State Genealogical Society

## Illinois State Genealogical Society           http://smtp.tbox.com/isgs/

| | |
|---|---|
| P.O. Box 10195 | Phone   (217) 789-1968 |
| Springfield, IL 62791-0195 | E-mail   c-wilmot@uiuc.edu |

Library
   [http://smtp.tbox.com/isgs/LIBRARY.HTM]
Quarterly
   [http://smtp.tbox.com/isgs/SUBMTQRT.HTM]

# State Historical Society

## Illinois State Historical Society           http://www.prairienet.org/ishs/

| | |
|---|---|
| 1 Old State Capitol Plaza | Phone   (217) 782-2635 |
| Springfield, IL 62701-1507 | Fax     (217) 524-8042 |
| | E-mail   ishs@eosinc.com |

Links, Illinois Genealogical Resources
   [http://www.prairienet.org/ishs/research.htm]
Links, Illinois Historical Resources
   [http://www.prairienet.org/ishs/heritage.htm]
Links, Illinois Historical Societies
   [http://www.prairienet.org/ishs/histtour.htm]
Publications
   [http://www.prairienet.org/ishs/publctns.htm]

# Other State Sites

## Augustana College           http://www.augustana.edu

| | |
|---|---|
| Special Collections Department | Phone   (309) 794-7317 |
| 639 38th Street | E-mail   alijb@augustana.edu |
| Rock Island, IL  61201-2273 |          alidh@augustana.edu |

| | |
|---|---|
| Swenson Swedish Immigration Research  Center | Phone   (309) 794-7204 |
| 639 38th Street | Fax     (309) 794-7443 |
| Rock Island, IL  61201-2273 | E-mail   swsa@Augustana.edu |

Civil War Diaries
   [http://www.augustana.edu:80/library/civil.html]
Library Guide
   [http://viking.augustana.edu/admin/swenson/guide.htm]
Native American: Biographies
   [http://www.augustana.edu:80/library/nabiog.html]
Pioneer Biography
   [http://www.augustana.edu:80/library/bio.html]
Special Collections Department
   [http://www.augustana.edu:80/library/index.html]
Swedish-American Genealogy
   [http://viking.augustana.edu/admin/swenson/fhguide.htm]

Swenson Swedish Immigration Research Center
[http://viking.augustana.edu/admin/swenson/]

## Carl Sandburg College
http://csc.techcenter.org

2232 South Lake Storey Road
Galesburg, IL 61401

Phone   (309) 344-2518

Genealogy Classes and Workshops
[http://csc.techcenter.org/~mneill/csc.html]

## Chicago Historical Society
http://www.chicagohs.org/

Library
Clark Street at North Avenue
Chicago, IL 60614-6099

Phone   (312) 642-5035, ext. 356
Fax     (312) 266-2077
E-mail  ziemer@chicagohs.org

Archives and Manuscripts
[http://www.chicagohs.org/MANUSCRIPTS.html]
Genealogical Research
[http://www.chicagohs.org/GENEALOGICAL.html]
Prints and Photographs
[http://www.chicagohs.org/PRINTS&PHOTOS.html]

## McLean County Historical Society
http://www.dave-world.net/community/mchs/mchs.html

200 North Main Street
Bloomington, IL 61701

Phone   (309) 827-0428
Fax     (309) 827-0100
E-mail  mchs@dave-world.net

Civil War Era Correspondence
[http://www.dave-world.net/community/mchs/cwletter.html]
Genealogy
[http://www.dave-world.net/community/mchs/genhome.html]
Photograph Indexes
[http://www.dave-world.net/community/mchs/librhome.html]

*Outstanding Site*

## Newberry Library
http://www.newberry.org/

60 West Walton Street
Chicago, IL 60610

Phone   (312) 255-3506 Reference
        (312) 255-3512 Genealogy

Bohemian Genealogy
[http://www.NEWBERRY.ORG:80/ISC77]
Chicago Genealogy Sources
[http://www.NEWBERRY.ORG:80/ISC105.HTM]
Connecticut Genealogy
[http://www.NEWBERRY.ORG:80/ISC115.HTM]
French Canadian Genealogy
[http://www.NEWBERRY.ORG:80/ISC116.HTM]

Illinois Genealogy
[http://www.NEWBERRY.ORG:80/ISC117.HTM]
Irish Genealogy
[http://www.NEWBERRY.ORG:80/ISC118.HTM]
Jewish Genealogy
[http://www.NEWBERRY.ORG:80/ISC119.HTM]
Newberry Newsletter
[http://www.NEWBERRY.ORG:80/ISC190]
Ohio Genealogy
[http://www.NEWBERRY.ORG:80/ISC120.HTM]
Ontario Genealogy
[http://www.NEWBERRY.ORG:80/ISC121.HTM]
Polish Genealogy
[http://www.NEWBERRY.ORG:80/ISC122.HTM]
Revolutionary War Patriots
[http://www.NEWBERRY.ORG:80/ISC112]
Virginia Genealogy
[http://www.NEWBERRY.ORG:80/ISC113]

## *Outstanding Site*

## North Park College
http://www.northpark.edu/

Archives Department
Library
3225 West Foster Avenue
Chicago, IL 60625

Phone (312) 244-6224
Fax (312) 267-2362
E-mail tjohnso1@gumby.npcts.edu

Covenant Archives
[http://www.northpark.edu/library/Covenant_Archives/index.html]
LIBRAS Archives
[http://www.northpark.edu/library/LIBRA_Archives/anniversoire.html]
Society for the Advancement of Scandinavian Study Archives
[http://www.northpark.edu/library/Archives/index.html#anchor65975]
Swedish-American Archives, of Greater Chicago
[http://www.northpark.edu/library/Archives/index.html#anchor66256]
Swedish American Historical Society
[http://www.northpark.edu/library/Swedish-American_History/index.html]

## Southern Illinois University
http://www.lib.siu.edu/

Special Collections Department
Morris Library
Carbondale, IL 62901-6632

Phone (618) 453-2516
Fax (618) 453-3451
E-mail dkoch@lib.siu.edu

American Conference for Irish Studies    Phone (618) 453-6851

American Conference for Irish Studies, Newsletter
[http://www.lib.siu.edu/projects/irish/resource.htm]
American Conference for Irish Studies, Research Report, History
[http://www.lib.siu.edu/projects/irish/hist95.htm]
Irish and Irish Immigration Studies
[http://www.lib.siu.edu/projects/irish/index.htm]

Special Collections Department
    [http://www.lib.siu.edu/hpage/spcol.html]

# INDIANA

## State Home Page

| Indiana State HomePage | http://www.state.in.us/ |
| --- | --- |

Access Indiana Information Network
    [http://www.ai.org/other/premium.html]
Directory, Local Health Departments
    [http://www.ai.org/doh/vital/local.html]
Driver's License Records, Registration Records, etc.
    [http://www.ai.org/cgi-bin/aiin/cgi-bin/quest.pl]
Indiana Government Offices
    [http://www.ai.org/stateag.html]
Indiana National Guard. History
    [http://www.ai.org/guard/]
Vital Records, Birth and Death
    [http://www.ai.org/doh/vital/vr1.html]
WWII Recollections of Sergeant Ed Andros
    [http://www.ai.org/guard/history/macarth.html]

## State Archives

| Indiana State Archives | http://www.ai.org/icpr/index.html |
| --- | --- |

| State Library Building | Phone | (317) 232-3660 |
| 140 North Senate Avenue | Fax | (317) 233-1085 or 232-0002 |
| Indianapolis, IN 46204 | E-mail | willever@icprlan.state.in.us |

Central State Hospital
    [http://www.ai.org/icpr/docs/cstate/chs.html]
Civil War
    [http://www.ai.org/icpr/archives/civilwar.html]
Constitution, 1816
    [http://www.ai.org/icpr/1816int.html]
County Records
    [http://www.ai.org/icpr/archives/cntyrecs.html]
Indiana Historical Societies
    [http://www.ai.org/icpr/docs/society.html]
Land Records
    [http://www.ai.org/icpr/archives/land_off.html]
Native Americans
    [http://www.ai.org/icpr/archives/indians.html]
Photographs
    [http://www.ai.org/icpr/html/photos.html]
School Records
    [http://www.ai.org/icpr/archives/schlrecd.html]
Trademarks
    [http://www.ai.org/icpr/archives/trademarks.html]
Vital Records
    [http://www.ai.org/icpr/html/whatsnot.html#VR]

# State Library

| Indiana State Library | http://www.statelib.lib.in.us/ |
|---|---|

| 140 North Senate Avenue<br>Indianapolis, IN 46204 | Phone | (317) 232-3670 Reference<br>(317) 232-3689 Genealogy<br>(317) 232-3668 Indiana Division<br>(317) 232-3671 Manuscripts<br>(317) 232-3664 Newspapers |
|---|---|---|
| | Fax | (317) 232-3728 |
| | TDD | (317) 232-7763 |
| | E-mail | cfaunce@statelib.lib.in.us Manuscripts |

Genealogy
[http://www.statelib.lib.in.us/WWW/INDIANA/GENEALOGY/genmenu.HTML]
Indiana Documents
[http://www.statelib.lib.in.us/WWW/INDIANA/state_documents.HTML]
Indiana Section
[http://www.statelib.lib.in.us/WWW/INDIANA/ABOUTIND.HTML]
Newspaper Holdings Guide
[http://www.statelib.lib.in.us/WWW/INDIANA/NEWSPAPER/HOLD.HTML]
Newspaper Section
[http://www.statelib.lib.in.us/WWW/INDIANA/NEWSPAPER/NEWSMENU.HTML]
Online Library Catalog
[http://libvax.STATELIB.LIB.IN.US/drabin/niso_forms]

# State Genealogical Society

| Indiana Genealogical Society, Inc. | http://www.fgs.org/~fgs/soc0087.htm |
|---|---|

P.O. Box 10507
Fort Wayne, IN 46852

Overview
[http://www.fgs.org/~fgs/soc0087.htm]

# State Historical Society
*Outstanding Site*

| Indiana Historical Society | http://www.ihs1830.org/ |
|---|---|

| Indiana State Library and Historical Building<br>315 West Ohio Street<br>Indianapolis, IN 46202-3299 | Phone | (317) 232-1874 |
|---|---|---|
| | Fax | (317) 233-3109 |
| | E-mail | rboomhower@statelib.lib.in.us<br>agressitt@statelib.lib.in.us<br>ldarbee@statelib.lib.in.us |

African American History Collections
[http://www.spcc.com/ihsw/aahc.htm]
Agricultural History Project
[http://www.spcc.com/ihsw/libag.htm]
Bass Photo Collection
[http://www.spcc.com/ihsw/bass.htm]
Bridge, Newsletter
[http://www.spcc.com/ihsw/bridge.htm]
Genealogical Societies in Indiana
[http://www.spcc.com/ihsw/genedir.htm]

Governors of Indiana
  [http://www.spcc.com/ihsw/ingov.htm]
Guide to Ethnic History Collections
  [http://www.spcc.com/ihsw/libeth.htm]
Hoosier Genealogist, Journal
  [http://www.spcc.com/ihsw/thg.htm]
Hoosier Heritage. Essays, Talks etc.
  [http://www.spcc.com/ihsw/heritage.htm]
Indiana's County Historians
  [http://www.spcc.com/ihsw/cohist.htm]
Local Historical Societies in Indiana
  [http://www.spcc.com/ihsw/historg.htm]
Manuscripts
  [http://www.spcc.com/ihsw/mguides.htm]
Monthly Lists of New Acquisitions
  [http://www.spcc.com/ihsw/newcat.htm]
Pioneer Heritage by Dr. James H. Madison
  [http://www.spcc.com/ihsw/pioneer.htm]
Traces of Indiana and Midwestern History, Journal
  http://www.spcc.com/ihsw/traces.htm]
Traveling Exhibits
  [http://www.spcc.com/ihsw/tel.htm]

# Other State Sites
*Outstanding Site*

## Allen County Public Library                http://www.acpl.lib.in.us

Fred J. Reynolds Historical Genealogy Department
900 Webster Street                         Phone    (219) 424-7241
Fort Wayne, IN 46802-3699

Biographical Sources
  [http://www.acpl.lib.in.us/Readers_Services/biographical_sources.html]
Genealogy Department
  [http://www.acpl.lib.in.us/Genealogy/genealogy_resources.html]
Getting Started
  [http://www.acpl.lib.in.us/Genealogy/researching_family.html]
Guide to the Collections
  [http://www.acpl.lib.in.us/Genealogy/genealogy_resources.html]
Links by Country
  [http://www.acpl.lib.in.us/Genealogy/genealogy_countries.html]
Links by State
  [http://www.acpl.lib.in.us/Genealogy/genealogy_sites.html]
Links by Subject
  [http://www.acpl.lib.in.us/Genealogy/genealogy_rtopics.html]

## Indiana Historical Bureau      http://www.statelib.lib.in.us/WWW/ihb/ihb.HTML

140 North Senate Avenue, Room 408    Phone   (317) 232-2535
Indianapolis, IN 46204-2296          Fax     (317) 232-3728
                                     E-mail  ihb@statelib.lib.in.us
Indiana Governors
  [http://www.statelib.lib.in.us/WWW/ihb/govlist.html]

Indiana Heritage Research Grants
    [http://www.statelib.lib.in.us/WWW/ihb/ihrg93.html]
Indiana Historian, Journal
    [http://www.statelib.lib.in.us/WWW/ihb/historian.html]
Indiana Historical Markers
    [http://www.statelib.lib.in.us/WWW/ihb/marklist.html]
Indiana History Bulletin. Indexes
    [http://www.statelib.lib.in.us/WWW/ihb/ihbull.html]

# Indiana University-Purdue University at Fort Wayne

| | |
|---|---|
| Department of History | Phone   (219) 481-6686 |
| Classroom-Medical 209 | Fax     (219) 481-6985 |
| 2101 East Coliseum Boulevard | |
| Fort Wayne, IN 46805-1499 | |
| | |
| Walter E. Helmke Library | Phone   (219) 481-6514 |
| 2101 East Coliseum Boulevard | Fax     (219) 481-6509 |
| Fort Wayne, IN 46805-1499 | |

Department of History
    [http://cvax.ipfw.indiana.edu/www/depts/history/homepage.html]
Fort Wayne History
    [http://cvax.ipfw.indiana.edu/www/depts/history/fortwayn.html]
Helmke Library
    [http://www-lib.ipfw.indiana.edu/index.html]
Historic Events
    [http://cvax.ipfw.indiana.edu/www/depts/history/indiana/events.html]
Historical Documents
    [http://cvax.ipfw.indiana.edu/www/depts/history/indiana/document.html]
Indiana Biography
    [http://cvax.ipfw.indiana.edu/www/depts/history/indiana/biog.html]
Indiana Business History
    [http://cvax.ipfw.indiana.edu/www/depts/history/indiana/business.html]
Indiana Catholic Page
    [http://cvax.ipfw.indiana.edu/www/depts/history/indicath.html]
Indiana Civil War
    [http://cvax.ipfw.indiana.edu/www/depts/history/indiana/civilwar.html]
Indiana Genealogy
    [http://cvax.ipfw.indiana.edu/www/depts/history/indiana/genealog.html]
Indiana Historical Societies
    [http://cvax.ipfw.indiana.edu/www/depts/history/indiana/museums.html]
Indiana History Groups
    [http://cvax.ipfw.indiana.edu/www/depts/history/indiana/institut.html]
Indiana History Links
    [http://cvax.ipfw.indiana.edu/www/depts/history/indihist.html]
Indiana Index
    [http://www-lib.ipfw.indiana.edu/pirs/state/inbysubj.html]
Library Catalogs
    [http://www-lib.ipfw.indiana.edu/libraries/libraries.html#Indiana]
Links, Indiana History
    [http://cvax.ipfw.indiana.edu/www/depts/history/indiana/otherind.html]
Links, Indianapolis History
    [http://cvax.ipfw.indiana.edu/www/depts/history/indiana/indianap.html]

## Monroe County Public Library          http://www.monroe.lib.in.us/

Indiana Room                              Phone   (812) 349-3080
303 East Kirkwood Avenue                  E-mail  ddevore@monroe.lib.in.us
Bloomington, IN 47408

Genealogy Collection
    [http://www.monroe.lib.in.us/indiana_room/genealogy.html]

## St. Joseph County Public Library       http://sjcpl.lib.in.us/homepage/

304 South Main Street                     Phone   (219) 282-4621
South Bend, IN 46601                      E-mail  m.waterson@gomail.sjcpl.lib.in.us

Genealogy
    [http://sjcpl.lib.in.us/homepage/LocalHist/Genealogy.html]
Links, Genealogy
    [http://sjcpl.lib.in.us/homepage/Reference/genealogy.html]
Links, Public Libraries, Worldwide
    [http://sjcpl.lib.in.us/Databases/PubLibServFind.html]
Local History and Genealogy Services
    [http://sjcpl.lib.in.us/homepage/LocalHist/LocalHistory.html]
Necrology Index
    [http://sjcpl.lib.in.us/homepage/LocalHist/Necrology.html]
Online Catalog
    [http://sjcpl.lib.in.us/homepage/dialacat.html]
South Bend Tribune Index, 1990- .
    [http://sjcpl.lib.in.us/Databases/TribIndexFindLinks.html]

## Society of Indiana Archivists         http://cawley.archives.nd.edu/sia/

Indiana State Archives                    E-mail  Cawley.1@nd.edu
315 West Ohio
Indianapolis, IN 46202

Overview
    [http://cawley.archives.nd.edu/sia/]
SIA Newsletter. Fulltext.
    [http://cawley.archives.nd.edu/sia/sianews.html]

## University of Notre Dame             http://www.nd.edu/

Rare Books and Special Collections        Phone   (219) 631-5636
102 Hesburgh Library                      Fax     (219) 631-6772
Notre Dame, IN 46556                      E-mail  Library.rarebook.1@nd.edu

Archives Guide
    [http://archives1.archives.nd.edu/guidecon.htm]
Online Catalog
    [http://www3.nd.edu/~rarebook/Dept/Text/references.html]
Parish History Collection
    [http://thorplus.lib.purdue.edu/]
Rare Books and Special Collections Department
    [http://www.nd.edu/~rarebook/]

# IOWA

## State Home Page

### Iowa State Home Page                    http://www.state.ia.us

Iowa Department of Public Health          Phone   (515) 281-4944
Bureau of Vital Records                   E-mail  webmaster@idph.state.ia.us
Lucas State Office Building, 1st Floor
Des Moines, IA 50319-0075

Bureau of Vital Records
    [http://idph.state.ia.us/pa/vr.htm]
Links to Iowa Sites
    [http://www.iowa.net/]
Links to Iowa State and Local Government
    [http://www.state.ia.us/government/index.html]
Vital Records
    [http://idph.state.ia.us/pa/vr/add-info.htm]

## State Library

### State Library of Iowa                   http://www.silo.lib.ia.us/

East 12th and Grand Streets               Phone   (515) 281-4102
Des Moines, IA 50319                      Fax     (515) 281-3384
                                                  (515) 281-6191
                                          E-mail  nhaigh@mail.lib.state.ia.us
                                                  siloweb@www.silo.lib.ia.us

Iowa Library Directory
    [http://www.silo.lib.ia.us/lib-dir.html]
Iowa Online Card Catalog
    [http://www.silo.lib.ia.us/cgi-bin/z3950/zform.CGI?SILO]
Links to Iowa Online Libraries
    [http://www.silo.lib.ia.us/web-dir.html]

## State Genealogical Society

### Iowa Genealogical Society               http://www.digiserve.com/igs/igs.htm

P.O. Box 7735                             Phone   (515) 276-0287
Des Moines, IA 50322-7735                 Fax     (515) 276-0287

County Chapters
    [http://www.digiserve.com/igs/county.htm]
Iowa Pioneers Project
    [http://www.digiserve.com/ladyhawk/IPL/ipl_main.htm]
Links, Genealogy
    [http://www.digiserve.com/ladyhawk/IPL/links.htm]

## State Historical Society

### State Historical Society of Iowa         http://www.uiowa.edu/~shsi/library/library.htm

600 East Locust                           Phone   (515) 281-6412
Des Moines, IA 50319

Historic Sites Program
    [http://www.uiowa.edu/~shsi/sites/sites.htm]
Library and Collections
    [http://www.uiowa.edu/~shsi/library/library.htm#3000]
Links to Iowa and Historical Sites
    [http://www.uiowa.edu/~shsi/jump/jump.htm]

# Other State Sites

## Iowa State University                http://www.iastate.edu/

Parks Library, Room 403                 Phone    (319) 294-6672
Ames, IA 50011                          E-mail   twalters@iastate.edu

History of Agriculture and Rural Life
    [http://www.lib.iastate.edu/spcl/agri/tc.html]
The Road I Grew Up On, Virtual Tour
    [http://www.lib.iastate.edu/spcl/road/road.html]
Special Collections Department
    [http://www.lib.iastate.edu/spcl/spcl.html]

## University of Iowa                http://www1.arcade.uiowa.edu/

100 Main Library                        Phone    (319) 335-5921 Archives
Iowa City, IA 52242-1420                E-mail   earl-rogers@uiowa.edu  Archives

Iowa Women's Archives                   Phone    (319) 335-5068
                                                 (319) 335-5921
                                        E-mail   karen-mason@uiowa.edu

John Martin Rare Book Room              Phone    (319) 335-9154
Hardin Library for the Health Sciences  E-mail   richard-eimas@uiowa.edu

Electronic Reference Form
    [http://www1.arcade.uiowa.edu/forms/e-ref.html]
Iowa Women's Archives Holdings
    [http://www1.arcade.uiowa.edu/iwa/holdings.htm]
John Martin Rare Book Room
    [http://www.arcade.uiowa.edu/hardin-www/bull12.html]
Newsletter
    [http://www1.arcade.uiowa.edu/lib/newsletter.html]
Special Collections Department
    [http://www1.arcade.uiowa.edu/spec-coll/]

## University of Northern Iowa             http://www.uni.edu

Special Collections and University Archives   Phone   (319) 273-6307
Rod Library, 3rd Floor                        Fax     (319) 273-2913
Cedar Falls, IA 50613-3675                    E-mail  gerald.peterson@uni.edu

Collections Guide
    [http://www.uni.edu/petersog/collguid.html]
Newspaper Collection
    [http://www.uni.edu/petersog/msc24nws.html]
Special Collections and University Archives
    [http://www.uni.edu/petersog/]

# KANSAS

## State Home Page

| State of Kansas HomePage | http://www.state.ks.us/ |
|---|---|

Links to Kansas Government
[http://skyways.lib.ks.us/kansas/kan_govt.html]

## State Library

| Kansas State Library | http://skyways.lib.ks.us/kansas/ |
|---|---|

State Capitol Building, 3rd Floor
Topeka, KS 66612

Phone    (913) 296-3296
        (800) 432-3919 Kansas
Fax       (913) 296-6650
E-mail   Cindy Roupe,KSST13LB@INK.ORG

Kansas Libraries, Newsletter
[http://skyways.lib.ks.us/kansas/KSL/admin/kansas_libraries.html]

## State Historical Society
### *Outstanding Site*

| Kansas State Historical Society | http://history.cc.ukans.edu/heritage/kshs/kshs1.html |
|---|---|

6425 S.W. Sixth Avenue
Topeka, KS 66615

Phone    (913) 272-8681
Fax       (913) 272-8682
TTY      (913) 272-8683
E-mail   user@hspo.wpo.state.ks.us
       Archives@hspo.wpo.state.ks.us
       Referenc@hspo.wpo.state.ks.us

Biography
[http://history.cc.ukans.edu/heritage/kshs/resource/bio.htm]
Census, Non-Kansas. Indexes
[http://history.cc.ukans.edu/heritage/kshs/resource/osindx.htm]
Census, Non-Kansas. 1790-1820
[http://history.cc.ukans.edu/heritage/kshs/resource/17901820.htm]
Census, Non-Kansas. 1830-1850
[http://history.cc.ukans.edu/heritage/kshs/resource/18301850.htm]
Census, Non-Kansas. 1860-1910
[http://history.cc.ukans.edu/heritage/kshs/resource/18601910.htm]
Census, Special Census
[http://history.cc.ukans.edu/heritage/kshs/resource/specen.htm]
Census, Territorial and State 1855-1875. Guide
[http://history.cc.ukans.edu/heritage/kshs/resource/18551875.htm]
Census, Territorial and State 1855-1925. Indexes.
[http://history.cc.ukans.edu/heritage/kshs/resource/cenindx.htm]
Census, Territorial and State 1880-1900. Guide.
[http://history.cc.ukans.edu/heritage/kshs/resource/18801900.htm]
Census, Territorial and State 1905-1925. Guide.
[http://history.cc.ukans.edu/heritage/kshs/resource/19051925.htm]
City Directories A-L
[http://history.cc.ukans.edu/heritage/kshs/resource/cdira-l.htm]
City Directories M-Z
[http://history.cc.ukans.edu/heritage/kshs/resource/cdirm-z.htm]

Indian Census Rolls
     [http://history.cc.ukans.edu/heritage/kshs/resource/indian1.htm]
Indian Enrollment Cards
     [http://history.cc.ukans.edu/heritage/kshs/resource/dawes.htm]
Kansas Heritage Magazine
     [http://history.cc.ukans.edu/heritage/kshs/products/heritage.htm]
Kansas Historical Quarterly
     [http://history.cc.ukans.edu/heritage/kshs/resource/khquart.htm]
Kansas History: a Journal
     [http://history.cc.ukans.edu/heritage/kshs/products/kshist.htm]
Kansas History: a Journal. Index
     [http://www.ukans.edu/carrie/kancoll/kbibl/khmag.html]
Kansas Museum of History
     [http://history.cc.ukans.edu/heritage/kshs/places/museum.htm]
Library
     [http://history.cc.ukans.edu/heritage/kshs/resource/lib.htm]
Military Records
     [http://history.cc.ukans.edu/heritage/kshs/resource/soldiers.htm]
Newspapers
     [http://history.cc.ukans.edu/heritage/kshs/resource/news.0.htm]
Newspapers, African-American
     [http://history.cc.ukans.edu/heritage/kshs/resource/blcknspr.htm]
Photographs
     [http://history.cc.ukans.edu/heritage/kshs/resource/photocol.htm]
State Archives
     [http://history.cc.ukans.edu/heritage/kshs/resource/archives.htm]

# Other State Sites

## Kansas Press Association                  http://www.kspress.com/

5423 S.W. 7th                               Phone    (913) 271-5304
Topeka, KS 66606                            E-mail   cwright@kspress.com

Kansas Newspapers, Directory
     [http://www.kspress.com/KPS/abclist.html]

## *Outstanding Site*

## University of Kansas

Kansas Collection                           Phone    (913) 864-4274
Spencer Research Library, Room 220          E-mail   lhnelson@raven.cc.ukans.edu
Lawrence, KS 66045-2800                              husker@sky.net
                                                     susancs@awod.com

Thomas R. Smith Map Collection              Phone    (913) 864-4420
Level 1, Anschutz Library                   Fax      (913) 864-5380
                                            E-mail   maps-ref@ukans.edu

Kansas Heritage Center for Family and       E-mail   lhnelson@ukanaix.cc.ukans.edu
     Local History. Kansas Data and Links.           chinn@ctrvax.vanderbilt.edu

**Kansas Collection**
Articles, Essays on Kansas History
     [http://kuhttp.cc.ukans.edu/carrie/kancoll/articles/]

Bibliography, A-L
    [http://kuhttp.cc.ukans.edu/carrie/kancoll/kbibl/kanhistory.a-l]
Bibliography, M-Z
    [http://kuhttp.cc.ukans.edu/carrie/kancoll/kbibl/kanhistory.m-z]
Biography
    [http://kuhttp.cc.ukans.edu/carrie/kancoll/kbibl/kanbiog.html]
Census
    [http://kuhttp.cc.ukans.edu/carrie/kancoll/research.htm#census]
City Directories
    [http://kuhttp.cc.ukans.edu/carrie/kancoll/research.htm#directories]
Collection Guide
    [http://kuhttp.cc.ukans.edu/cwis/units/kulib/kanscol.html]
Cutler, William G. History of Kansas. 1883.
    [http://raven.cc.ukans.edu/~hisite/kancoll/books/cutler/cutler.html]
Early Kansas Imprint Scanners
    [http://kuhttp.cc.ukans.edu/carrie/ekis/]
Graphics
    [http://kuhttp.cc.ukans.edu/carrie/kancoll/graphics/]
Kansas Collection
    http://kuhttp.cc.ukans.edu/carrie/kancoll/index.html
Kansas POWs in TX 1863-65
    [http://kuhttp.cc.ukans.edu/carrie/kancoll/articles/powlist.htm#list]
Links
    [http://kuhttp.cc.ukans.edu/carrie/kancoll/links.htm]
Military Records
    [http://kuhttp.cc.ukans.edu/carrie/kancoll/research.htm#military]
Newspapers
    [http://kuhttp.cc.ukans.edu/carrie/kancoll/kbibl/kanhistory.m-z]
Orphan Trains
    [http://www.ukans.edu/carrie/kancoll/articles/orphans/index.html]
Post Card Collections
    [http://kuhttp.cc.ukans.edu/carrie/kancoll/galwin.htm]
Research Sources. Extensive
    [http://kuhttp.cc.ukans.edu/carrie/kancoll/research.htm]
Smith Map Collection
    [http://kuhttp.cc.ukans.edu/cwis/units/kulib/maps/collect.html]
Voices, Online Magazine
    [http://www.ukans.edu/carrie/kancoll/voices/]
**Kansas Heritage Center for Family and Local History**
    [http://history.cc.ukans.edu/heritage/heritage_main.html]
County Organization Dates
    [http://history.cc.ukans.edu/heritage/research/coorgdat.html]
Cowboys
    [http://history.cc.ukans.edu/heritage/old_west/cowboy.html]
Forts
    [http://history.cc.ukans.edu/heritage/research/kansfort.html]
Genealogical and Historical Societies
    [http://history.cc.ukans.edu/heritage/heritage_main.html]
Gunfighters
    [http://history.cc.ukans.edu/heritage/research/gunfighters.html]
Highways
    [http://history.cc.ukans.edu/heritage/highway.html]

Historic Trails
[http://history.cc.ukans.edu/heritage/research/trail.html]
Kansas Family History
[http://history.cc.ukans.edu/heritage/families/families_main.html]
Kansas Peoples
[http://history.cc.ukans.edu/heritage/old_west/kspeoples.html]
Kansas Pioneers Project
[http://history.cc.ukans.edu/heritage/pioneers/pion_main.html]
Kansas Timeline
[http://history.cc.ukans.edu/heritage/research/timeline.html]
Methodists
[http://history.cc.ukans.edu/heritage/um/um.html]
Native Americans
[http://history.cc.ukans.edu/heritage/old_west/indian.html]
Nature Links
[http://history.cc.ukans.edu/heritage/prairie/prairie.html]
One Room Schoolhouse Project
[http://history.cc.ukans.edu/heritage/orsh/orsh_main.html]
Railroads
[http://history.cc.ukans.edu/heritage/research/rr/railroads.html]

# KENTUCKY

## State Home Page

| Kentucky State Page | http://www.state.ky.us/ |
|---|---|
| Kentucky Department of Military Affairs | E-mail  military@dayglo.state.ky.us |

Kentucky Military History Museum
[http://www.state.ky.us/agencies/military/milhist.htm]
Military Records and Research Branch
[http://www.state.ky.us/agencies/military/mrrb.htm]

## State Library and Archives
### *Outstanding Site*

**Kentucky Department for Libraries and Archives**
    http://www.kdla.state.ky.us/

| 300 Coffee Tree Road | Phone  (502) 564-8300 |
|---|---|
| P.O. Box 537 | E-mail  minder@a1.kdla.state.ky.us |
| Frankfort, KY 40602-0537 | |

Archives Reading Room                    Phone · (502) 564-8704

Adoption Records
[http://www.kdla.state.ky.us/arch/adoption.htm]
African American Sources
[http://www.kdla.state.ky.us/arch/Africa.htm]
Annual Reports
[http://www.kdla.state.ky.us/intro/annual.htm]
Birth and Death Records Request Form
[http://www.kdla.state.ky.us/arch/Bdvital.htm]
Census Records
[http://www.kdla.state.ky.us/arch/kentcens.htm]

Civil War Records
[http://www.kdla.state.ky.us/arch/civil.htm]
County Clerks in Kentucky
[http://www.kdla.state.ky.us/arch/pubson.htm]
Directory of Kentucky Public Libraries
[http://www.kdla.state.ky.us/libserv/publdir.htm]
Genealogical Correspondence Policy
[http://www.kdla.state.ky.us/arch/corpolic.htm]
Genealogical Reference Request Form
[http://www.kdla.state.ky.us/arch/genrefrq.htm]
Historical and Genealogical Sources
[http://www.kdla.state.ky.us/arch/sources.htm]
Kentucky Guide Project
[http://www.kdla.state.ky.us/arch/guidwebe.htm]
Kentucky Public Library Newsletter
[http://www.kdla.state.ky.us/libserv/pubnews.htm]
Kentucky State Archives
[http://www.kdla.state.ky.us/arch/arch.htm]
Land Record Information
[http://www.kdla.state.ky.us/arch/land.htm]
Links, Other Kentucky Archives
[http://www.kdla.state.ky.us/arch/refaddrs.htm]
Local Records Program
[http://www.kdla.state.ky.us/pubrec/lrmiss.htm]
Managing Kentucky Government Records
[http://www.kdla.state.ky.us/pubrec/manwrit.htm]
Native American Sources
[http://www.kdla.state.ky.us/arch/Indian.htm]
Naturalization Records
[http://www.kdla.state.ky.us/arch/naturali.htm]
Online Public Access Catalog
[http://www.kdla.state.ky.us/libserv/libserv.htm]
Professional Researchers
[http://www.kdla.state.ky.us/arch/reselist.htm]
Public Records
[http://www.kdla.state.ky.us/pubrec/pubrecs.htm]
State Archives and Records Commission
[http://www.kdla.state.ky.us/pubrec/sarcomm.htm]
State Historical Records Advisory Board
[http://www.kdla.state.ky.us/pubrec/strecadv.htm]
State Publications Online
[http://www.kdla.state.ky.us/arch/pubson.htm]
State Publications Program
[http://www.kdla.state.ky.us/arch/Statpub.htm]
Vital Records
[http://www.kdla.state.ky.us/arch/vital.htm]

# State Genealogical Society

## Kentucky Genealogical Society

http://members.aol.com/bdharney2/bh3.htm

P.O. Box 153
Frankfort, KY 40602

E-mail   bdharney2@aol.com

Bluegrass Roots
    [http://members.aol.com/bdharney2/bh3e.htm]
KGS News
    [http://members.aol.com/bdharney2/bh3a.htm]

# State Historical Society

## Kentucky Historical Society            http://www.state.ky.us/agencies/khs

Old State Capitol Annex, 3rd Floor        Phone    (502) 564-3016
P.O. Box 1792                             Fax      (502) 564-4701
Frankfort, KY 40602-1792

Counties
    [http://www.state.ky.us/agencies/khs/research/list_counties.htm]
Counties, Formation
    [http://www.state.ky.us/agencies/khs/research/county_formation.htm]
Kentucky History Museum
    [http://www.state.ky.us/agencies/khs/museums/history_museum.htm]
Kentucky Oral History Commission
    [http://www.state.ky.us/agencies/khs/outreach/oral_history.htm]
Library
    [http://www.state.ky.us/agencies/khs/research/research_index.htm]
Special Collections
    [http://www.state.ky.us/agencies/khs/research/special_collections1.htm]

# Other State Sites

## Centre College                         http://www.centre.edu

600 West Walnut Street                    Phone    (606) 238-5272
Danville, KY 40422                        Fax      (606) 236-7925

Family and Local History
    [http://www.centre.edu/academic/library/archives/cc120.html]
Kentucky College for Women
    [http://www.centre.edu/academic/library/archives/cc100.html]
Newspapers
    [http://www.centre.edu/academic/library/archives/cc123.html]
Special Collections
    [http://www.centre.edu/academic/library/archives/specoll.html]

## Eastern Kentucky University            http://acs.eku.edu

Crabbe Library, Room 126                  Phone    (606) 622-1792
Richmond, KY 40475-3121                   Fax      (606) 622-1174
                                          E-mail   ARCHIVE@ACS.EKU.EDU
Collections
    [http://acs.eku.edu:70/0disk$acs%3a%5b006006.gopherd.gopher_data.library.archive.
    intro%5d_res.%3b1]
Special Collections and Archives Section
    [http://acs.eku.edu:70/0disk$acs%3a%5b006006.gopherd.gopher_data.library.archive.
    intro%5d_intro.%3b1]

## Kentucky Civil War, Confederate States of America, Orphan Brigade
http://bl-12.rootsweb.com/~orphanhm/

E-mail  orphans1@mc.net
        walden@Octagon.TACOM.army.mil

Battle Flags
    [http://bl-12.rootsweb.com/~orphanhm/flags.htm]
Orphan Brigade Photo Gallery
    [http://bl-12.rootsweb.com/~orphanhm/photogal.htm]
Roster of Brigades
    [http://bl-12.rootsweb.com/~orphanhm/rosters.htm]
Uniforms
    [http://bl-12.rootsweb.com/~orphanhm/uniforms.htm]

## Kentucky Explorer                    http://www.win.net/kyexmag/KEhome.html

P.O. Box 227                         Phone   (606) 666-5060
Jackson, KY 41339                    Fax     (606) 666-7018
                                     E-mail  kyexgen@harold.eastky.com

Genealogy Help Line
    [http://www.win.net/kyexmag/KEgen.html]
Kentucky Explorer Index
    [http://www.win.net/kyexmag/KEindex.html]
Kentucky Historical Societies, Directory
    [http://www.win.net/kyexmag/KEsociety.html]

## Northern Kentucky University         http://www.nku.edu/~refdept/archives.htmlx

Special Collections and Archives Department    Phone   (606) 572-6158
Library                                        Fax     (606) 572-5390
Highland Heights, KY 41099-6101                E-mail  ADAMSR@NKU.EDU

Christopher Gist Historical Society Collection
    [http://www.nku.edu/~refdept/gist.html]
Collection Guides
    [http://www.nku.edu/~refdept/collections.html]

### *Outstanding Site*

## University of Kentucky                http://www.uky.edu/

Margaret I. King Library             Phone   (606) 257-8371
Lexington, KY 40506                  E-mail  wjmars01@ukcc.uky.edu

Genealogy Resources
    [http://www.uky.edu/Subject/genealogy.html]
Kentucky Place Names
    [http://www.uky.edu/KentuckyPlaceNames/]
Kentucky Vital Records Indexes
    [http://ukcc.uky.edu/~vitalrec/]
Library Newsletter
    [http://www.uky.edu/Libraries/ln.html]
Links by Subject
    [http://www.uky.edu/Subject/subject-catalog.html]

Links to Libraries Worldwide
    [http://www.uky.edu/Subject/libraries.html]
Special Collections Department
    [http://www.uky.edu/Libraries/Special/]

## University of Louisville          http://www.louisville.edu/library/uarc/

Special Collections Department, Room G17
Ekstrom Library                          Phone    (502) 852-6752
Louisville, KY 40292                     Fax      (502) 852-8734

University Archives and Records Center   Phone    (502) 852-6674
                                         Fax      (502) 852-6673
                                         E-mail   archives@ulkyvm.louisville.edu
Finding Aids
    [gopher://ulkyvm.louisville.edu:70/11/ularc/uarc]
Links, Kentucky Archives
    [http://www.louisville.edu/library/uarc/kyarchiv.html]
Online Archives Catalog
    [http://www.louisville.edu/library/uarc/archcat.html]
Oral History Project
    [http://www.louisville.edu/library/uarc/ohc.html]
Photographic Archives
    [http://www.louisville.edu/library/ekstrom/special/pa_info.html]
Special Collections Department
    [http://www.louisville.edu/library/ekstrom/special/]
University Archives and Records Center
    [http://www.louisville.edu/library/uarc/]
Women's Manuscript Collections
    [http://www.luisville.edu/library/uarc/womcoll.html]

## Western Kentucky University     http://www2.wku.edu

Department of Library Special Collections   Phone    (502) 745-5083
The Kentucky Building                       Fax      (502) 745-4878
1 Big Red Way
Bowling Green, KY 42101-3576

Kentucky Library, Room 206                  Phone    (502) 745-5083
                                                     (502) 745-6263
                                            E-mail   Nancy.Baird@wku.edu

Kentucky Museum                             Phone    (502) 745-2592
                                                     (502) 745-6434

Manuscripts and Folklife Archives           E-mail   hodgepm@wkuvx1.wku.edu

Kentucky Library
    [http://www2.wku.edu/www/Library/dlsc/ky_lib.htm]
Kentucky Museum
    [http://www2.wku.edu/www/Library/museum/index.htm]
Manuscripts and Folklife
    [http://www2.wku.edu/www/Library/dlsc/mscripts.htm#mailing]
Special Collections
    [http://www2.wku.edu/www/Library/dlsc/index.htm]

# LOUISIANA

## State Home Page

### Info Louisiana
http://www.state.la.us/

Links, Local Government
[http://www.state.la.us/local/locindx.htm]

## State Archives

### Louisiana State Archives
http://www.sec.state.la.us/arch.htm

Archives and Records Section
Essen Lane
P.O. Box 94125
Baton Rouge, LA 70804-9125

Phone   (504) 342-3389
Fax      (504) 342-3547

Louisiana Governors
[http://www.sec.state.la.us/gov-1.htm]
Louisiana History
[http://www.sec.state.la.us/brief-1.htm]

## State Library

### Louisiana State Library
http://smt.state.lib.la.us/

760 North Third Street
P.O. Office Box 131
Baton Rouge, LA 70821-0131

Phone   (504) 342-4913
Fax      (504) 342-3547
TDD     (504) 342-2476
E-mail  mschroth@pelican.state.lib.la.us

Genealogy Guides
[http://smt.state.lib.la.us/flaan.htm]
Links, Louisiana
[http://smt.state.lib.la.us/flasite.htm]
Links, Louisiana Libraries
[http://smt.state.lib.la.us/flibdlis.htm]
Louisiana Genealogical Societies
[http://smt.state.lib.la.us/genlist.htm]

## Other State Sites

### Beauregard Parish Library
http://www.beaulib.dtx.net/

E-mail  jamey@beaulib.dtx.bet

Genealogical Resources
[http://www.beaulib.dtx.net/genie.htm]

### Historic New Orleans Collection
http://www.hnoc.org/

533 Royal Street
New Orleans, LA 70130

Phone   (504) 523-4662
Fax      (504) 598-7108

Williams Research Center
410 Chartres Street
New Orleans, LA 70130

Phone   (504) 598-7171
Fax      (504) 598-7168

Publications
    [http://www.hnoc.org/hnocpubs.htm]

# Louisiana Archives and Manuscripts Association
    http://home.gnofn.org/~nopl/links/archives/lama.htm

P.O. Box 51213
New Orleans, LA 70151-1213

Newsletter
    [http://home.gnofn.org/~nopl/links/archives/fall96.htm]

# Louisiana State University Libraries        http://www.lsu.edu/

Special Collections Department               Phone    (504) 388-6551
Hill Memorial Library, Room 201              E-mail   notvfp@unix1.sncc.lsu.edu
Baton Rouge, LA 70803-3300

Louisiana and Lower Mississippi              Phone    (504) 388-6501
    Valley Collections                       E-mail   gmcmull@unix1.sncc.lsu.edu

Louisiana Newspaper Project                  Phone    (504) 388-6559
                                             E-mail   notlbs@lsuvm.sncc.lsu.edu

Williams Center for Oral History            Phone    (504) 388-6577
                                             E-mail   notped@lsuvm.sncc.lsu.edu
Civil War Sesquicentennial News
    [http://www.cwc.lsu.edu/projects/sesqui.htm]
Library
    [http://www.lib.lsu.edu/]
Links to Louisiana Sites
    [http://www.lsu.edu/guests/poli/public_html/newla.html]
Louisiana and Lower Mississippi Valley Collections
    [http://www.lib.lsu.edu/special/llmvc.html]
Louisiana Newspaper Project
    [http://www.lib.lsu.edu/special/lnp.html]
Oral History
    [http://www.lib.lsu.edu/special/thwcoh.html]
Special Collections Department
    [http://www.lib.lsu.edu/special/]
U.S. Civil War Center
    [http://www.cwc.lsu.edu/]

## *Outstanding Site*

# New Orleans Public Library        http://home.gnofn.org/~nopl/nutrias.htm

Louisiana Division                   Phone   (504) 596-2610
219 Loyola Avenue
New Orleans, LA 70112-2044

African-American Genealogy
    [http://home.gnofn.org/~nopl/guides/black.htm]
Census, 1850. Hints
    [http://home.gnofn.org/~nopl/info/louinfo/louinfo5.htm]

Census, 1860-1920
    [http://home.gnofn.org/~nopl/info/louinfo/census2.htm]
City Archives and Special Collections
    [http://home.gnofn.org/~nopl/spec/speclist.htm]
Genealogical Materials, 3rd Edition
    [http://home.gnofn.org/~nopl/guides/genguide/ggcover.htm]
House and Building Research
    [http://home.gnofn.org/~nopl/guides/house/title.htm]
Louisiana Division
    [http://home.gnofn.org/~nopl/info/louinfo/louinfo.htm]
Manuscript Collections
    [http://home.gnofn.org/~nopl/mss/mss.htm]
Naturalization Records
    [http://home.gnofn.org/~nopl/inv/crimnat.htm]
Passenger Lists
    [http://home.gnofn.org/~nopl/info/louinfo/louinfo3.htm]

## *Outstanding Site*

| Tulane University | http://www.tulane.edu |
|---|---|

| | |
|---|---|
| Louisiana Collection<br>Tilton Memorial Library<br>6823 St. Charles Avenue<br>New Orleans, LA 70118-5682 | Phone  (504) 865-5643<br>Fax      (504) 865-6773 |
| Amistad Research Center | Phone  (504) 865-5535<br>Fax      (504) 865-5580<br>E-mail  amistad@tulane.edu<br>            ddevore@tulane.edu |
| Special Collections Division | Phone  (504) 865-5685<br>Fax      (504) 865-6773<br>E-mail  meneray@mailhost.tcs.tulane.edu |
| Manuscripts Department | Phone  (504) 865-5685<br>Fax      (504) 865-6773<br>E-mail  lmiller@mailhost.tcs.tulane.edu |
| Southeastern Architectural Archive | Phone  (504) 865-5699<br>Fax      (504) 856-6773<br>E-mail  vanzante@ mailhost.tcs.tulane.edu |

African American Genealogy
    [gopher://rs11.tcs.tulane.edu:1070/00/Tulane%20Departments/Amistad%20Research%20
    Center/6.%20%20RESOURCES/Genealogy]
Amistad Case
    [gopher://rs11.tcs.tulane.edu:1070/00/Tulane%20Departments/Amistad%20Research%20
    Center/6.%20%20RESOURCES/BIBLIOGRAPHIES/AMISTAD%20%26AMA%20
    BIB LIOGRAPHY]
Amistad Research Center
    [http://www.arc.tulane.edu/]
Architectural Archives
    [http://www.tulane.edu/~lmiller/SEAAHome.html]
Black Cowboy Bibliography
    [gopher://rs11.tcs.tulane.edu:1070/00/Tulane%20Departments/Amistad%20Research%20
    Center/6.%20%20RESOURCES/BIBLIOGRAPHIES/BLACK%20COWBOYS]

Blacks in the Military
  [gopher://rs11.tcs.tulane.edu:1070/00/Tulane%20Departments/Amistad%20Research%20
  Center/6.%20%20RESOURCES/BIBLIOGRAPHIES/BLACKS%20IN%20US%20MILITARY]
Family History Collections
  [http://www.tulane.edu/~lmiller/FamilyHistory.html]
Jewish Heritage Collections
  [http://www.tulane.edu/~lmiller/JewishStudiesIntro.html]
Library Collections
  [gopher://rs11.tcs.tulane.edu:1070/11/Tulane%20Departments/Amistad%20Research%20
  Center/3.%20%20HOLDINGS/PERIODICALS]
Louisiana Collection
  [http://www.tulane.edu/~lmiller/LaCollection.html]
Manuscript Collections, Armistad Research Center
  [gopher://rs11.tcs.tulane.edu:1070/11/Tulane%20Departments/Amistad%20Research%20
  Center/3.%20%20HOLDINGS/LIST%20COLLECTIONS]
Manuscripts Department
  [http://www.tulane.edu/~lmiller/ManuscriptsHome.html]
Military Records
  [http://www.tulane.edu/~lmiller/Military.html]
Social Agency Records
  [http://www.tulane.edu/~lmiller/SocialAgencies.html]
Social and Civic Organizations
  [http://www.tulane.edu/~lmiller/Civic.html]
Special Collections Division
  [http://www.tulane.edu/~lmiller/Civic.html]
Writings Based on Research at the Center
  [gopher://rs11.tcs.tulane.edu:1070/00/Tulane%20Departments/Amistad%20Research%20
  Center/6.%20%20RESOURCES/BIBLIOGRAPHIES/WRITINGS%20BASED%20ON%20
  RESEARCH%20AT%20THE%20CENTER]

## University of New Orleans          http://www.uno.edu/Welcome.shtml

Long Library                          Phone   (504) 280-7275
Lakefront Campus
New Orleans, LA 70148

Archives and Special Collections
  [http://www.uno.edu/~lirf/archive.html]
Louisiana Collection
  [http://www.uno.edu/~lirf/lacoll.html]

# MAINE

## State Home Page

## Maine State HomePage          http://www.state.me.us/

Directory of Courts
  [http://www.courts.state.me.us/directory.html]
Historic Preservation Commission
  [http://www.state.me.us/mhpc/homepag1.htm]
Judicial Branch
  [wysiwyg://199/http://www.courts.state.me.us/]

Links to Maine Sites
    [http://www.destek.net/Maps/ME.shtml]
Maine Library Commission
    [http://www.state.me.us/msl/libcom.htm]
Maine Medal of Honor Memorial
    [http://www.state.me.us/va/defense/moh.htm]
Maine Military Historical Society Museum
    [http://www.state.me.us/va/defense/museum.htm]

# State Archives

## Maine State Archives
    http://www.state.me.us/sos/arc/general/admin/mawww001.htm

| | |
|---|---|
| Station # 84<br>Augusta, ME 04333-0084 | Phone  (207) 287-5795<br>Fax    (207) 287-5739<br>E-mail  jbrown@saturn.caps.maine.edu |

Civil War Records
    [http://www.state.me.us/sos/arc/archives/military/civilwar/civilwar.htm]
Genealogy Resources
    [http://www.state.me.us/sos/arc/archives/genealog/genealog.htm]
Judicial Records
    [http://www.state.me.us/sos/arc/archives/judicial/judicial.htm]
Legislative Records
    [http://www.state.me.us/sos/arc/archives/legislat/legislat.htm]
Local Government Records
    [http://www.state.me.us/sos/arc/recmgmt/localgov/localhom.htm]
Marriage Index 1892-1966
    [http://www.state.me.us/sos/arc/archives/genealog/marriage.htm]
Military Records
    [http://www.state.me.us/sos/arc/archives/military/military.htm]
Searchable Databases
    [http://www.state.me.us/sos/arc/general/admin/database.htm]

# State Library

## Maine State Library                http://www.state.me.us/msl/mslhome.htm

| | |
|---|---|
| State House Station #64<br>Augusta, ME 04333 | Phone  (207) 287-5600<br>Fax    (207) 287-5615<br>E-mail  slgnich@state.me.us<br>        sldwhit@state.me.us |

Links to Maine Libraries
    [http://www.state.me.us/msl/melibson.htm]
Maine Guide, Useful Links
    [http://www.state.me.us/msl/mgintro.htm]
Maine Libraries, Newsletter
    [http://www.state.me.us/msl/mlo.htm]
Maine Library Association, MLA
    [http://wwwsgi.ursus.maine.edu/mla/]
Maine Memo, MLA Newsletter
    [http://wwwsgi.ursus.maine.edu/mla/mainememo2.html]
MAINECAT, Online Catalog
    [http://maine.library.net/]

Reference Department
    [http://www.state.me.us/msl/ref.htm]

## State Historical Society

| Maine Historical Society | http://www.simmons.edu/~glass/mhs_home.html |
|---|---|
| 485 Congress Street<br>Portland, ME 04101 | Phone   (207) 774-1822 |

Library
    [http://www.simmons.edu/~glass/library.html]
Maine History Gallery
    [http://www.simmons.edu/~glass/gallery.html]

## Other State Sites

| University of Maine | http://www.ume.maine.edu/ |
|---|---|
| Special Collections Department<br>5729 Fogler Library<br>Orono, ME 04469-5729 | Phone   (207) 581-1686<br>Fax       (207) 581-1653<br>E-mail   muriels@ursus1.ursus.maine.edu |
| Maine Folklife Center<br>South Stevens 5773<br>Orono, ME 04469-5773 | Phone   (207) 581-1891<br>E-mail   Pauleena_MacDougall@voyager.umeres.maine.edu<br>Alaric_Faulkner@voyager.umeres.maine.edu |

Canadian Studies Collection
    [http://www.ume.maine.edu/~canam/library.html]
Maine Collection
    [http://libinfo.ume.maine.edu/Speccoll/mainecol.htm]
Maine Folklife Center
    [http://www.ume.maine.edu/~folklife/]
Maine State Documents
    [http://libinfo.ume.maine.edu/Speccoll/statdocs.htm]
Special Collections Department
    [http://libinfo.ume.maine.edu/Speccoll/speccol.htm]
University Collection
    [http://libinfo.ume.maine.edu/Speccoll/univcol.htm]

# MARYLAND

## State Home Page

| Maryland Electronic Capitol—Maryland State Home Page<br>    http://www.mec.state.md.us/mec/ | |
|---|---|
| State Department of Education<br>Department of Library Development Services<br>200 West Baltimore Street<br>Baltimore, MD 21201 | Phone   (410) 767-0437<br>Fax       (410) 333-2507<br>E-mail   sailor@mail.pratt.lib.md.us |

Links, SAILOR, Online Catalog
    [http://sailor.lib.md.us/]

# State Archives

## Maryland State Archives
http://www.mdarchives.state.md.us/msa/homepage/html/homepage.html

350 Rowe Boulevard
Annapolis, MD 21401-1686

Phone   (410) 974-3914
         (800) 235-4045 in Maryland
Fax     (410) 974-2525
E-mail  archives@mdarchives.state.md.us

Admiralty Court
[http://www.mdarchives.state.md.us/msa/speccol/4646/html/title.html]
Adoption Records
[http://www.mdarchives.state.md.us/msa/refserv/html/adopt.html]
Bank Records
[http://www.mdarchives.state.md.us/msa/speccol/4313/html/0000.html]
Biographical Initiative
[http://www.mdarchives.state.md.us/msa/mm95_96/html/histleg.html]
Checklist of Indexes
[http://www.mdarchives.state.md.us/msa/refserv/html/index.html]
Church Records
[http://www.mdarchives.state.md.us/msa/speccol/html/0002.html]
County Information
[http://www.mdarchives.state.md.us/msa/refserv/html/counties.html]
Courses in History Online
[http://www.mdarchives.state.md.us/msa/educ/html/courses.html]
Maps
[http://www.mdarchives.state.md.us/msa/speccol/maps/html/collect.html]
Maryland Government
[http://www.mdarchives.state.md.us/msa/homepage/html/mm95_96.html]
Maryland Government Records
[http://www.mdarchives.state.md.us/msa/refserv/html/series.html]
Maryland History Coloring Book
[http://www.mdarchives.state.md.us/msa/stagser/s1259/121/7575/html/colorbk.html]
Maryland Manual 1996-97
[http://www.mdarchives.state.md.us/msa/mdmanual/html/mm96-97.html]
Maryland Newspaper Project
[http://www.mdarchives.state.md.us/msa/speccol/html/0003.html]
Newsletter
[http://www.mdarchives.state.md.us/msa/refserv/html/bulldogs.html]
Newspaper Guide
[http://www.mdarchives.state.md.us/msa/speccol/news/html/news.html]
State Agency Records
[http://www.mdarchives.state.md.us/msa/refserv/pubs/staghist/html/intro.html]
Vital Records
[http://www.mdarchives.state.md.us/msa/refserv/html/vitalrec.html]

# State Historical Society

## Maryland Historical Society
http://www.mcps.k12.md.us/curriculum/socialstd/FT/MD_Historic_Soc.html

201 West Monument Street
Baltimore, MD 21201

Phone  (410) 685-3750

Overview
   [http://www.mcps.k12.md.us/curriculum/socialstd/FT/MD_Historic_Soc.html]


# Other State Sites

## Baltimore County Genealogical Society      http://www.serve.com/bcgs/bcgs.html

P.O. Box 10085                          Phone   (410) 750-9315
Towson, MD 21285-0085                   E-mail  peeples@erols.com

Bible Records
   [http://www.serve.com/bcgs/bible.html]
Knightsmith Family
   [http://www.serve.com/bcgs/ascii/knghtsmt.txt]
Surname Files
   [http://www.serve.com/bcgs/ascii/bcgsvfff.txt]


## Baltimore County Library      http://204.255.212.10/centers/history/history.html

320 York Road                           Phone   (410) 887-6100
Towson, MD 21204                        E-mail  webmaster@mail.bcpl.lib.md.us

Genealogy Resources
   [http://204.255.212.10/centers/history/geneal.html]
Local History Resources
   [http://204.255.212.10/centers/history/local.html]
Passenger Lists
   [http://gopher.nara.gov:70/0/genealog/holdings/catalogs/ipcat/rg36.html]
Passenger Lists 1891-1957
   [http://gopher.nara.gov:70/0/genealog/holdings/catalogs/ipcat/rg85.html]


## Johns Hopkins University      http://archives.mse.jhu.edu:8000/

Milton S. Eisenhower Library            Phone   (410) 516-8348
3400 North Charles Street               Fax     (410) 516-7202
Baltimore, MD 21218                     E-mail  James.Stimpert@jhu.edu

Early Americana Collections: 1600-1800
   [http://archives.mse.jhu.edu:8000/sc-ameri.html]
Family and Children's Society Records
   [gopher://musicbox.mse.jhu.edu:70/00/mss/ms360.txt]
Loyalist Confiscation Records
   [gopher://musicbox.mse.jhu.edu:70/00/mss/ms380.txt]
Manuscripts Register and Index
   [gopher://musicbox.mse.jhu.edu:70/11/mss]
Maps
   [http://archives.mse.jhu.edu:8000/peabmaps.html]
Milton S. Eisenhower Library
   [http://milton.mse.jhu.edu:8001.html/milton.html]
Special Collections and Archives
   [http://archives.mse.jhu.edu:8000/index.html]

# University of Maryland, College Park
http://www.itd.umd.edu/UMS/UMCP/RARE/797hmpg.html

| | |
|---|---|
| Marylandia and Rare Book Department | Phone   (301) 405-9212 |
| McKeldin Library | E-mail   karenfis@wam.umd.edu |
| College Park, MD 20742 | |

Baltimore News American Photo Collection
[http://www.itd.umd.edu/UMS/UMCP/RARE/797hmpg3.html]
Maps
[http://www.itd.umd.edu/UMS/UMCP/RARE/797hmpg2.html]
Maryland State Publications
[http://www.itd.umd.edu/UMS/UMCP/RARE/797hmpg1.html]\

# MASSACHUSETTS

## State Home Page

### Commonwealth of Massachusetts HomePage          http://www.state.ma.us/

| | |
|---|---|
| Massachusetts Historical Commission | Phone   (617) 727-8470 |
| 220 Morrissey Boulevard | Fax      (617) 727-5128 |
| Boston, MA  02125 | TDD      (800) 392-6090 |

Constitution
[http://www.state.ma.us/legis/const.htm]
Links, Massachusetts Cities and Towns
[http://www.state.ma.us/cc/]
Local Preservation Update, Newsletter
[http://www.magnet.state.ma.us/sec/mhc/mhclpu/lpuidx.htm]
Maps, Acrobat Reader
[http://www.state.ma.us/sec/cis/cismap/mapidx.htm]
Massachusetts Court System
[http://www.state.ma.us/courts/courts.htm]
Massachusetts Historical Commission
[http://www.magnet.state.ma.us/sec/mhc/]
Massachusetts Historical Commission, Newsletter
[http://www.state.ma.us/sec/mhc/mhcpa/paidx.htm]

## State Archives

### Massachusetts State Archives          http://www.magnet.state.ma.us/sec/arc/

| | |
|---|---|
| 220 Morrissey Boulevard | Phone   (617) 727-2816 |
| Boston, MA  02125 | Fax      (617) 288-4505 |

Archives Advisory Commission
[http://www.magnet.state.ma.us/sec/arc/arcaac/aacintro.htm]
Ethnic History/Genealogy
[http://www.magnet.state.ma.us/sec/arc/arcarc/hol3.htm]
Holdings
[http://www.magnet.state.ma.us/sec/arc/arcarc/hol.htm]
Researching Your Family History
[http://www.magnet.state.ma.us/sec/arc/arcfam/famidx.htm]

# State Library
## *Outstanding Site*

## Massachusetts Board of Library Commissioners
http://www.mlin.lib.ma.us/mblc.htm

648 Beacon Street
Boston, MA 02215

Phone   (617) 267-9400
        (800) 952-7403 in Massachusetts
Fax     (617) 421-9833
E-mail  info@mlin.lib.ma.us

Links, Massachusetts Libraries
[http://www.mlin.lib.ma.us/homepage.htm]
Links, U.S. Libraries, etc.
[http://www.mlin.lib.ma.us/fsl.htm]
\MLIN, Online Gopher
[http://www.mlin.lib.ma.us/]
Massachusetts Library Catalogs Online
[http://www.mlin.lib.ma.us/catalogs.htm]
Massachusetts State Union List of Serials
[http://www.mlin.lib.ma.us/mag.htm]

# Other State Sites

## American Antiquarian Society          gopher://mark.mwa.org/

185 Salisbury Street
Worcester, MA 01609-1634

Phone   (508) 752-5813
Fax     (508) 754-9069
E-mail  nhb@mwa.org

Guide, Under Its Generous Dome
[gopher://mark.mwa.org:70/1dome.dir]
Online Catalog
[gopher://mark.mwa.org:70/1catdesc.dir]

## Andover Harvard Theological Seminary          http://divweb.harvard.edu

45 Francis Avenue
Cambridge, MA 02138

Phone   (617) 496-1618
Fax     (617) 496-4111
E-mail  cwillard@div.harvard.edu

Library
[http://divweb.harvard.edu/library/]
Manuscript Registers (Church Records)
[http://divweb.harvard.edu/library/bms/bmsind1.htm]
Unitarian-Universalist Bibliography
[http://divweb.harvard.edu/library/biblio/uure.htm]

## Boston Public Library          http://www.bpl.org/

666 Boylston Street
Copley Square
Boston, MA 02117

Phone   (617) 536-5400

Genealogy Resources at the BPL
[gopher://bpl.org:70/00gopher_root%3A%5Bbpl_info.services.researchlib.soc_sci%5
Dgenealogy_resources.doc]
Obituary Database, 1990-1995
[http://www.bpl.org/WWW/Obits.html]

## *Outstanding Site*

# Historical Records of Dukes County, Massachusetts
http://www.vineyard.net/vineyard/history/

RR2 Box 247                                   E-mail  cbaer@vineyard.net
Vineyard Haven, MA 02568

Allen Family Project
   [http://www.vineyard.net/vineyard/history/allen/allenhp.htm]
Census, 1790- , Population Figures
   [http://www.vineyard.net/vineyard/history/dukes/pop.htm]
Census, 1790, Index
   [http://www.vineyard.net/vineyard/history/cen1790i.htm]
Census, 1790, Original Arrangement
   [http://www.vineyard.net/vineyard/history/cen1790.htm]
Census, 1850, Chilmark, Original Arrangement
   [http://www.vineyard.net/vineyard/history/chilcen50.htm]
Census, 1850, Dukes County Index
   [http://www.vineyard.net/vineyard/history/cz50ind.htm]
Census, 1850, Edgartown, Original Arrangement
   [http://www.vineyard.net/vineyard/history/edgcen50.htm]
Census, 1850, Tisbury, Original Arrangement
   [http://www.vineyard.net/vineyard/history/tiscen50.htm]
Census, 1860, Tisbury, Index
   [http://www.vineyard.net/vineyard/history/cen60.htm]
Census, 1870, Tisbury, Index
   [http://www.vineyard.net/vineyard/history/cen70.htm]
Census, 1910, Tisbury, Original Arrangement
   [http://www.vineyard.net/vineyard/history/cen10.htm]
Census, 1910, Tisbury, Index
   [http://www.vineyard.net/vineyard/history/cen10ndx.htm]
Chilmark Records
   [http://www.vineyard.net/vineyard/history/dukes/chilmark.htm]
City Directory, 1897, Tisbury
   [http://www.vineyard.net/vineyard/history/td1897.htm]
Deaths, 1850-1875
   [http://www.vineyard.net/vineyard/history/deathpag.htm]
Draft List, 1862
   [http://www.vineyard.net/vineyard/history/draftpag.htm]
Edgartown Records
   [http://www.vineyard.net/vineyard/history/dukes/edgtown.htm]
Map, Dukes County, 1784
   [http://www.vineyard.net/vineyard/history/dukes/mv1784.gif]
Marriage Records Index, 1850-1875
   [http://www.vineyard.net/vineyard/history/tmindex.htm]
Mayhew Family
   [http://www.vineyard.net/vineyard/history/dukes/bnk1_104.htm]
Oral and Written Histories
   [http://www.vineyard.net/vineyard/history/history.htm]
Queries
   [http://www.vineyard.net/vineyard/history/queries.htm]
Vineyard Gazette Indexes Death Notices, 1850-1875
   [http://www.vineyard.net/vineyard/history/gazdeath.htm]

Vineyard Gazette Indexes Death Notices, 1884-1939, A-K
    [http://www.vineyard.net/vineyard/history/vgind1.htm]
Vineyard Gazette Indexes Death Notices, 1884-1939, L-Z
    [http://www.vineyard.net/vineyard/history/vgind2.htm]
Vineyard Gazette Indexes Marriages Index. 1853-1863
    [http://www.vineyard.net/vineyard/history/gazmar63.htm]
West, Jeruel Family
    [http://www.vineyard.net/vineyard/history/jernotes.htm]
Yale, Leroy Milton Biography
    [http://www.vineyard.net/vineyard/history/leroy.htm]

## Natick Historical Society Museum     http://www.ixl.net/~natick/

58 Eliot Street                 Phone   (508) 647-4841
South Natick, MA 01760        E-mail  eliot@ixl.net

Annals of Elm Bank, the Cheney Estate
    [http://www.ixl.net/~natick/ElmBank.html]
Natick History
    [http://www.ixl.net/~natick/Natick_History_Brief.html]
Natick Inns and Taverns
    [http://www.ixl.net/~natick/Inns_&_Taverns.html]
Natick Manufacturing
    [http://www.ixl.net/~natick/Business_and_Industry.html]

## New England Historic Genealogical Society     http://www.nehgs.org/

99-101 Newbury Street        Phone   (617) 536-5740
Boston, MA 02116             Fax     (617) 536-7307
                             E-mail  nehgs@nehgs.org
Circulating Library Catalog
    [http://www.nehgs.org/circcat.htm]
Guide to German Resources
    [http://www.nehgs.org/germans.htm]
Guide to Irish Resources
    [http://www.nehgs.org/irish.htm]
NEHGS as a Family History Center
    [http://www.nehgs.org/lds.htm]

## Simmons College     http://www.simmons.edu/

Library                          Phone   (617) 521-2440
300 The Fenway          E-mail  beatley@artemis.simmons.edu
Boston, MA 02115

Archives
    [http://www.simmons.edu/resources/libraries/archives/record.html]
Archives and Special Collections
    [http://www.simmons.edu/resources/libraries/archives/archives.html]
Library
    [http://www.simmons.edu/resources/libraries/]

Manuscripts
[http://www.simmons.edu/resources/libraries/archives/manuscript.html]

# MICHIGAN
## State Home Page

| Michigan State Government | http://www.migov.state.mi.us/ |
|---|---|

Military History
[http://www.voyager.net/goguard/history.htm]
Vital Records
[http://www.mdch.state.mi.us/PHA/OSR/frame.ssi]

## State Archives
*Outstanding Site*

| State Archives of Michigan | http://www.sos.state.mi.us |
|---|---|

| Michigan Library and Historical Center | Phone | (517) 373-1408 |
|---|---|---|
| 717 West Allegan Street | Fax | (517) 373-0851 |
| Lansing, MI 48918-1805 | | |

Archival Circulars, Finding Aids
[http://www.sos.state.mi.us/history/archive/circular.html]
Census Records, Special
[gopher://gopher.sos.state.mi.us:70/00/history/archives/c45]
Census Records, State
[gopher://gopher.sos.state.mi.us:70/00/history/archives/c9]
County Clerks Genealogy Directory
[http://www.sos.state.mi.us/history/archive/archgene.html]
Court Records
[gopher://gopher.sos.state.mi.us:70/00/history/archives/c37]
Civil War Manuscripts
[gopher://gopher.sos.state.mi.us:70/00/history/archives/c20]
Land Records
[gopher://gopher.sos.state.mi.us:70/00/history/archives/c2]
Military, Local Records
[gopher://gopher.sos.state.mi.us:70/00/history/archives/c27]
Military, Post War Records
[gopher://gopher.sos.state.mi.us:70/00/history/archives/c7]
Military, War Records
[gopher://gopher.sos.state.mi.us:70/00/history/archives/c4]
Naturalization Records
[gopher://gopher.sos.state.mi.us:70/00/history/archives/c10]
Photographs
[http://www.sos.state.mi.us/history/archive/archphot.html]
Probate Records
[gopher://gopher.sos.state.mi.us:70/00/history/archives/c6]
School Records
[gopher://gopher.sos.state.mi.us:70/00/history/archives/c11]
Vital Records
[gopher://gopher.sos.state.mi.us:70/00/history/archives/c19]

# State Library

## Library of Michigan
http://www.libofmich.lib.mi.us/index.html

P.O. Box 30007
717 West Allegan Street
Lansing, MI 48909-1805

Phone   (517) 373-1580
E-mail   info@libofmich.lib.mi.us

Abrams Foundation Historical Collection    Phone   (517) 373-1300

African-American Research
   [http://www.libofmich.lib.mi.us/citizens/collections/genealogy/afroamer.html]
Basic Michigan Books
   [http://www.libofmich.lib.mi.us/libraries/collections/genealogy/basictitles.html]
Diaries and Autobiographies
   [http://www.libofmich.lib.mi.us/libraries/collections/genealogy/midiaries.html]
Fur Trade
   [http://www.libofmich.lib.mi.us/citizens/collections/genealogy/mifurtrade.html]
Genealogy Sources
   [http://www.libofmich.lib.mi.us/libraries/collections/genealogy/misources.html]
How To Guides
   [http://www.libofmich.lib.mi.us/citizens/collections/genealogy/genealogy.html]
Library Directory
   [http://www.libofmich.lib.mi.us/libraries/libraries.html]
Lighthouses
   [http://www.libofmich.lib.mi.us/citizens/collections/genealogy/milighthouses.html]
Lumbering
   [http://www.libofmich.lib.mi.us/citizens/collections/genealogy/milumbering.html]
Maps
   [http://www.libofmich.lib.mi.us/citizens/collections/microformmaps.html]
Native Americans
   [http://www.libofmich.lib.mi.us/citizens/collections/genealogy/minatamerbib.html]
Passenger Lists
   [http://www.libofmich.lib.mi.us/citizens/collections/genealogy/immigration.html]
Search Our Website
   [http://www.libofmich.lib.mi.us/cgi-bin/cgiwrap/lmwebsit/search]

# State Historical Society

## Michigan Historical Center
http://www.sos.state.mi.us/history/museum/explore/explore.html

Michigan Department of State
717 West Allegan Street
Lansing, MI 48918-1805

Phone   (517) 373-3559
        (800) 366-3703
E-mail   webspinners@sosmail.state.mi.us

Michigan History Magazine

Phone   (517) 373-1645
        (800) 366-3703

Historic Preservation
   [http://www.sos.state.mi.us/history/preserve/preserve.html]
Michigan History Magazine
   [http://www.sos.state.mi.us/history/mag/mag.html]
Museums
   [http://www.sos.state.mi.us/history/museum/explore/museums/musems.html]

State Archaeologist
  [http://www.sos.state.mi.us/history/archeol/archeol.html]

# Other State Sites

## Detroit Public Library    http://www.detroit.lib.mi.us/

| | |
|---|---|
| Burton Historical Collection | Phone   (313) 833-1480 |
| 5201 Woodward Avenue | Fax      (313) 832-0877 |
| Detroit, MI 48202 | E-mail  nvangor@cms.cc.wayne.edu |

Burton Historical Collection
  [http://www.detroit.lib.mi.us/special_collections.htm]

## Detroit Society for Genealogical Research    http://www.fgs.org/~fgs/soc0042.htm

| | |
|---|---|
| Burton Historical Collection | Phone   (313) 833-1480 |
| Detroit Public Library | Fax      (313) 832-0877 |
| 5201 Woodward Avenue | E-mail  nvangor@cms.cc.wayne.edu |
| Detroit, MI 48202 | |

Overview
  [http://www.fgs.org/~fgs/soc0042.htm]

## Michigan State University    http://pilot.msu.edu/unit/msuarhc/

| | |
|---|---|
| University Archives and Historical Collections | Phone   (517) 355-2330 |
| 101 Conrad Hall | Fax      (517) 353-9319 |
| East Lansing, MI 48824-1327 | E-mail  (frye@pilot.msu.edu) |
| | (goulds@pilot.msu.edu) |
| | (honhart@pilot.msu.edu) |

Collection Guide
  [http://pilot.msu.edu/unit/msuarhc/intro.html]
Links to Other Libraries
  [http://zweb.cl.msu.edu/]
Submit an Online Reference Questions
  [http://pilot.msu.edu/unit/msuarhc/archvreq.html]

## Michigan Technological University    http://www.lib.mtu.edu/jrvp/index.htm

| | |
|---|---|
| MTU Archives and Copper Country | Phone   (906) 487-3209 |
|    Historical Collections | Fax      (906) 487-2357 |
| J.R. Van Pelt Library | E-mail  copper@mtu.edu |
| 1400 Townsend Drive | |
| Houghton, MI 49931-1295 | |

Collections Guide
  [http://www.lib.mtu.edu/jrvp/history.htm]

## University of Michigan-Dearborn    http://www.umd.umich.edu/

| | |
|---|---|
| 4901 Evergreen Road | E-mail  rfraser@umich.edu |
| Dearborn, MI 48128-1491 | |

| | |
|---|---|
| Armenian Research Center | E-mail  gottenbr@umich.edu |

Armenian Research Center
    [http://www.umd.umich.edu/dept/armenian/]
Holocaust Survivor Oral History Project
    [http://www.umd.umich.edu/lib/holo/]


## *Outstanding Site*

| University of Michigan | http://www.umd.umich.edu/ |
| --- | --- |

| Bentley Historical Library | Phone | (313) 764-3482 |
| --- | --- | --- |
| 1150 Beal Avenue | Fax | (313) 936-1333 |
| Ann Arbor, MI 48109-2113 | E-mail | bentley.ref@umich.edu |

| William L. Clements Library | Phone | (313) 764-2347 |
| --- | --- | --- |
| 909 South University Avenue | Fax | (313) 647-0716 |
| Ann Arbor, MI 48109-1190 | E-mail | clements.library@umich.edu |

| Special Collections Library | Phone | (313) 764-9377 |
| --- | --- | --- |
| 711 Harlan Hatcher Graduate Library | Fax | (313) 763-5080 |
| Ann Arbor, MI 48109-1205 | E-mail | Peggy.Daub@umich.edu |

Civil War Collection
    [http://www.clements.umich.edu/Schoff.html]
Civil War Collection Name Index
    [http://www.clements.umich.edu/Webguides/Schoff/ScGuidesA.html]
Civil War Collection Regimental Index
    [http://www.clements.umich.edu/Webguides/Schoff/Regndx.html]
Clements Library Associates
    [http://www.clements.umich.edu/Associates.html]
Clements Library Associates Quarto, Newsletter
    [http://www.clements.umich.edu/quarto.html]
Manuscripts Division
    [http://www.clements.umich.edu/Manuscripts.html]
Manuscripts Index
    [http://www.clements.umich.edu/MsGuides/MsGuidesA.html]
Map Division
    [http://www.clements.umich.edu/Maps.html]
Michigan Historical Collections
    [http://www.umich.edu/~bhl/bhl/mhchome/mhchome.htm]
Michigan in the Olympics. Virtual Tour
    [http://www.umich.edu/~bhl/bhl/olymp2/oltitle.htm]
Music Division
    [http://www.clements.umich.edu/Music.html]
Photographic Division
    [http://www.clements.umich.edu/Photos.html]
Photographic Terms
    [http://www.clements.umich.edu/Photogal/def.html#tin]
Prints Division
    [http://www.clements.umich.edu/Prints.html]
Special Collections
    [http://www.lib.umich.edu/libhome/SpecColl.lib/collections.html#humanities]
University of Michigan Archives
    [http://www.umich.edu/~bhl/bhl/uarphome/uarphome.htm]

# MINNESOTA
## State Home Page

North Star!
Minnesota Government Information and Services
   http://www.state.mn.us/mainmenu.html

                               E-mail  info@state.mn.us

Constitution
   [http://www.house.leg.state.mn.us/cco/rules/mncon/preamble.htm]
Court System
   [http://www.courts.state.mn.us/]
Library Directory
   [http://www.metronet.lib.mn.us/mnlibs/publib.htm]
Links, Local Government
   [http://www.state.mn.us/govtoffice/index.html#80]
State Statutes
   [http://www.leg.state.mn.us/leg/statutes.htm]

## State Library

Department of Library Services
   http://www.sos.state.mi.us/history/archive/archive.html

Department of Minnesota Children,              Phone   (612) 296-6104
   Families and Learning                       E-mail  children@state.mn.us
Capitol Square Building
550 Cedar Street
St. Paul, MN 55101

Minnesota Libraries, Newsletter. Fulltext
   [http://www.educ.state.mn.us/libry/libunit/plnews.htm]

## State Genealogical Society

Minnesota Genealogical Society           http://www.mtn.org/mgs/

1650 Carroll Avenue                      Phone   (612) 645-3671
P.O. Box 16069                           E-mail  mgsdec@mtn.org
St. Paul, MN 55116-0069

Links, Genealogy, Minnesota
   [http://www.mtn.org/mgs/othersoc/]

## State Historical Society

Minnesota Historical Society             http://www.mnhs.org/

345 Kellogg Boulevard West               Phone   (612) 296-2143
St. Paul, MN 55102-1906

Building and House History
   [http://www.mnhs.org/research/rh1.htm]
Business Records
   [http://www.mnhs.org/research/c3.htm]
City Directories
   [http://www.mnhs.org/research/c4.htm]

Genealogy
   [http://www.mnhs.org/research/rg1.htm]
Legislative History Research
   [http://www.mnhs.org/research/rl1.htm]
Manuscripts
   [http://www.mnhs.org/research/c10.htm]
Map Collections
   [http://www.mnhs.org/research/c17.htm]
Minnesota State Archives
   [http://www.mnhs.org/research/c18.htm]
Naturalizataion Records
   [http://www.mnhs.org/research/c19.htm]
Newspapers
   [http://www.mnhs.org/research/c14.htm]
Oral Histories
   [http://www.mnhs.org/research/c8.htm]
Organizational Records
   [http://www.mnhs.org/research/c9.htm]
Photographs
   [http://www.mnhs.org/research/c11.htm]
Portraits
   [http://www.mnhs.org/research/c13.htm]
Tax and Assessment Rolls
   [http://www.mnhs.org/research/c2.htm]

# Other State Sites

## Minnesota Library Association
http://www.lib.mankato.msus.edu:2000/

1315 Lowry Avenue North
Minneapolis, MN 55411-1398

Phone   (612) 521-1735
Fax      (612) 529-5503
E-mail   mnla@augsburg.edu

Newsletter
   [http://www.lib.mankato.msus.edu:2000/mla/news.html]

### Outstanding Site

## Minnesota Obituaries
http://www.pconline.com/~bortsch/mnobits/index.html

E-mail   bortsch@pconline.com

Data Format
   [http://www.pconline.com/~bortsch/mnobits/format.html]
Newspapers Indexed
   [http://www.pconline.com/~bortsch/mnobits/papers.html]
Obituaries, September 1995–.
   [http://www.pconline.com/~bortsch/mnobits/index.html]
Unknown, Incomplete Names
   [http://www.pconline.com/~bortsch/mnobits/samples.html]

### Outstanding Site

## University of Minnesota Libraries
http://www.umn.edu/tc/

Manuscripts Division
826 Berry Street
Saint Paul, MN 55114

Phone   (612) 624-3855
E-mail   a-lath1@vm1.spcs.umn.edu

Special Collections and Rare Books        Phone    (612) 624-1528
James Ford Bell Library                   E-mail   c-urne@vm1.spcs.umn.edu

Center for Austrian Studies (CAS)         Phone    (612) 624-7321
314 Social Sciences Building              Fax      (612) 626-2242
267 19th Avenue South                     E-mail   danpink@gold.tc.umn.edu
Minneapolis MN 55455                               ander441@gold.tc.umn.edu

Center for European Studies              Phone    (612) 625-1557
309 Social Sciences Building             Fax      (612) 626-2242
297-19th Avenue South                    E-mail   cesiis@gold.tc.umn.edu
Minneapolis, MN 55455

Immigration History Research Center (IHRC)   Phone    (612) 627-4208
826 Berry Street                             Fax      (612) 627-4190
Saint Paul, MN 55114                         E-mail   ihrc@gold.tc.umn.edu

Social Welfare History Archives (SWHA)    Phone    (612) 624-6394
101 Walter Library                        Fax      (612) 625-5525
Minneapolis, MN 55455                     E-mail   david.j.klaassen-1@tc.umn.edu

British Periodicals, 19th Century
    [http://mh.cla.umn.edu/britper.html]
Center for Austrian Studies Austrian History Yearbook
    [http://www.socsci.umn.edu/cas/ahy.htm]
Center for Austrian Studies Austrian Studies Newsletter
    [http://www.socsci.umn.edu/cas/newslet.htm]
Center for Austrian Studies European Links
    [http://www.socsci.umn.edu/cas/links.htm]
Center for Austrian Studies Working Papers
    [http://www.socsci.umn.edu/cas/workp.htm]
Center for Austrian Studies
    [http://www.socsci.umn.edu/cas/us.htm]
Center for European Studies
    [http://cla-net.cla.umn.edu/europe/]
Genealogical Sources at the IHRC
    [http://www.umn.edu/ihrc/genealog.htm]
Immigration History Research Center (IHRC)
    [http://www.umn.edu/ihrc/]
Immigration History Research Center News
    [http://www.umn.edu/ihrc/publ.htm]
Special Collections
    [http://mh.cla.umn.edu/speccoll.html]
Social Welfare History Archives Guides
    [http://archon.lib.umn.edu/swha.htm]
University Libraries
    [http://www.lib.umn.edu/]

## University of St. Thomas Libraries        http://www.lib.stthomas.edu/

Department of Special Collections          Phone    (612) 962-5468
O'Shaughnessy-Frey Library, Mail #5004     Fax      (612) 962-5406
2115 Summit Avenue                         E-mail   jbdavenport@stthomas.edu
St. Paul, MN  55105-1096

Archbishop Ireland Memorial Library      Phone   (612) 962-5453
2260 Summit Avenue      E-mail   j9malcheski@stthomas.edu
St. Paul, MN 55105      memartin@a1.stthomas.edu

Celtic Collection
    [http://www.lib.stthomas.edu/special/index.htm#celtic]
Collections
    [http://www.lib.stthomas.edu/ireland/]
French Memoir Collection
    [http://www.lib.stthomas.edu/special/index.htm#French]
Links to Catholic Sites
    [http://www.lib.stthomas.edu/ireland/pages/catholic/catholic.htm]
Luxembourg Collection
    [http://www.lib.stthomas.edu/special/index.htm#luxem]
University Archives
    [http://www.lib.stthomas.edu/special/index.htm#Archives]

## Upsala Obituary, Marriage and Cemetery Index
    http://www.upstel.net/~johns/CemIndex/CemIndex.html

E-mail   johns@upstel.net.

Upsala News Tribune 1917-1940
    [http://www.upstel.net/~johns/CemIndex/CemIndex2.html]

# MISSISSIPPI

## State Home Page

### Mississippi State Government HomePage     http://www.state.ms.us/

Links, Mississippi Government
    [http://www.state.ms.us/]

## State Library

### Mississippi Library Commission     http://www.mlc.lib.ms.us

1221 Ellis Avenue      Phone   (601) 359-1036
P.O. Box 10700
Jackson, MS 29289-0700

Overview
    [http://www.mlc.lib.ms.us]

## Other State Sites

### Mississippi Genealogy     http://www.insolwwb.net/~rholler/ms/

E-mail   rholler@insolwwb.net

U.S. GenWeb Project
    [http://www.insolwwb.net/~rholler/ms/]

### University of Mississippi     http://www.olemiss.edu/

Archives and Special Collections      Phone   (601) 234-6091
University, MS 38677      Fax     (601) 234-6381
     E-mail   ulverich@vm.cc.olemiss.edu

Mississippi Collection                          E-mail   ullandi@sunset.backbone.olemiss.edu

Center for the Study of Southern Culture        Phone   (601) 232-5993
                                                Fax      (601) 232-5814
                                                E-mail   webmaster@www.cssc.olemiss.edu

Center for Population Studies                   E-mail   saholley@sunset.backbone.olemiss.edu

Archives and Special Collections
    [http://www.olemiss.edu/depts/general_library/files/archhome.htm]
Libraries
    [http://www.olemiss.edu/depts/general_library/]
Maps, Population
    [http://www.olemiss.edu/depts/population_studies/maps.htm]
Southern Media Archives
    [http://imp.cssc.olemiss.edu/sma/sma.html]
Southern Register, Newsletter
    [http://imp.cssc.olemiss.edu/register/96/summ_fall/contents.html]

## University of Southern Mississippi         http://www.usm.edu/

Center for Oral History and Culture             Phone   (601) 266-4575
Suite J, McClesky Hall                          E-mail   cbolton@whale.st.usm.edu
Hattiesburg, MS 39406-5175

McCain Library and Archives                     Phone   (601) 266-4348
P.O. Box 5148                                   Fax      (601) 266-4409
Hattiesburg, MS 39406-5148                      E-mail   btusa@ocean.st.usm.edu
                                                         yarnold@whale.st.usm.edu

Center for Oral History and Culture
    [http://www.usm.edu/~ocach/]
Civil War Materials
    [http://www.lib.usm.edu/civilwar.html]
deGrummond Children's Literature Collection
    [http://www.lib.usm.edu/degrumm.htm]
Links, Mississippi Archives
    [http://www.lib.usm.edu/archives.html]
McCain Library
    [http://www.lib.usm.edu/mccain.html]
Manuscript Collections
    [http://www.lib.usm.edu/summlist.html]
Manuscripts and Archives Department
    [http://www.lib.usm.edu/archives.html]
Women
    [http://www.lib.usm.edu/women.html]

# MISSOURI
## State Home Page

## Missouri State Government Web          http://www.state.mo.us/

County Officials
    [http://mosl.sos.state.mo.us/ofman/mocount1.html]
Historical Records Management
    [http://mosl.sos.state.mo.us/gov-ser/sosrecma.html]

Local Records Preservation
   [http://mosl.sos.state.mo.us/gov-ser/soslorec.html]
Missouri Court Automation Project
   [http://www.state.mo.us/sca/ec2004.htm]
Official Manual of the State of Missouri, 1995-96
   [http://mosl.sos.state.mo.us/ofman/ofman.html]
Vital Records
   [http://www.health.state.mo.us/cgi-bin/uncgi/BirthAndDeathRecords]

## State Archives

| Missouri State Archives | http://mosl.sos.state.mo.us/gov-ser/arch.html |
|---|---|

| State Information Center | Phone | (573) 751-4717 |
|---|---|---|
| 600 West Main Street | | (573) 751-4717 |
| P.O. Box 778 | | (573) 751-4717 |
| Jefferson City, MO 65102 | E-mail | archref@mail.more.net |
| | | jperkins@mail.more.net |

Friends of the Missouri State Archives
   [http://mosl.sos.state.mo.us/gov-ser/arch.html]
Local Records Grants Program
   [http://mosl.sos.state.mo.us/gov-ser/archlrg.html]

## State Library

| Missouri State Library | http://mosl.sos.state.mo.us/lib-ser/libser.html |
|---|---|

| 600 West Main Street | Phone | (573) 751-3615 |
|---|---|---|
| P.O. Box 387 | Fax | (573) 751-3612 |
| Jefferson City, MO 65102-0387 | E-mail | sparker@mail.sos.state.mo.us |

Biographical Files, Missouri Officials
   [http://mosl.sos.state.mo.us/lib-ser/libref/www_hist.html]
Library Directory
   [http://mosl.sos.state.mo.us/lib-ser/libdir.html]
Missouri Center for the Book
   [http://mosl.sos.state.mo.us/lib-ser/libpub/mcb/mcb.html]
Missouri Libraries on the Internet
   [http://mosl.sos.state.mo.us/linkpgs/molib.html]
Newspaper Clipping Collection
   [http://mosl.sos.state.mo.us/lib-ser/libref/papclip.html]
Official Manual of the State of Missouri, 1995-96
   [http://mosl.sos.state.mo.us/ofman/ofman.html]
Online Newsletter
   [http://mosl.sos.state.mo.us/newsline/newsline.html]

## State Genealogical Society

| Missouri State Genealogical Association | http://www.umr.edu/~mstauter/mosga/ |
|---|---|

P.O. Box 833
Columbia, MO 65205-0833

Overview
   [http://www.umr.edu/~mstauter/mosga/]

# Other State Sites

## Kansas City Area Archivists
http://cctr.umkc.edu/WHMCKC/KCAA/KCAAHOME.HTM

Western Historical Manuscript Collection     Phone   (816) 235-1543
302 Newcomb Hall     E-mail   WHMCKC@smtpgate.umkc.edu
University of Missouri-Kansas City
5100 Rockhill Road
Kansas City, MO 64110-2499

Directory of Area Archives
    [http://cctr.umkc.edu/WHMCKC/KCAA/KCAADIR.htm]

## Mid-Continent Public Library
http://www.mcpl.lib.mo.us/

317 West 24 Highway     Phone   (816) 252-0950
Independence, MO 64050     E-mail   ge@mcpl.lib.mo.us

Genealogy and Local History Department
    [http://www.mcpl.lib.mo.us/gen.htm]

## University of Missouri-Kansas City
http://cctr.umkc.edu/whmckc/index.html

Western Historical Manuscript Collection     Phone   (816) 235-1543
302 Newcomb Hall     E-mail   WHMCKC@smtpgate.umkc.edu
5100 Rockhill Road
Kansas City, MO 64110-2499

Area Organization Records
    [http://cctr.umkc.edu/WHMCKC/Collections/cframe.htm]
Church Records
    [http://cctr.umkc.edu/WHMCKC/Collections/cframe.htm]
Genealogy and Family Collections
    [http://cctr.umkc.edu/WHMCKC/Collections/cframe.htm]
Military Records
    [http://cctr.umkc.edu/WHMCKC/Collections/cframe.htm]

## Webster University
http://library2.websteruniv.edu/webdata/libhome.html

Eden-Webster Library     Phone   (314) 961-3627
475 East Lockwood Avenue     Fax     (314) 961-9063
St. Louis, MO 63119     E-mail   edward@library2.websteruniv.edu

Church Records, Microfilm
    [http://library2.websteruniv.edu/webdata/congrega.html]
Eden Theological Seminary Archives
    [http://library2.websteruniv.edu/webdata/edenarch.html]
Webster University Archives
    [http://library2.websteruniv.edu/webdata/webuarch.html]

## William Jewell College
http://www.jewell.edu/

Curry Library     Phone   (816) 781-7700, ex 5465
500 College Hill     Fax     (816) 415-5027
Liberty, MO 64068-1896     E-mail   knaussb@william.jewell.edu

Puritan Writings Collection
    [http://www.jewell.edu/Curry/collections/puritanbib.html]
Special Collections Department
    [http://www.jewell.edu/Curry/collections/special.html]
Spurgeon Archives
    [http://www.spurgeon.org/mainpage.htm]
Spurgeon Collection,  Religion
    [http://www.jewell.edu/Curry/collections/spurgeon.html]


# MONTANA

## State Home Page

| Montana State Home Page | http://www.mt.gov/ |
|---|---|

Links, Montana Government
    [http://www.mt.gov/]

## State Archives

| Records Management Bureau | http://www.mt.gov/sos/sectst.htm#anchor360717 |
|---|---|

| Secretary of State<br>P.O. Box 202801<br>Helena, MT 59620-2801 | Phone  (406) 444-2716<br>Fax     (406) 444-3976<br>E-mail  sos@mt.gov |
|---|---|

Overview
    [http://www.mt.gov/sos/sectst.htm#anchor360717]

## State Library

| Montana State Library | http://msl.mt.gov/ |
|---|---|

| 1515 East 6th Avenue<br>P.O. Box 201800<br>Helena, MT 59620-1800 | Phone  (406) 444-3115<br>          (406) 444-5374 Reference<br>Fax     (406) 444-5612<br>E-mail  mwhite@msl.mt.gov<br>          kstrege@msl.mt.gov |
|---|---|

Collections
    [http://msl.mt.gov/slr/slrdata.html]
Montana Government Links
    [http://msl.mt.gov/slr/govlink.html]
Montana Library Directory
    [http://msl.mt.gov/slr/slrpubs.html]
Montana Links
    [http://msl.mt.gov/slr/mtlinks.html]
Montana Public Library Links
    [http://msl.mt.gov/slr/otherlbs.html]
Montana Schools Links
    [http://msl.mt.gov/slr/schllink.html]
Online Catalog
    [http://msl.mt.gov/catalog.html]

# State Historical Society

## Montana Historical Society                http://www.his.mt.gov

225 North Roberts                  Phone   (406) 444-2681
Helena, MT 59601                   Fax     (406) 444-2696

Overview
    [http://www.his.mt.gov]

# Other State Sites

## Montana State University-Bozeman          http://www.lib.montana.edu/index.html

Special Collections and Archives   Phone   (406) 994-4242
P.O. Box 173320                    Fax     (406) 994-2851
Bozeman, MT 59717-3320             E-mail  User Name @msu.oscs.montana.edu

Manuscript Finding Aids
    [http://www.lib.montana.edu/SPCOLL/findaid.html]
Montana History
    [http://www.lib.montana.edu/SPCOLL/findaid.html#montana]
Native Americans
    [http://www.lib.montana.edu/SPCOLL/findaid.html#native]
Special Collections and Archives
    [http://www.lib.montana.edu/LIBGUIDE/guide14.html]

## *Outstanding Site*

## Lewis and Clark Library                   http://www.mth.mtlib.org/homepage.html

120 South Last Chance Gulch        Phone   (406) 447-1690
Helena, MT 59601-4133              Fax     (406) 447-1687

Helena Area Libraries
    [http://www.mth.mtlib.org/LCLHomepage/Local/HelenaLibs.html]
Helena Organization List©
    [http://www.mth.mtlib.org/LCLHomepage/MainList/NEWRefPoint.html]
Independent Record, Newspaper Index
    [http://www.mth.mtlib.org/LCLHomepage/MainList/NewIRSearch.html]

## University of Montana                     http://www.lib.umt.edu/

Mansfield Library                  Phone   (406) 243-6866 Reference
Missoula, MT 59812                 Fax     (406) 243-2060
                                   E-mail  root@entity.lib.umt.edu
K. Ross Toole Archives             E-mail  archives@selway.umt.edu
Special Collections Department     E-mail  mullin@selway.umt.edu

Griznet Online Library Catalog
    [http://www.lib.umt.edu/catalog1.htm]
K. Ross Toole Archives
    [http://www.lib.umt.edu/archive/web.htm]
Manuscripts Guides
    [http://www.lib.umt.edu/archive/web.htm]

# NEBRASKA

## State Home Page

| Nebraska State HomePage | http://www.state.ne.us/ |
|---|---|

Drivers License Records
 [http://nol.nol.org/home/DMV/index.html]
 [http://www.nol.org/tour/tour_13.htm]
NebraskaLink, Links
 [http://www.neblink.com/]
Nebraska Online (NOL)
 [http://www.nol.org/NLA/]
Unicameral, Nebraska Legislature
 [http://unicam1.lcs.state.ne.us/]

## State Library

| Nebraska Library Commission | http://www.nlc.state.ne.us/ |
|---|---|

The Atrium
1200 North Street, Suite 120
Lincoln, NE 68508-2023

Libraries on the Internet
 [http://www.nlc.state.ne.us/nelib/nelib.html]
NCompass, Quarterly Newsletter
 [http://www.nlc.state.ne.us/public/ncom.html]
N3, Networking News
 [http://www.nlc.state.ne.us/netserv/n3.html]
Nebraska Libraries
 [http://www.nlc.state.ne.us/libraries/library.html]
Nebraska Library Association
 [http://www.nol.org/NLA/]
NLCommunicator, Monthly Newsletter
 [http://www.nlc.state.ne.us/public/nlcom.html]
State Publications
 [http://www.nlc.state.ne.us/public/newslet.html]
What's Up Doc?, Documents Newsletter
 [http://www.nlc.state.ne.us/docs/whatsup.html]

Phone   (402) 471-2045
        (800) 307-2665 Nebraska
Fax     (402) 471-2083
E-mail  webspinner@neon.nlc.state.ne.us

## State Genealogical Society

| Nebraska State Genealogical Society | http://www.fgs.org/~fgs/soc0371.htm |
|---|---|

P.O. Box 5608
Lincoln, NE 68505-0608

Overview
 [http://www.fgs.org/~fgs/soc0371.htm]

## Other State Sites

| Creighton University | http://www.creighton.edu/ |
|---|---|

Carl M. Reinert/Alumni Memorial Library
2500 California Plaza
Omaha, NE 68178

Phone   (402) 280-2927
Fax     (402) 280-2435
E-mail  davids@creighton.edu

Dominican Republic Collection
[http://reinert.creighton.edu/drweb.htm]
Libraries
[http://www.creighton.edu/libraries.html]
Rare Book Room
[http://reinert.creighton.edu/Rarebkrm.htm]
Special Collections Department
[http://reinert.creighton.edu/Special.htm]

## University of Nebraska-Lincoln
http://www.unl.edu/lovers/home.html

Archives and Special Collections Department
South Love Library
Rooms 310-311
Lincoln, NE 68588-0410

Phone (402) 472-2531
E-mail infomail@unllib.unl.edu

Archives and Special Collections Department
[http://www.unl.edu/lovers/spec.html]
Collections
[http://www.unl.edu/lovers/spec.html#major]
Libraries
[http://www.unl.edu/lovers/logito.html]
Western Americana Collection
[http://www.unl.edu/lovers/spec.html#west]

# NEVADA

## State Home Page

### State of Nevada
http://www.state.nv.us/

Links, Nevada Government
[http://www.state.nv.us/]
Nevada Historical Marker Index
[http://www.state.nv.us/cnr/ndwp/markers/hist_map.htm]

## State Library and Archives

### Nevada State Library and Archives
http://www.clan.lib.nv.us/docs/arc-rec.htm

100 North Stewart Street
Carson City, NV 89710

Phone (702) 687-5160
(702) 687-5210
E-mail webmstr@clan.lib.nv.us

Carson Appeal Newspaper Index
[http://www.clan.lib.nv.us/docs/appeal.htm]
Genealogical Resources
[http://www.clan.lib.nv.us/docs/geneal.htm]
Governors' Records
[http://www.clan.lib.nv.us/docs/govrec.htm]
Historical Societies and Museums List
[http://www.clan.lib.nv.us/docs/histsoc.htm]
Local Governments Records Manual
[http://www.clan.lib.nv.us/docs/recman.htm]

Mining Claims
[http://www.clan.lib.nv.us/docs/mining.htm]
Naturalization Records
[http://www.clan.lib.nv.us/docs/natural.htm]
NSLA Vertical File Index
[http://www.clan.lib.nv.us/docs/vertfile.htm#Inventory]
Nevada Bibliographies
[http://www.clan.lib.nv.us/docs/nvbiblio.htm]
Vital Records
[http://www.clan.lib.nv.us/docs/birth.htm]
Vital Records Management
[http://www.clan.lib.nv.us/docs/recman.htm#Vital]

# State Historical Society

## Nevada State Museum and Historical Society
http://www.clan.lib.nv.us/docs/mus-lv.htm

| | |
|---|---|
| 700 Twin Lakes Drive | Phone   (702) 486-5205 |
| Las Vegas, NV 89107 | |

Overview
[http://www.clan.lib.nv.us/docs/mus-lv.htm]

# Other State Sites

## University of Nevada, Las Vegas
http://www.nscee.edu/unlv/UNLV_Home_Page/OpenFolder.html

| | |
|---|---|
| James R. Dickinson Library | Fax     (702) 895-3850 |
| 4505 Maryland Parkway | E-mail  michelp@nevada.edu |
| Las Vegas, NV 89154-7010 | (libraryweb@ccmail.nevada.edu) |

| | |
|---|---|
| Nevada Women's Archives | Phone   (702) 895-3954 |
| | E-mail  corbett@nevada.edu |

Nevada Women's Archives
[http://www.nscee.edu/unlv/Libraries/women/womarch.html]
Special Collections Department
[http://www.nscee.edu/unlv/Libraries/services/speccol/sc.html]

## University of Nevada, Reno          http://www.unr.edu/

| | |
|---|---|
| Getchell Library, Room 291 | Phone   (702) 784-6500 Ext. 327 |
| Reno, NV 89557-0044 | Fax     (702) 784-4529 |
| | E-mail  specarch@unr.edu |

Collection Guides
[http://www.library.unr.edu/~specoll/colls.html]
Nevada Women's Archives
[http://www.library.unr.edu/~specoll/womarchp.html]
Special Collections Department
[http://www.library.unr.edu/~specoll/index.html]
University Archives
[http://www.library.unr.edu/~univarch/]

# NEW HAMPSHIRE

## State Home Page

| Webster, NH Government Online | http://webster.state.nh.us/nhsl/ |
|---|---|

New Hampshire Almanac
[http://webster.state.nh.us/nhinfo/nhinfo.html]
New Hampshire Cities and Towns
[http://webster.state.nh.us/localgovt/cities.htm]

## State Archives

**New Hampshire Division of Records Management and Archives**
http://www.state.nh.us/state/archives.htm

| 71 South Fruit Street | Phone | (603) 271-2236 |
|---|---|---|
| Concord, NH 03301 | Fax | (603) 271-2272 |
| | E-mail | FMEVERS@lilac.nhsl.lib.nh.us |
| | | BBURFORD@lilac.nhsl.lib.nh.us |

Guide to the New Hampshire State Archives
[http://www.state.nh.us/state/guidemnu.htm]
Perley Survey Fieldbook Index (1914 - 1961)
[http://www.state.nh.us/state/prly_int.htm]

## State Library

| New Hampshire State Library | http://webster.state.nh.us/nhsl/ |
|---|---|

| 20 Park Street | Phone | (603) 271-6823 Genealogy Desk |
|---|---|---|
| Concord, NH 03301-6314 | Fax | (603) 271-6826 |
| | E-mail | tepare@lilac.nhsl.lib.nh.us |

Reference Services
[http://webster.state.nh.us/nhsl/cadstaff.html]

## State Genealogical Society

| New Hampshire Society of Genealogists | http://www.tiac.net/users/nhsog/ |
|---|---|

| P.O. Box 2316 | E-mail milliken@tiac.net |
|---|---|
| Concord, NH 03302-2316 | |

New Hampshire Genealogical Record, Table of Contents
[http://www.tiac.net/users/nhsog/prod04.htm]
Newsletter, Fulltext
[http://www.tiac.net/users/nhsog/prod05.htm]
Publications
[http://www.tiac.net/users/nhsog/publica.htm]

## State Historical Society
### *Outstanding Site*

| New Hampshire Historical Society | http://newww.com/org/nhhs/ |
|---|---|

| 30 Park Street | Phone 603) 271-2236 |
|---|---|
| Concord, NH 03301-6384 | E-mail nhhslib@aol.com |

Abbott-Downing Photographs
[http://newww.com/org/nhhs/databases/adowning.html]
Book Collection
[http://newww.com/org/nhhs/printed.html]
Civil War Photographs
[http://newww.com/org/nhhs/databases/civil.html]
Library
[http://newww.com/org/nhhs/library.html]
Manuscripts
[http://newww.com/org/nhhs/manuscript.html]
New Hampshire Currency Database
[http://newww.com/org/nhhs/databases/currency.html]
Searchable Databases
[http://newww.com/org/nhhs/databases/index.html]

# Other State Sites

## Association Canado-Américaine                    http://www.acafraternal.org/~aca/

P.O. Box 989                                        Phone    (800) 222-8577
Manchester, NH 03105-0989

Directory, Chapters and Officers
[http://www.acafraternal.org/~aca/direct.htm]

## Dartmouth College                               http://www.dartmouth.edu/

Baker Library                                       Phone   (603) 646-2560
Hinman Box 6025                                     E-mail  Baker.Library.Reference@dartmouth.edu
Hanover, NH 03755-3590

Library
[http://www.dartmouth.edu/~library/]

## Londonderry Project
http://jefferson.village.virginia.edu/~ensp482/erc2g/thesis/text/thshome.html

History of Londonderry
[http://jefferson.village.virginia.edu/~ensp482/erc2g/thesis/text/thshome.html]

## *Outstanding Site*

## Lane Memorial Library                           http://www.hampton.lib.nh.us/

2 Academy Avenue                                    Phone   (603) 926-3368
Hampton, NH 03842-2280                              Fax     (603) 926-1348
                                                    E-mail  bteschek@hampton.lib.nh.us
Cemetery Records
[http://www.hampton.lib.nh.us/hampton/graves/graves.htm]
Hampton Genealogies Online
[http://www.hampton.lib.nh.us/hampton/history.html]
History Sources
[http://www.hampton.lib.nh.us/hampton/history.htm]

## New Hampshire Legacy Magazine     http://www.nh.com/legacy/index.shtml

Phone   (603) 883-3344
E-mail   publisher@nh.com

Issues, Fulltext
[http://www.nh.com/legacy/index.shtml]

### *Outstanding Site*

## The Old Man of the Mountains     http://mutha.com/oldmanmt.html

Cannon Mountain
Franconia Notch, NH 03580

Phone   (603) 823-5563

Detroit Publishing Company Photographs
[http://rs6.loc.gov/cgi-bin/query/r?detr:@band(United+States--New+Hampshire--
White+Mountains.)]
Historic Photographs
[http://www.cs.dartmouth.edu/whites/photos/old/oldman.jpg]
Photograph Collection
[http://www.cs.dartmouth.edu/whites/old_man.html]

## Strawbery Banke Museum     http://wwwsc.library.unh.edu/specoll/Sbanke/homepag.htm

P.O. Box 300
454 Court Street
Portsmouth, NH 03802-0300

Phone   (603) 433-1101

Library and Archives
[http://wwwsc.library.unh.edu/specoll/Sbanke/library.htm]

### *Outstanding Site*

## University of New Hampshire     http://unhinfo.unh.edu/

Diamond Library
18 Library Way
Durham, NH 03824-3592

Phone   (603) 862-2714

Artists and Photographers Collection
[http://wwwsc.library.unh.edu/specoll/mancoll/artists.htm]
Book Collections
[http://wwwsc.library.unh.edu/specoll/bookcoll.htm]
Civil War Collection
[http://wwwsc.library.unh.edu/specoll/mancoll/civwar.htm]
Durham, New Hampshire Area Records
[http://wwwsc.library.unh.edu/specoll/mancoll/durhmrec.htm]
Libraries
[http://wwwsc.library.unh.edu/]
Links, New Hampshire
[http://wwwsc.library.unh.edu/specoll/nhother.htm]
Manuscripts
[http://wwwsc.library.unh.edu/specoll/mancoll/mancoll.htm]
New Hampshire Newspapers
[http://wwwsc.library.unh.edu/specoll/mancoll/nhnews.htm]
New Hampshire Old Graveyard Association Records
[http://wwwsc.library.unh.edu/specoll/mancoll/nhoga.htm]

New Hampshire State Documents
    [http://wwwsc.library.unh.edu/specoll/stdocs.htm]
Shaker Materials
    [http://wwwsc.library.unh.edu/specoll/mancoll/shaker.htm]
Special Collections Department
    [http://wwwsc.library.unh.edu/specoll/izaak.htm]

# NEW JERSEY
## State Home Page

### State of New Jersey Home Page            http://www.state.nj.us/

Links, New Jersey County and Local Government
    [http://www.state.nj.us/localgov.htm]
Links, New Jersey Libraries
    [http://www.state.nj.us/statelibrary/njlib.htm]

## State Archives

### Division of Archives and Records Management
    http://www.state.nj.us/state/darm/darmidx.html

| | |
|---|---|
| State Library Building | Phone  (609) 292-6260 |
| 185 West State Street - Level 2 | Fax    (609) 396-2454 |
| CN 307 | E-mail  feedback@sos.state.nj.us |
| Trenton, NJ  08625-0307 | |

Overview
    [http://www.state.nj.us/state/darm/darmidx.html]

## State Library

### New Jersey State Library            http://www.state.nj.us/statelibrary/njlib.htm

| | |
|---|---|
| 185 West State Street | Phone  (201) 292-6274 Genealogy |
| CN 520 | Fax    (609) 984-7901 |
| Trenton, NJ  08625-0520 | |

Jerseyana Collection
    [http://www.state.nj.us/statelibrary/libjersy.htm]
Links, New Jersey Libraries
    [http://www.state.nj.us/statelibrary/njlib.htm]
Overview
    [http://www.state.nj.us/statelibrary/njlib.htm]

## Other State Sites

### League of Historical Societies of New Jersey
    http://scils.rutgers.edu/~macan/leaguelist.html

P.O. Box 909
Madison, NJ  07940

Links, Societies, Agencies, Groups
    [http://scils.rutgers.edu/~macan/leaguelist.html]

## Newark Public Library    http://www.npl.org/

New Jersey Information Center                    Phone    (201) 733-7775
3rd floor, Main Library
5 Washington Street
Newark, NJ 07102

New Jersey Information Center
    [http://www.npl.org/aboutnpl/division/njic.html]
Overview
    [http://www.npl.org/aboutnpl/division/njiccol.html]

## New Jersey History Online    http://scils.rutgers.edu/~macan/nj.history.html

E-mail   macan@scils.rutgers.edu

Bibliographies
    [http://scils.rutgers.edu/~macan/njhb.html]
Links, Libraries
    [http://scils.rutgers.edu/~macan/library.html]
Links, New Jersey Museums & Sites
    [http://scils.rutgers.edu/~macan/museums.html]

## *Outstanding Site*

## Princeton University    http://infoshare1.princeton.edu:2003/

Princeton University Library                    Phone    (609) 258-3184
One Washington Road                             E-mail   wljoyce@firestone.princeton.edu
Princeton, NJ  08544-2098                                mmsherry@princeton.edu

Population Research Library                      Phone    (609) 258-4874
21 Prospect Avenue                              E-mail   popindex@opr.princeton.edu
Princeton, NJ  08544-2091

Delafield Family Papers
    [http://infoshare1.princeton.edu:2003/libraries/firestone/rbsc/aids/delafield.html]
New Jerseyana
    [http://www.princeton.edu/~ferguson/h-mo-pr.html#njana]
Office of Population Research
    [http://opr.princeton.edu/]
Online Catalog
    [http://infoshare1.princeton.edu:2003/online/Catalog2.html]
Population Index
    [http://popindex.princeton.edu/]
Population Research Library
    [http://opr.princeton.edu/library/library.html]
Rare Books and Special Collections Department
    [http://infoshare1.princeton.edu:2003/libraries/firestone/rbsc/about_rbsc.html]

## Seton Hall University    http://www.shu.edu/library/speccoll.html

Special Collections Center                      Phone    (201) 761-9476
Walsh Library                                   E-mail   brownsam@pirate.shu.edu
South Orange, NJ  07079-2696

New Jersey Catholic Historical Records Commission
History Department
South Orange, NJ 07079-2696

Archdiocese of Newark
    [http://www.shu.edu/library/speccoll.html]
New Jersey Catholic Records Newsletter
    [http://www.shu.edu/library/catholicrec/index.html]

## University of Medicine and Dentistry of New Jersey
    http://www3.umdnj.edu/~libcwis/univlibs.html

| Department of Special Collections | Phone | (201) 982-6293 |
|---|---|---|
| 30 12th Street | Fax | (201) 982-7474 |
| Newark, NJ 07103-2754 | E-mail | irwin@umdnj.edu |

Department of Special Collections
    [http://www3.umdnj.edu/~libcwis/speccoll.html]
New Jersey Medical History Collection
    [http://www3.umdnj.edu/~libcwis/manuscrt.html]
Online Catalog
    [http://www3.umdnj.edu/~libcwis/ulhin.html]
Oral History Collection
    [http://www3.umdnj.edu/~libcwis/oralhist.html]

# NEW MEXICO

## State Home Page

| State of New Mexico Government Information | http://www.state.nm.us/ |
|---|---|

Overview
    [http://www.state.nm.us/]

## State Archives

| State Archives and Records Center | http://www.state.nm.us/ |
|---|---|

| 404 Montezuma | Phone | (505) 827-7332 |
|---|---|---|
| Santa Fe, NM 87503 | Fax | (505) 827-7331 |

Overview
    [http://www.state.nm.us/]

## State Library

| New Mexico State Library | http://www.stlib.state.nm.us/ |
|---|---|

| 325 Don Gaspar | Phone | (505) 827-4083 |
|---|---|---|
| Santa Fe, NM 87501-2777 | Fax | (505) 827-3888 |
| | E-mail | mccallan@stlib.state.nm.us |

Genealogical Societies in New Mexico
    [http://www.stlib.state.nm.us/sw.rm-info/geneasoc.html]
Hitchhiker, Newsletter
    [http://www.stlib.state.nm.us/hiker/current.html]

New Mexico Library Directory
    [http://www.stlib.state.nm.us/email.html]
People of New Mexico
    [http://www.stlib.state.nm.us/sw.rm-info/famous.html]

## Other State Sites

### New Mexico State University         http://www.nmsu.edu/

NMSU Library                          Phone   (505) 646-6928
P.O. Box 30006, Dept. 3475            E-mail  library@lib.nmsu.edu
Las Cruces, NM 88003-8006

Border Research Institute
    [http://www.nmsu.edu/~bri/briprof.html]
New Mexico Cities, Links
    [mccallan@stlib.state.nm.us ]

# NEW YORK

## State Home Page

### New York State HomePage            http://www.state.ny.us/

Department of Vital Records
    [http://www.health.state.ny.us/nysdoh/consumer/vr.htm]

## State Archives
### *Outstanding Site*

### State Archives and Records Administration (SARA)
    http://www.sara.nysed.gov/

New York State Archives               Phone   (518) 474-8955
New York State Education Department   Fax     (518) 473-7573
Albany, NY 12230                      E-mail  gosys@unix6.nysed.gov
                                              refserv@unix6.nysed.gov

Canal Records
    [http://unix6.nysed.gov/holding/aids/canal/content.htm]
Corrections Department
    [http://unix6.nysed.gov/holding/aids/correct/content.htm]
Electronic Records in SARA
    [http://unix6.nysed.gov/holding/fact/er-fact.htm]
Finding Aids
    [http://unix6.nysed.gov/pubs/findaids.htm]
Genealogical Sources in SARA
    [http://unix6.nysed.gov/holding/fact/genea-fa.htm]
Guide to Records
    [http://unix6.nysed.gov/pubs/guideabs.htm]
Historical Resources in New York Repositories
    [http://unix6.nysed.gov/services/grant/guides.htm]
ILL Requests
    [http://unix6.nysed.gov/services/research/inter.htm]

In the Field, Newsletter
    [http://www.sara.nysed.gov/new.htm]
Local Records Management
    [http://unix6.nysed.gov/pubs/lgrtip.htm]
Local Records, Microfilm
    [http://unix6.nysed.gov/holding/fact/local-mi.htm]
Military Records
    [http://unix6.nysed.gov/holding/fact/mil-fact.htm]
Military Records, Request Form
    [http://unix6.nysed.gov/holding/fact/pform.htm]
Military Records, Request Form, Online
    [http://unix6.nysed.gov/holding/fact/mil-req.htm]
Military Records, Revolutionary War
    [http://unix6.nysed.gov/holding/aids/rev/content.htm]
Military Records, WWI
    [http://unix6.nysed.gov/holding/aids/wwi/content.htm]
Motion Picture Scripts Index
    [http://www.sara.nysed.gov:9999/]
Native Americans
    [http://unix6.nysed.gov/holding/aids/native/content.htm]
Naturalization Records
    [http://unix6.nysed.gov/holding/fact/natur-fa.htm]
New York Cities and Counties. Links
    [http://nyslgti.gen.ny.us/]
New York House of Refuge
    [http://unix6.nysed.gov/holding/aids/school/content.htm]
New York State Government History
    [http://unix6.nysed.gov/holding/guide/content.htm]
NYHIST-L, E-mail Listserv
    [http://unix6.nysed.gov/services/listserv.htm]
Online Catalog
    [http://www.sara.nysed.gov/default.html]
Online Website Search
    [http://www.sara.nysed.gov/search.htm]
Probate Records
    [http://unix6.nysed.gov/holding/fact/prob-fac.htm]
Public Access Systems, New York Historical Records
    [http://unix6.nysed.gov/services/grant/systems.htm#sara]
Publications List
    [http://unix6.nysed.gov/pubs/publist.htm]
Statewide Access to Historical Records
    [http://unix6.nysed.gov/new/accessr.htm]
Teaching with Historical Records
    [http://unix6.nysed.gov/services/teachers/ctspromo.htm]
Virtual Tour
    [http://www.sara.nysed.gov/virtual/virtual.html]
Vital Records
    [http://unix6.nysed.gov/holding/fact/vital.htm]
War Council, New York State
    [http://unix6.nysed.gov/holding/aids/wwii/content.htm]
Women, Records Pertaining to
    [http://unix6.nysed.gov/holding/fact/women-fa.htm]

# State Library

| New York State Library | http://www.nysl.nysed.gov/ |
|---|---|

Empire State Plaza
Cultural Education Center
Albany, NY 12230

Phone  (518) 474-6282
E-mail  refserv@unix2.nysed.gov

African American Bibliographies
    [gopher://unix2.nysed.gov:70/11/nyslpubs/afambibliog]
Census
    [http://www.nysl.nysed.gov/uscensus.htm]
    [http://www.nysl.nysed.gov/fedcen.htm]
Census, New York State
    [http://www.nysl.nysed.gov/nyscens.htm]
DAR Records
    [http://www.nysl.nysed.gov/dar.htm]
Family Records Preservation
    [http://www.nysl.nysed.gov/hints.htm]
Genealogy
    [http://www.nysl.nysed.gov/gengen.htm]
Genealogy, Beginning
    [http://www.nysl.nysed.gov/famtree.htm]
Genealogy Card Indexes
    [http://www.nysl.nysed.gov/cardind.htm]
Geographic Information System, GIS
    [http://www.nysl.nysed.gov/gis.htm]
ILL Services
    [http://www.nysl.nysed.gov/ill.htm]
Immigrant Search
    [http://www.nysl.nysed.gov/tracimmi.htm]
Local Histories
    [http://www.nysl.nysed.gov/lochist.htm]
Loyalist Records
    [http://www.nysl.nysed.gov/loyalist.htm]
Manuscripts and Special Collections Department
    [http://www.nysl.nysed.gov/mssdesc.htm]
Microforms
    [http://www.nysl.nysed.gov/humamicr.htm]
Military Records, Civil War on
    [http://www.nysl.nysed.gov/milipost.htm]
Military Records, Pre-Civil War
    [http://www.nysl.nysed.gov/miliante.htm]
Newspapers, Early American
    [gopher://unix2.nysed.gov:70/11/nyslpubs/ea.newspaper.coll]
Newspapers, New York State
    [gopher://unix2.nysed.gov:70/11/nyslpubs/nys.newspaper]
New York State Documents
    [http://unix2.nysed.gov/edocs/education/check96.htm]
Probate Records
    [http://www.nysl.nysed.gov/nywills.htm]
Surnames
    [http://www.nysl.nysed.gov/surnames.htm]

Vital Records
   [http://www.nysl.nysed.gov/vitrec.htm]

# Other State Sites
*Outstanding Site*

| New York Public Library | http://www.nypl.org/ |
|---|---|

| 5th Avenue and 42nd Street<br>New York, NY 10018-2788 | Phone   (212) 930-0830 |
|---|---|

| Jewish Division, Room 84 | Phone   (212) 930-0601 |
| Map Division, Room 117 | Phone   (212) 930-0587 |
| Oriental Division, Room 219 | Phone   (212) 930-0716 |
| Rare Books and Manuscripts, Room 328 | Phone   (212) 930-0801 |
|  | Fax      (212) 302-4815 |

| Slavic and Baltic Division, Room 216-7 | Phone   (212) 930-0714 |
|---|---|
|  | Fax      (212) 930-0940 |
|  | Email    slavicref@nypl.org |

| U.S. History, Local History and<br>   Genealogy Division, Room 315S | Phone   (212) 930-0828 |
|---|---|

| Schomburg Center for Research<br>   in Black Culture<br>515 Malcolm X Boulevard<br>New York, NY 10037-1801 | Phone   (212) 491-2200 |
|---|---|

Baltic, Slavic Links
   [http://www.nypl.org/research/chss/slv/sites.html]
Bibliography of Slavic, Baltic Materials
   [http://www.nypl.org/research/chss/slv/slvbib.html]
Biographical Sources
   [http://www.nypl.org/research/chss/grd/resguides/biog.html]
CATNYP, Online Catalog
   [http://www.nypl.org/research/chss/grd/resguides/catnyp.html]
Genealogy Links
   [http://www.nypl.org/research/chss/lhg/genguide.html]
Genealogy Resources
   [http://www.nypl.org/research/chss/lhg/research.html]
History Links
   [http://www.nypl.org/research/chss/lhg/hisguide.html]
LEO, Online Branch Libraries Catalog
   [http://www.nypl.org/catalogs/catalogs.html]
Manuscripts List
   [http://www.nypl.org/research/chss/spe/rbk/faids/majorjo.html#alpha]
Map Division
   [http://www.nypl.org/research/chss/map/map.html]
Military History Collections
   [http://www.nypl.org/research/chss/subguides/milhist/home.html]
Modern European History
   [http://www.nypl.org/research/chss/grd/resguides/eurhist.html]
Mormon History
   [http://www.nypl.org/research/chss/grd/resguides/mormon.html]

New York City History Links
    [http://www.nypl.org/research/chss/lhg/nycguide.html]
New York Links
    [http://www.nypl.org/branch/subguides/branchref.html#OTHER LIBRARIES AND LIBRARY
    CATALOGS]
Obituaries
    [http://www.nypl.org/research/chss/grd/resguides/obit.html]
Oriental Division
    [http://www.nypl.org/research/chss/ort/ort.html]
Rare Books and Manuscripts
    [http://www.nypl.org/research/chss/spe/rbk/rare.html]
Schomburg Center
    [http://www.nypl.org/research/sc/sc.html]
U.S. History, Local History and Genealogy
    [http://www.nypl.org/research/chss/lhg/genea.html]
Women's Studies
    [http://www.nypl.org/research/chss/grd/resguides/women.html]

## State University of New York, Oswego      http://www.oswego.edu/library/

Penfield Library                    Phone   (315) 341-3537
Oswego, NY  13126                   E-mail  sturr@oswego.edu

Manuscripts
    [gopher://gopher.Oswego.EDU:70/77/library/speccoll/.mostindxs/manuscripts]
Newspaper Index
    [gopher://gopher.Oswego.EDU:70/77/library/speccoll/.newspp/newspp]
Oswego County Historical Society Journal Index
    [gopher://gopher.Oswego.EDU:70/00/library/speccoll/about.ochsj]
Special Department Collections
    [http://www.oswego.edu/library/speccoll.html]
SUNY Online Catalogs
    [http://olis.sysadm.suny.edu/lib_tel.htm]

## Westchester County Clerk        http://nyslgti.gen.ny.us/Westchester/

110 Grove Street                    Phone   (914) 285-3080
White Plains, NY 10601              E-mail  dwc1@ofs.co.westchester.ny.us

Land Records Division               Phone   (914) 285-3070
110 Grove Street
White Plains, NY 10601

Westchester County Archives         Phone   (914) 592-1925
2199 Saw Mill River Road
Elmsford, NY 10523

Collection Guide
    [http://nyslgti.gen.ny.us/Westchester/gdintro.html]
Genealogy Guide
    [http://nyslgti.gen.ny.us/Westchester/genies.html]
Genealogy Guide, Bronx
    [http://nyslgti.gen.ny.us/Westchester/bronx.html]
Vital Records
    [http://nyslgti.gen.ny.us/Westchester/vital.html]

## Western New York Library Resources Council     http://www.wnylrc.org/

4455 Genesee Street              Phone   (716) 633-0705
P.O. Box 400                     Fax     (716) 633-1736
Buffalo, NY 14225-0400           E-mail  bsywetz@wnylrc.org
                                         hbamford@wnylrc.org

Directory of Genealogy Collections
    [http://freenet.buffalo.edu/~library/local/localcoll.html]

# NORTH CAROLINA
## State Home Page

North Carolina HomePage        http://www.sips.state.nc.us/nchome.html

North Carolina National Guard History
    [http://vger.gcc.dcc.state.nc.us/home/ng/nghist.htm]

## State Library and Archives
### Outstanding Site

North Carolina Division of Archives and
History State Library of North Carolina      http://www.ah.dcr.state.nc.us/

Division of Archives and History    Phone   (919) 733-7305
109 East Jones Street               Fax     (919) 733-8807
Raleigh, NC 27601-2807              E-mail  sprcsmail@ncsl.dcr.state.nc.us

North Carolina Newspaper Project    Phone   (919) 733-2570
                                    E-mail  jwelch@hal.dcr.state.nc.us)

North Carolina State Archives       Phone   (919) 733-3952
                                    E-mail  jsorrell@ncsl.dcr.state.nc.us

State Public Records Cataloging Service   Phone   (919) 733-7305
                                    Fax     (919) 733-8807
                                    E-mail  sprcsmail@ncsl.dcr.state.nc.us

Archives and Records Section
    [http://www.ah.dcr.state.nc.us/archives/]
County Government, History of
    [http://hal.dcr.state.nc.us/NC/CNTYOUT/PRECOUNT.HTM]
County Records
    [http://www.ah.dcr.state.nc.us/archives/arch/county.htm]
Federal Archives Relating to North Carolina
    [http://www.ah.dcr.state.nc.us/archives/arch/federal.htm]
Foreign Archives Relating to North Carolina
    [http://www.ah.dcr.state.nc.us/archives/arch/foreign.htm]
Genealogical Records
    [http://www.ah.dcr.state.nc.us/archives/arch/miscel.htm]
Genealogical Research, North Carolina
    [http://hal.dcr.state.nc.us/iss/gr/genealog.htm]
Historical Records
    [http://www.ah.dcr.state.nc.us/archives/arch/hist-res.htm]
Laws Relating To Archives and History
    [http://www.spr.dcr.state.nc.us/ncgs/gs121.htm]

Military Records
[http://www.ah.dcr.state.nc.us/archives/arch/military.htm]
North Carolina Encyclopedia
[http://hal.dcr.state.nc.us/ncslnew.map?428,91]
North Carolina Newspaper Project
[http://www.dcr.state.nc.us/tss/newspape.htm]
North Carolina State Archives, Accession Lists
[http://www.ah.dcr.state.nc.us/archives/arch/access.htm]
North Carolina State Records
[http://www.ah.dcr.state.nc.us/archives/arch/state.htm]
Newspapers, by City
[http://www.dcr.state.nc.us/ncnp/cities.htm]
Newspapers, by County
[http://www.dcr.state.nc.us/ncnp/counties.htm]
Newspapers on Microfilm
[http://www.dcr.state.nc.us/tss/newspape.htm]
Public Records Law, North Carolina State
[http://www.spr.dcr.state.nc.us/ncgs/ncgs132.htm]
Public Records, North Carolina Guidelines for
[http://www.spr.dcr.state.nc.us/manrecrd/manrecrd.htm]
State Library of North Carolina
[http://hal.dcr.state.nc.us/ncslhome.htm]
Tar Heel Tracks, Journal
[http://hal.dcr.state.nc.us/iss/gr/general.htm]

# State Genealogical Society

## North Carolina Genealogical Society
http://www.moobasi.com/genealogy/ncgs/homepage.html

P.O. Box 1492
Raleigh, NC 27602

E-mail  ncgs.info@moobasi.com

NCGS
[http://www.fgs.org/~fgs/soc0131.htm]
Overview
[http://www.moobasi.com/genealogy/ncgs/homepage.html]

# Other State Sites

## Appalachian State University
http://www.acs.appstate.edu/dept/library/belklib.html

Belk Library
Boone, NC 28608

Phone  (704) 262-4041
Fax  (704) 262-2553
E-mail  hayfj@appstate.edu

Appalachian Studies Bibliography
[http://www.acs.appstate.edu/dept/library/appcoll/apsbib.html]
Eury Appalachian Collection
[http://www.acs.appstate.edu/dept/library/appcoll/history.html]

## Charlotte, Mecklenburg County Public Library
http://www.plcmc.lib.nc.us/branch/main/carolina/collecti.htm

Robinson-Spangler Carolina Room
310 North Tryon Street
Charlotte, NC 28202

Phone  (704) 336-2980
Fax  (704) 336-2677
E-mail  ncr@plcmc.lib.nc.us

Charlotte's Attic, Newsletter
    [http://www.plcmc.lib.nc.us/branch/main/carolina/news.htm]
Collections
    [http://www.plcmc.lib.nc.us/branch/main/carolina/collecti.htm]

# Davidson University
    http://www.davidson.edu/administrative/library/little.htm

| | |
|---|---|
| P.O. Box 1837 | Phone    (704) 892-2331 |
| Davidson, NC 28036 | Fax       (704) 892-2625 |

Archives
    [http://www.davidson.edu/administrative/library/archives1.htm]
Civil War
    [http://www.davidson.edu/administrative/library/mancol6.htm#Civil War]
Manuscripts
    [http://www.davidson.edu/administrative/library/mancol6.htm]

# Duke University                     http://www.lib.duke.edu/

| | |
|---|---|
| Special Collections Library | Phone    (919) 660-5822 |
| P.O. Box 90185 | Fax       (919) 684-2855 |
| Durham, NC 27708-0185 | E-mail  specoll@mail.lib.duke.edu |

Broadside, Newsletter
    [http://scriptorium.lib.duke.edu/broadside/]
Civil War Women
    [http://scriptorium.lib.duke.edu/collections/civil-war-women.html]
Collections
    [http://scriptorium.lib.duke.edu/specoll/collections.html]
Special Collections Library
    [http://scriptorium.lib.duke.edu/]

# East North Carolina University     http://www.ecu.edu/

| | |
|---|---|
| J.Y. Joyner Library | Phone    (919) 328-6601 |
| Greenville, NC 27858-4353 | Fax       (919) 328-0268 |

Manuscripts
    [http://fringe.lib.ecu.edu/JoynerLib/LibraryDepts/SpclColl/Manuscript/man.html]
North Carolina Collection
    [http://fringe.lib.ecu.edu/JoynerLib/LibraryDepts/SpclColl/NCColl/ncc.html]
North Carolina Periodical Index
    [http://fringe.lib.ecu.edu/Periodicals/scope.html]
Special Collections
    [http://fringe.lib.ecu.edu/JoynerLib/LibraryDepts/SpclColl/special.html]

# North Carolina Association of County Clerks
    http://ncinfo.iog.unc.edu/clerks/ncacc.htm

| | |
|---|---|
| c/o Institute of Government | Phone    (704) 884-3107 |
| CB#3330 KNAPP Building | E-mail  bell.iog@mhs.unc.edu |
| UNC-Chapel Hill | |
| Chapel Hill, NC 27599-3330 | |

Minute by Minute, Newsletter
    [http://ncinfo.iog.unc.edu/clerks/accmts.htm]
North Carolina Clerks Reference Guide
    [http://ncinfo.iog.unc.edu/clerks/iog1.htm]
Public Records Law
    [http://ncinfo.iog.unc.edu/clerks/lb2.htm]
Retention Schedules
    [http://ncinfo.iog.unc.edu/clerks/comgr.htm]

# North Carolina Association of Municipal Clerks
    http://ncinfo.iog.unc.edu/clerks/ncamc.htm

| | |
|---|---|
| c/o Institute of Government<br>CB#3330 KNAPP Building<br>UNC-Chapel Hill<br>Chapel Hill, NC 27599-3330 | E-mail  bell.iog@mhs.unc.edu |

Directory of Municipal Clerks
    [http://ncinfo.iog.unc.edu/clerks/citydr.htm]

# North Carolina Association Registers of Deeds
    http://ncinfo.iog.unc.edu/regdeeds/

| | |
|---|---|
| Yancey County Courthouse<br>Burnsville, NC 28714 | Phone  (704) 682-2174<br>Fax  (704) 682-4520 |

Directory, North Carolina Registers of Deeds
    [http://ncinfo.iog.unc.edu/regdeeds/rod.htm]
Land Records Bulletin, Series
    [http://ncinfo.iog.unc.edu/gopher/pubs/other/land_records/]
Maps and Plats, Preliminary Checklist
    [http://ncinfo.iog.unc.edu/regdeeds/check.htm]

# Society of North Carolina Archivists    http://www.duke.edu/~rkoonts/index.htm

| | |
|---|---|
| P.O. Box 20448<br>Raleigh, NC 27619-0448 | E-mailpaul_kiel@ncsu.edu |

Links, Archival, North Carolina and U.S.
    [http://www.duke.edu/~rkoonts/links.htm]
North Carolina Archivist, Newsletter. Fulltext
    [http://www.duke.edu/~rkoonts/news46.htm]

## *Outstanding Site*

# University of North Carolina, Chapel Hill    http://www.unc.edu/

| | |
|---|---|
| Institute of Government<br>CB 3330 Knapp Building<br>Chapel Hill, NC 27599-3330 | Phone  (919) 966-4347<br>E-mail  podhajsk.iog@mhs.unc.edu |
| Manuscripts Department<br>CB 3926 Wilson Library<br>Chapel Hill, NC 27514-8890 | Phone  (919) 962-1345<br>Fax  (919) 962-4452<br>E-mail  mss@email.unc.edu |

North Carolina Collection                    Phone   (919) 962-1172
CB 3930 Wilson Library                       E-mail  nccref@email.unc.edu
Chapel Hill, NC 27514-8890

Southern Oral History Program                Phone   (919) 962-0455
Department of History                        Fax     (919) 962-1403
CB 3195, 406 Hamilton Hall                   E-mail  kac@email.unc.edu
Chapel Hill, NC 27599-3195

African-American Documentary Resources in North Carolina
    [http://www.upress.virginia.edu/epub/pyatt/]
Directory, State and County Government
    [http://www.secstate.state.nc.us/secstate/toc.htm]
Documenting the American South
    [http://sunsite.unc.edu/docsouth/]
Institute of Government
    [http://ncinfo.iog.unc.edu/]
Institute of Government Library
    [http://ncinfo.iog.unc.edu/library/index.html]
Libraries
    [http://sunsite.unc.edu/reference/top.html]
Links, City and County Government
    [http://ncinfo.iog.unc.edu/localgvt.html]
Manuscripts Department
    [http://www.unc.edu/lib/mssinv/]
North Carolina Collection
    [http://www.unc.edu/lib/ncc/]
Photograph Archives
    [http://www.unc.edu/lib/ncc/photos.html]
Publishing Archives
    [http://www.unc.edu/lib/mssinv/pub.html]
Southern Historical Collection, Guides
    [http://www.unc.edu/lib/mssinv/dir/]
Southern Legal History
    [http://www.unc.edu/depts/csas/srr5.htm]
Southern Oral History Program
    [http://www.unc.edu/depts/sohp/]
Southern Oral History Program Collection Interviews
    [http://www.unc.edu/depts/sohp/coll.html]
Southern Oral History Program, Links
    [http://www.unc.edu/depts/sohp/links.html]
Southern Research Reports, Publications
    [http://www.unc.edu/depts/csas/srr.htm]

# NORTH DAKOTA

## State Home Page

North Dakota HomePage            http://www.state.nd.us/

Links, North Dakota Cities and Counties
    [http://www.tradecorridor.com/cities.htm]
North Dakota Court System
    [http://sc3.court.state.nd.us/]

# State Library

| | |
|---|---|
| ## North Dakota State Library | http://www.sendit.nodak.edu/ndsl/index.html |

604 East Boulevard Avenue
Bismarck, ND 58505-0800

Phone   (701) 328-4622

Reference Services
[http://www.sendit.nodak.edu/ndsl/ref_loan.html]

# State Historical Society

| | |
|---|---|
| ## State Historical Society of North Dakota | http://www.state.nd.us./hist/ |

612 East Boulevard Avenue
Bismarck, ND 58505-0830

Phone   (701) 328-2666
Fax     (701) 328-3710
E-mail  ccmail.histsoc@ranch.state.nd.us

State Archives and State Research Library

Phone   (701) 328-2091
Fax     (701) 328-3710

State Historical Records Advisory Board

Phone   (701) 328-2668
E-mail  ccmail.gnewborg@ranch.state.nd.us

Biography
[http://www.state.nd.us./hist/infwpa.htm]
Census
[http://www.state.nd.us./hist/infcens.htm]
Genealogical Resources
[http://www.state.nd.us./hist/infgen.htm]
History
[http://www.state.nd.us./hist/history.htm]
Land Records
[http://www.state.nd.us./hist/infland.htm]
Museum Divison
[http://www.state.nd.us./hist/mus.htm]
Naturalization Records
[http://www.state.nd.us./hist/infnat.htm]
Newspapers
[http://www.state.nd.us./hist/infnews.htm]
North Dakota Governors
[http://www.state.nd.us./hist/ndgov.htm]
Oral Histories
[http://www.state.nd.us./hist/infoh.htm]
State Archives and Historical Research Library
[http://www.state.nd.us./hist/sal.htm]
State Historical Records Advisory Board
[http://www.state.nd.us./hist/shrab.htm]
Vital Records
[http://www.state.nd.us./hist/infvit.htm]

# Other State Sites

| | |
|---|---|
| ## North Dakota State University | http://www.ndsu.nodak.edu/ |

North Dakota State University Libraries
Fargo, ND 58105

Phone   (701) 231-8886
Fax     (701) 231-7138
E-mail  nulibarc@plains.nodak.edu

Germans from Russia Heritage Collection        Phone   (701) 231-8416
P.O. Box 5599                                  Fax     (701) 231-7138
Fargo, ND 58105-5599                           E-mail  mmmiller@badlands.nodak.edu

Institute for Regional Studies                 Phone   (701) 231-8914
P.O. Box 5599                                  Fax     (701) 231-7138
Fargo, ND 58105-5599                           E-mail  mmmiller@badlands.nodak.edu

Bibliography
    [http://www.lib.ndsu.nodak.edu/gerrus/#books]
Biography Files
    [http://www.lib.ndsu.nodak.edu/ndirs/biograph.html]
Census Records
    [http://www.lib.ndsu.nodak.edu/ndirs/census.html]
Databases and Indexes
    [http://www.lib.ndsu.nodak.edu/ndirs/instind.html]
Forum Obituaries Index
    [http://www.lib.ndsu.nodak.edu/ndirs/obithome.html]
Germans from Russia Heritage Collection
    [http://www.lib.ndsu.nodak.edu/gerrus/]
Institute for Regional Studies
    [http://www.lib.ndsu.nodak.edu/ndirs/]
Journey to the Homeland, Newsletter
    [http://www.lib.ndsu.nodak.edu/gerrus/#journey]
Lawrence Welk Collection
    [http://www.lib.ndsu.nodak.edu/welk/]
Library
    [http://www.lib.ndsu.nodak.edu/]
Links, North Dakota
    [http://www.lib.ndsu.nodak.edu/ndakota.html]
Manuscripts
    [http://www.lib.ndsu.nodak.edu/ndirs/manuscrp.html]
North Dakota Biography Index
    [http://www.lib.ndsu.nodak.edu/ndirs/ndbi.html]
Other Repositories
    [http://www.lib.ndsu.nodak.edu/ndirs/gensoc.html]

# University of North Dakota        http://www.und.nodak.edu/

Chester Fritz Library                 Phone   (701) 777-4629 Reference
P.O. Box 9000                                 (701) 777-4625 Special Collections
Grand Forks, ND 58202                 Fax     (701) 777-3319
                                      E-mail  slater@plains.nodak.edu Special Coll.
Genealogy Collection
    [http://www.und.nodak.edu/dept/library/Collections/famhist.html]
Library
    [http://www.und.nodak.edu/dept/library/]
Library Newsletter
    [http://www.und.nodak.edu/dept/library/Libpub/libnews.html]
Special Collections Department
    [http://www.und.nodak.edu/dept/library/Collections/spk.html]

# OHIO

## State Home Page

| State of Ohio Government | http://www.state.oh.us/ |
|---|---|
| State Government | [http://www.state.oh.us/] |

## State Library

| State Library | http://winslo.ohio.gov/ |
|---|---|

| State Library of Ohio | Phone (614) 644-7061 |
|---|---|
| 65 South Front Street | Fax (614) 644-7004 |
| Columbus, OH 43215-0334 | E-mail chordusk@mail.slonet.ohio.gov |

Links, Ohio Libraries
  [http://winslo.ohio.gov/stgvlib.html]
Links, Ohio Newspapers
  [http://winslo.ohio.gov/ohnews.html]
Links, Online Library Journals
  [http://winslo.ohio.gov/libjour.html]
Ohio Library Directory
  [http://winslo.ohio.gov/pubdir.html]

## State Genealogical Society

| Ohio Genealogical Society | http://www.ogs.org/public/default.htm |
|---|---|

| 34 Sturges Avenue | Phone (419) 522-9077 |
|---|---|
| P.O. Box 2625 | E-mail ogs@freeland.richland.oh.us |
| Mansfield, OH 44906-0625 | |

Directory OGS Chapters
  http://www.ogs.org/public/chap.htm]
OGS, BBS
  http://www.ogs.org/public/bbs.htm]
Teleconferences
  http://www.ogs.org/public/tele.htm]

## State Historical Society

| Ohio Historical Society | http://winslo.ohio.gov/ohswww/ohshome.html |
|---|---|

| 1982 Velma Avenue | Phone (614) 297-2300 |
|---|---|
| Columbus, Ohio 43211-2497 | E-mail ohswww@winslo.ohio.gov |
| | |
| Archives and Library | Phone (614) 297-2510 |
| | E-mail ohsref@winslo.ohio.gov |
| | |
| OHS Local History Office | Phone (614) 297-2340 |
| | Fax (614) 297-2318 |
| | E-mail jdbritton@msn.com |

Archives and Library
  http://winslo.ohio.gov/ohswww/arch_lib.html]

Census Records
    http://winslo.ohio.gov/ohswww/census.html]
Civil War Collection
    [http://winslo.ohio.gov/ohswww/civilwar/fact.html]
County Courthouse Directory
    http://winslo.ohio.gov/ohswww/cthouse.html]
Land Records
    http://winslo.ohio.gov/ohswww/landentr.html]
Laws about Ohio Records
    [http://winslo.ohio.gov/ohswww/resource/statearc/orc.html]
Links, Ohio American History Research Centers
    [http://winslo.ohio.gov/ohswww/lgr/networkl.html]
Links, Outside OH
    [http://winslo.ohio.gov/ohswww/links/index.html]
Local Government Records
    [http://winslo.ohio.gov/ohswww/lgr/index.html]
Military Records
    http://winslo.ohio.gov/ohswww/military.html]
Naturalization Records
    [http://winslo.ohio.gov/ohswww/natural.html]
Newspaper, Indexes
    [http://winslo.ohio.gov/ohswww/newsindx.html]
Newspapers
    [http://winslo.ohio.gov/ohswww/newspape.html]
Ohio Association of Historical Societies and Museums (OAHSM)
    [http://winslo.ohio.gov/ohswww/resource/oahsm/index.html]
Ohio Historical Records Advisory Board
    [http://winslo.ohio.gov/ohswww/ohrab/index.html]
Other Records
    [http://winslo.ohio.gov/ohswww/othrgens.html]
Photograph Collections
    [http://winslo.ohio.gov/ohswww/textonly/resource/audiovis/pcoll.html]
Publications
  Local History Notebooks (Topics)
    [http://winslo.ohio.gov/ohswww/textonly/resource/oahsm/notebook.html]
  Timeline, Index, 1984-1993.
    [http://winslo.ohio.gov/ohswww/timeline/index.html]
State Archives
    [http://winslo.ohio.gov/ohswww/resource/statearc/index.html]
State Archives, Finding Aids
    [http://winslo.ohio.gov/ohswww/resource/statearc/agencies/index.html]
Vital Records, Birth and Death
    [http://winslo.ohio.gov/ohswww/brthdth1.html]
Vital Records, Marriage and Divorce
    [http://winslo.ohio.gov/ohswww/marriag1.html]

# Other State Sites

## Bowling Green State University             http://www.bgsu.edu/

| Jerome Library | Phone | (419) 372-9612 |
| Bowling Green, OH 43403-0175 | Fax | (419) 372-0155 |
| | E-mail | rgraham@bgnet.bgsu.edu |
| | | mbarnes@bgnet.bgsu.edu |

Center for Archival Collections
Jerome Library, 5th Floor

E-mail   scharte@bgnet.bgsu.edu

Institute for Great Lakes Research
Jerome Library, 6th Floor

Phone   (419) 372-9612
Fax      (419) 372-0155
E-mail   rgraham@bgnet.bgsu.edu
         mbarnes@bgnet.bgsu.edu

Archival Chronicle, Newsletter, Fulltext
    [http://www.bgsu.edu/colleges/library/cac/chron.html]
Center for Archival Collections
    [http://www.bgsu.edu/colleges/library/cac/cac.html]
Institute for Great Lakes Research
    [http://www.bgsu.edu/colleges/library/iglr/iglr.html]
Libraries
    [http://www.bgsu.edu/colleges/library/llr.html]
Links, Maritime History
    [http://www.bgsu.edu/colleges/library/iglr/links.html]
Naturalization Records
    [http://www.bgsu.edu/colleges/library/cac/ac1291.html#feature]
Newspapers
    [http://www.bgsu.edu/colleges/library/cac/howto.html]
Online Question Form
    [http://www.bgsu.edu/colleges/library/cac/askarch.html]
Special Collections and Services
    [http://www.bgsu.edu/colleges/library/special.html]

## Dayton and Montgomery County Public Library   http://www.dayton.lib.oh.us/

215 East Third Street
Dayton, OH 45402-2135

Phone   (513) 227-9500
Fax      (513) 227-9528
E-mail   ads_Elli@dayton.lib.oh.us

Dunbar, Paul Lawrence, Collection
    [http://www.dayton.lib.oh.us/~ads_elli/dunbar.htm#TOC]
Montgomery Historical Society Collection
    [http://www.dayton.lib.oh.us/~ads_elli/newcom2.htm#TOC]
Shaker Collections
    [http://www.dayton.lib.oh.us/~ads_elli/shakers.htm#TOC]
Women's Collections
    [http://www.dayton.lib.oh.us/~ads_elli/wsuff.htm#TOC]

## Kent State University                    http://www.kent.edu/

Special Collections Department
Main Library, 12th Floor
Kent, OH 44242

Phone   (330) 672-2270
E-mail   nbirk@kentvm.kent.edu
         jsomers@lms.kent.edu

Kent Family Papers
    [http://www.library.kent.edu/speccoll/kent/kentfam.html]
Libraries
    [http://www.library.kent.edu/]
Regional Historical Collections
    [http://www.library.kent.edu/speccoll/histmat.html]
Special Collections Department
    [http://www.library.kent.edu/speccoll/]

Trinity Lutheran Church Records (Kent, Ohio)
    [http://www.library.kent.edu/speccoll/kent/trinity.html]
Woodard Family Papers
    [http://www.library.kent.edu/speccoll/kent/woodard.html]

## Oberlin College                     http://www.oberlin.edu/

Oberlin College Library          Phone   (216) 775-8285
Mudd Center                      E-mail  whitney.pape@oberlin.edu
Oberlin, OH 44074

Architectural Records
    [http://www.oberlin.edu/~archive/WWW_files/arch_records_intro.html]
Archives Holdings
    [http://www.oberlin.edu/~archive/OCA_holdings.html]
Congregational Church Record
    [http://www.oberlin.edu/~archive/WWW_files/first_church_t.html]
Index to Lorain County News and Oberlin Weekly News1860
    [http://www.oberlin.edu/~library/dobnews.html]
Oberlin College Archives
    [http://www.oberlin.edu/~archive/]
Personal Papers
    [http://www.oberlin.edu/~archive/Personal_papers.html]
Special Collections Department
    [http://www.oberlin.edu/~library/speccol.html]
Women's History Sources
    [http://www.oberlin.edu/~archive/WWW_files/womens_history_intro.html]

## Ohio University                     http://www.ohiou.edu/

Archives and Special Collections   Phone   (614) 593-2710
Ohio University Library            Fax     (614) 593-0138
Park Place                         E-mail  gbain1@ohiou.edu
Athens, OH 45701-2978                      library@www.cats.ohiou.edu

Genealogical Resources
    [http://www.library.ohiou.edu/libinfo/depts/microforms/geneal.htm]
Library
    [http://www.library.ohiou.edu/index.htm]
Newspapers, Regional
    [http://www.library.ohiou.edu/libinfo/depts/microforms/reginwsp.htm]
Special Collections
    [http://www.library.ohiou.edu/LibInfo/depts/Archives/ArchSpecColl.htm]

## Wright State University             http://www.wright.edu/

Dunbar Library                   Phone   (937) 775-4125
3640 Colonel Glenn Highway               (937) 775-2092  Special Collections
Dayton, OH 45435                 Fax     (937) 775-2356
                                 E-mail  archive@library.wright.edu
African American Records
    [http://www.libraries.wright.edu/staff/dunbar/arch/afamer.htm]
Auglaize County Records
    [http://www.libraries.wright.edu/staff/dunbar/arch/aug.htm]

Champaign County Records
  [http://www.libraries.wright.edu/staff/dunbar/arch/champ.htm]
Church Records
  [http://www.libraries.wright.edu/staff/dunbar/arch/churches.htm]
Civil War Collection
  [http://www.libraries.wright.edu/staff/dunbar/arch/civwar.htm]
Clark County Records
  [http://www.libraries.wright.edu/staff/dunbar/arch/clark.htm]
Darke County Records
  [http://www.libraries.wright.edu/staff/dunbar/arch/darke.htm]
Greene County Records
  [http://www.libraries.wright.edu/staff/dunbar/arch/greene.htm]
Libraries
  [http://www.libraries.wright.edu/]
Local Government Records
  [http://www.libraries.wright.edu/staff/dunbar/arch/lgrimm.htm]
Logan County Records
  [http://www.libraries.wright.edu/staff/dunbar/arch/logan.htm]
Medical, Physicians Records
  [http://www.libraries.wright.edu/staff/dunbar/arch/locmed.htm]
Mercer County Records
  [http://www.libraries.wright.edu/staff/dunbar/arch/mercer.htm]
Miami County Records
  [http://www.libraries.wright.edu/staff/dunbar/arch/miami.htm]
Montgomery County Records
  [http://www.libraries.wright.edu/staff/dunbar/arch/montg.htm]
Preble County Records
  [http://www.libraries.wright.edu/staff/dunbar/arch/preble.htm]
Shelby County Records
  [http://www.libraries.wright.edu/staff/dunbar/arch/shelby.htm]
Special Collections Department
  [http://130.108.121.217/staff/dunbar/arch/schome.htm] 1
Women's Collections
  [http://www.libraries.wright.edu/staff/dunbar/arch/women.htm]

# OKLAHOMA

## State Home Page

Oklahoma State HomePage          http://www.state.ok.us/

Links, Oklahoma State Government Agencies
  [http://www.state.ok.us/osfdocs/agncs1.html]

## State Library

Oklahoma Department of Libraries          http://www.state.ok.us/~odl/

200 Northeast 18th Street                  Phone   (405) 521-2502
Oklahoma City, OK 73105-3298

Oklahoma Center for the Book                Phone   (405) 521-2502
                                            Fax     (405) 525-7804
                                            E-mail  gcarlile@oltn.odl.state.ok.us

Oklahoma Office of Archives and Records

Phone    (405) 521-2502
Fax      (405) 525-7804
         (405) 521-8803  Records Center
E-mail   tkremm@oltn.odl.state.ok.us

Links, Oklahoma Libraries
    [http://www.state.ok.us/~odl/servlibs/pldirect/index.htm]
Oklahoma Archives and Records Commission
    [http://www.state.ok.us/~odl/oar/arrccom.htm]
Oklahoma Center for the Book
    [http://www.state.ok.us/~odl/ocb/authors.htm]
Oklahoma State Historical Records Advisory Board
    [http://www.state.ok.us/~odl/oar/ohrab.htm]

# State Genealogical Society

## Oklahoma Genealogical Society          http://www.fgs.org/~fgs/soc0379.htm

P.O. Box 12986
Oklahoma City, OK 73157-2986

Overview
    [http://www.fgs.org/~fgs/soc0379.htm]

# State Historical Society

## Oklahoma Historical Society          http://www.keytech.com/~frizzell/ohspage.html

2100 North Lincoln Boulevard       Phone    (405) 522-5209
Oklahoma City, OK 73105-4997       Fax      (405) 521-2492

Biographical Research Request Form
    [http://www.keytech.com/~frizzell/libraryfees.html]
Newspaper Department
    [http://www.keytech.com/~frizzell/newspaperform.html]
Oral History Collection
    [http://www.keytech.com/~frizzell/oralhistoryform.html]
Photograph Department
    [http://www.keytech.com/~frizzell/photoarchproce.html]

# Other State Sites

## Cherokee Heritage Center
    http://www.powersource.com/powersource/heritage/center.html

P.O. Box 515                       Phone    (918) 456-6007
Tahlequah, OK 74465-0515           Fax      (918) 456-6165

Cherokee National Historical Society
    [http://www.powersource.com/powersource/heritage/default.html]
Cherokee National Museum
    [http://www.powersource.com/powersource/heritage/museum.html]
Columns, Newsletter
    [http://www.powersource.com/powersource/heritage/columns.html]

# Oklahoma State University      http://pio.okstate.edu/

204 Edmon Low Library
Stillwater, OK 74078

Phone  (405) 744-6311  Special Collections
E-mail  www-master@www.okstate.edu
       hmlloyd@okway.okstate.edu Special

Library
   [http://www.library.okstate.edu/index.htm]
Special Collections Department
   [http://www.library.okstate.edu/dept/scua/scuahp.htm]
Women's Archives Guide
   [http://www.library.okstate.edu/dept/scua/guide.htm]

# Southwest Oklahoma Genealogical Society      http://www.sirinet.net/~lgarris/swogs/

P.O. Box 148
Lawton, OK 73502-0148

E-mail  lgarris@sirinet.net

Bible Records
   [http://www.sirinet.net/~lgarris/swogs/bible.html]
Books Reviews
   [http://www.sirinet.net/~lgarris/swogs/reviews.html]
Federal Tract Books
   [http://www.sirinet.net/~lgarris/swogs/tract.html]
Queries
   [http://www.sirinet.net/~lgarris/swogs/okquery.html]
Southwest Oklahoma Genealogical Society Online Membership Directory
   [http://www.sirinet.net/~lgarris/swogs/memadd.html]

# University of Tulsa      http://www.utulsa.edu/

McFarlin Library
2933 East 6th Street
Tulsa, OK 74104-3123

Phone  (918) 631-2880
Fax    (918) 631-3791
E-mail  lib_ssk@centum.utulsa.edu

Cherokee Manuscripts
   [gopher://tured.pa.utulsa.edu:70/00/McFarlin%20Library/Historical%20Manuscripts/
   Cherokee%20Manuscripts%20and%20Documents]
Choctaw Manuscripts
   [gopher://tured.pa.utulsa.edu:70/00/McFarlin%20Library/Historical%20Manuscripts/
   Choctaw%20Manuscripts%20and%20Documents]
Creek Manuscripts
   [gopher://tured.pa.utulsa.edu:70/00/McFarlin%20Library/Historical%20Manuscripts/
   Creek%20Manuscripts%20and%20Documents]
Library
   [http://www.lib.utulsa.edu/general/mcfinfo.htm]
Links
   [http://www.lib.utulsa.edu/guides/libraryg.htm]
Manuscript Guides
   [gopher://tured.pa.utulsa.edu/11/McFarlin%20Library/Historical%20Manuscripts]
Oklahoma History
   [gopher://tured.pa.utulsa.edu:70/00/McFarlin%20Library/Historical%20Manuscripts/
   Oklahoma%20Historical%20Documents%20and%20Photographs]
Special Collections Department
   [http://www.lib.utulsa.edu/general/speccoll.htm]

# OREGON

## State Home Page

### Oregon Online, Oregon State HomePage          http://www.state.or.us/

Oregon Blue Book
    [http://www.sos.state.or.us/bsd/9596.blbook/9596orbb.htm]
Vital Records
    [gopher://gopher.state.or.us:70/00/.documents/ORHH0038.text]

## State Archives

### Oregon State Archives          http://arcweb.sos.state.or.us/

| 800 Summer Street, N.E. | Phone | (503) 373-0701 |
| Salem, OR 97310 | Fax | (503) 373-0953 |
| | E-mail | reference.archives@state.or.us |

Address List, Oregon Repositories
    [http://arcweb.sos.state.or.us/cpaddresslist.html]
Boundary Changes
    [http://arcweb.sos.state.or.us/cpmapboundary.html]
Census Records
    [http://arcweb.sos.state.or.us/census.html]
County Records Inventories
    [http://arcweb.sos.state.or.us/cpinventories.html]
Genealogical Information Locator, Database
    [http://arcweb.sos.state.or.us/databases/searchg]eneal.html]
Land Records
    [http://arcweb.sos.state.or.us/land.html]
Maps
    [http://arcweb.sos.state.or.us/cpmaps.html]
Military Records
    [http://arcweb.sos.state.or.us/milit.html]
Naturalization Records
    [http://arcweb.sos.state.or.us/natural.html]
Oregon Roots Listserv
    [http://arcweb.sos.state.or.us/listserv_roots.html]
Probate Records
    [http://arcweb.sos.state.or.us/prob.html]
Records Management Resources
    [http://arcweb.sos.state.or.us/recmgmt/defaultrecmgmt.html]
Territorial Records
    [http://arcweb.sos.state.or.us/territ.html]
Vital Records
    [http://arcweb.sos.state.or.us/vital.html]

## State Library

### Oregon State Library          http://www.osl.state.or.us/oslhome.html

| State Library Building | Phone | (503) 378-4277 X240 |
| Salem, OR 97310 | Fax | (503) 588-7119 |
| | E-mail | merrialyce.k.blanchard@state.or.us |

History of State Library
    [http://www.osl.state.or.us/oslhome/oslbegin.html]
Links, Oregon Guides
    [http://www.osl.state.or.us/oslhome/ortophome.html]
Links, Oregon Libraries
    [http://library.usask.ca/hytelnet/usa/OR.html]
Oregon Index, Newspapers, etc.
    [http://www.osl.state.or.us/orpac/orindwebhome.html]

# Other State Sites

## Genealogical Forum of Oregon, Inc.
http://www.rootsweb.com/~genepool/forum.htm

2130 S.W. 5th Avenue #220          Phone   (503) 227-2398
Portland, OR 97201-4934

Oregon Genealogical and Historical Societies
    [http://www.rootsweb.com/~genepool/orgeneal.htm]
Overview
    [http://www.rootsweb.com/~genepool/forum.htm]

## Oregon History and Genealogy Resources
http://www.rootsweb.com/~genepool/oregon.htm

Kindred Keepsakes              E-mail  jrabun@ix.netcom.com
P.O. Box 41552
Eugene, OR 97404-0369

Links, Oregon Historical Sites
    [http://www.rootsweb.com/~genepool/orhist.htm]
Links, Oregon Sites
    [http://www.rootsweb.com/~genepool/oregon.htm]

## Oregon State University          http://www.orst.edu/

Oregon State University Archives    Phone   (541) 737-2165
94 Kerr Administration Building     Fax     (541) 737-2400
Corvallis, OR 97331-2103            E-mail  archives@ccmail.orst.edu   Archives
                                            krishnar@ucs.orst.edu  Special Coll.

Archives
    [http://www.orst.edu/Dept/archives/]
Links, Archival
    [http://www.orst.edu/Dept/archives/links.html]
Manuscripts
    [http://www.orst.edu/Dept/archives/archive/arch130.html]
Photograph Collections
    [http://www.orst.edu/Dept/archives/archive/arch120.html]
Special Collections Department
    [http://www.orst.edu/Dept/Special_Collections/]

## University of Oregon          http://darkwing.uoregon.edu/

University of Oregon Library        Phone   (541) 346-3068
1299 University of Oregon           E-mail  bmctigue@oregon.uoregon.edu
Eugene, OR 97403-1299

Library
    [http://darkwing.uoregon.edu/]
Manuscripts
    [http://libweb.uoregon.edu/speccoll/mss/mss_inv.html]
Special Collections Department
    [http://darkwing.uoregon.edu/~bmctigue/spc.html]


# PENNSYLVANIA

## State Home Page

| Pennsylvania HomePage | http://www.state.pa.us/ |
|---|---|

History of Pennsylvania
    [http://www.state.pa.us/PA_History/]
Links, County and Local Government
    [http://www.state.pa.us/govlocal.html]

## State Archives

**State Archives of Pennsylvania**
    http://www.state.pa.us/PA_Exec/Historical_Museum/overview.html

Pennsylvania Historical and Museum Commission
P.O. Box 1026                          Phone    (717) 783-3281
Harrisburg, PA 17108-1026              E-mail  webmaster@state.pa.us

Land Office
    [http://www.state.pa.us/PA_Exec/Historical_Museum/DAM/lo.htm]
Manuscripts
    [http://www.state.pa.us/PA_Exec/Historical_Museum/DAM/mg/index.htm]
Record Groups
    [http://www.state.pa.us/PA_Exec/Historical_Museum/DAM/rg/index.htm]
State Archives of Pennsylvania
    [http://www.state.pa.us/PA_Exec/Historical_Museum/DAM/psa.htm]

## State Library

**State Library of Pennsylvania**      http://www.cas.psu.edu/docs/pde/LIBSTATE.HTML

P.O. Box 1601                          Phone    (717) 783-5950
Commonwealth and Walnut Streets        Fax      (717) 783-2070
Harrisburg, PA 17105-1601              E-mail  payne@shrsys.hslc.org

Census Records
    [http://www.cas.psu.edu/docs/pde/LIBCENS.HTML]
County Courthouses, Pennsylvania
    [http://www.cas.psu.edu/docs/pde/LIBCOURT.HTML#COURT]
Genealogical and Historical Societies
    [http://www.cas.psu.edu/docs/pde/LIBCOURT.HTML#HIST]
Genealogy Resources
    [http://www.cas.psu.edu/docs/pde/LIBGENREC.HTML]
Naturalization Records
    [http://www.cas.psu.edu/docs/pde/LIBNAT.HTML]

Published Pennsylvania Archives
   [http://www.cas.psu.edu/docs/pde/LIBGEN.HTML]

# State Genealogical Society

## Genealogical Society of Pennsylvania          http://libertynet.org/~gencap/gsp.html

1305 Locust Street                       Phone   (215) 545-0391
Philadelphia, PA 19107-5405              Fax     (215) 545-0936

Overview
   [http://libertynet.org/~gencap/gsp.html]

# State Historical Society

## Historical Society of Pennsylvania          http://www.libertynet.org/~pahist/index.html

1300 Locust Street                       Phone   (215) 732-6201
Philadelphia, PA 19107-5699              Fax     (215) 732-2680
                                         E-mail  hsppr@aol.com

Architectural Resources
   [http://www.libertynet.org/~pahist/arch.html]
Civil War Resources
   [http://www.libertynet.org/~pahist/civil.html]
Genealogy Resources
   [http://www.libertynet.org/~pahist/family.html]
Peale Family
   http://www.libertynet.org/~pahist/peale.html]
Pennsylvania Magazine of History and Biography, Table of Contents
   [http://www.libertynet.org/~pahist/pmhb.html]

# Other State Sites

## Atheneum                               http://www.libertynet.org/~athena/

219 South Sixth Street                   Phone   (215) 925-2688
Philadelphia, PA 19106-3794              Fax     (215) 925-3755
                                         E-mail  athena@libertynet.org

Architectural Archives
   [http://www.libertynet.org/~athena/archives.html]
Archives, Guide
   [http://www.libertynet.org/~athena/hold.html]
Biographical Dictionary of Philadelphia Architects, 1700-1930
   [http://www.libertynet.org/~athena/bio.html]
Links, Architectural
   [http://www.libertynet.org/~athena/links.html]
Photographs
   [http://www.libertynet.org/~athena/photo.html]
Roman Catholic Building Resources
   [http://www.libertynet.org/~athena/catholic.html]

## Balch Institute for Ethnic Studies          http://www.libertynet.org:80/~balch/

18 South 7th Street                      Phone   (215) 925-8090
Philadelphia, PA 19106                   E-mail  BALCHLIB@HSLC.ORG

Civil Rights Bibliography
    [http://www.libertynet.org:80/~balch/civil-rights-bib.html]
Guide to Holdings
    [http://www.libertynet.org:80/~balch/guide/balchgud.htm]

## Carnegie Library of Pittsburgh          http://alphaclp.clpgh.org/CLP/

4400 Forbes Avenue                    Phone    (412) 622-3114
Pittsburgh, PA  15213                 E-mail   padept@alphaclp.clpgh.org.

African-American Genealogy
    [http://alphaclp.clpgh.org/CLP/Pennsylvania/oak_penna32.html]
Allegheny County, Orphans
    [http://alphaclp.clpgh.org/exhibit/orphan.html]
Genealogy Resources
    [http://alphaclp.clpgh.org/CLP/Pennsylvania/oak_penna3.html]
Genealogy Resources, Pennsylvania
    [http://alphaclp.clpgh.org/CLP/Pennsylvania/oak_penna31.html]
Pennsylvania Department
    [http://alphaclp.clpgh.org/CLP/Pennsylvania/oak_penna.html]

## The Free Library of Philadelphia         http://www.library.phila.gov/

1901 Vine Street                      Phone    (215) 686-5322
Philadelphia, PA 19103

Birth Records
    [http://www.library.phila.gov/central/ssh/waltgen/bir.htm]
Census
    [http://www.library.phila.gov/central/ssh/waltgen/cens1.htm]
Death Records
    [http://www.library.phila.gov/central/ssh/waltgen/dea.htm]
Genealogy Pathfinder
    [http://www.library.phila.gov/central/ssh/waltgen/geneal1.htm]
Marriage Records
    [http://www.library.phila.gov/central/ssh/waltgen/mar.htm]
Military Records
    [http://www.library.phila.gov/central/ssh/waltgen/mil1.htm]
Other Records
    [http://www.library.phila.gov/central/ssh/waltgen/deedwill.htm]
Passenger Records
    [http://www.library.phila.gov/central/ssh/waltgen/pass1.htm]

## Genealogical Computing Association of Pennsylvania (GENCAP)
    http://libertynet.org/~gencap/

51 Hillcrest Road
Barto, PA 19504

Newsletter
    [http://libertynet.org/~gencap/newsletter.html]
Overview
    [http://libertynet.org/~gencap/]

## Haverford College

http://www.haverford.edu/

Magill Library
370 Lancaster Avenue
Haverford, PA 19041-1392

Phone    (610) 896-1274
E-mail   elapsans@haverford.edu

Archives, Finding Aids
[http://www.haverford.edu/library/sc/aids.html]
Library
[http://www.haverford.edu/library/web/library.html]
Quaker Collection
[http://www.haverford.edu/library/sc/qcoll.html]
Special Collections Department
[http://www.haverford.edu/library/sc/sc.html]

## PACSCL, Philadelphia Area Consortium of Special Collections Libraries

http://www.libertynet.org:80/~pacscl/

Van Pelt-Dietrich Library Center
3420 Walnut Street
Philadelphia, PA 19104-6206

Phone    (215) 985-1445
Fax      (215) 985-1446
E-mail   lblancha@pobox.upenn.edu

Links to PACSCL Member and Related Sites
[http://www.libertynet.org:80/~pacscl/dir.html]

## Philadelphia City Archives

http://phila.gov/phils/carchive.htm

401 North Broad Street, Room 942
Philadelphia, PA 19108

Phone    (215) 686-1581
Fax      (215) 574-4458
E-mail   archives@phila.gov

Deeds and Architectural Records
[http://phila.gov/phils/Docs/Inventor/deeds.htm]
Genealogical Resources
[http://phila.gov/phils/Docs/Inventor/genealgy.htm]
Mayors of Philadelphia
[http://phila.gov/phils/Mayorlst.htm]
Naturalization Records
[http://phila.gov/phils/Docs/Inventor/natz.htm]

## Temple University

http://www.temple.edu/

Paley Library
13th Street and Berks Mall
Philadelphia, PA 19122

Phone    (215) 204-8230
Fax      (215) 204-5201
E-mail   whitetm@astro.ocis.temple.edu

Biographical Dictionary Project
917 Gladfelter Hall (025-24)
12th Street and Berks Mall

Phone    (215) 204-3406
Fax      (215) 204-5891
E-mail   BDEPL@VM.TEMPLE.EDU

Blockson Afro-American Collection
Sullivan Hall, First Floor
12th Street and Berks Mall

Phone    (215) 204-6632
Fax      (215) 204-5197
E-mail   aberhanu@thunder.ocis.temple.edu

Urban Archives
Paley Library

Phone    (215) 204-8257
Fax      (215) 204-3681
E-mail   brightbi@astro.ocis.temple.edu

Biographical Dictionary of Early Pennsylvania Legislators
[http://www.temple.edu/history/]
Blockson Afro-American Collection
[http://www.library.temple.edu/blockson/]
Special Collections Department
[http://www.library.temple.edu/speccoll/]
Urban Archives
[http://www.library.temple.edu/urbana/]
Urban Archives Notes, Newsletter
[http://www.library.temple.edu/urbana/urbnot.htm]

# RHODE ISLAND

## State Home Page

### Rhode Island Public Information Kiosk          http://www.state.ri.us/

Rhode Island Cities and Towns
[http://www.state.ri.us/submenus/candt.htm]
Rhode Island History
[http://www.state.ri.us/submenus/rihstlnk.htm]

## State Archives

### Rhode Island State Archives          http://archives.state.ri.us/

337 Westminster Street                    Phone    (401) 277 2353
Providence, RI 02903

Census
[gopher://archives.state.ri.us:70/00/Electronic%20Brochure%3A%20%20State%20
Census%20Records]
Civil War Records
[gopher://archives.state.ri.us:70/00/RI%20Civil%20War%20Records]
Military Records
[gopher://archives.state.ri.us:70/00/Electronic%20Brochure%3A%20%20Military%20Records]
Overview
[http://archives.state.ri.us/]

## State Library

### Rhode Island Department of Library Services          http://www.dsls.state.ri.us/

300 Richmond Street                    Phone   (401) 277-2726
Providence, RI 02903-4222              Fax     (401) 277-4195

DSLS Newsletter
[http://www.dsls.state.ri.us/dept/news/vol2_96/news_962.htm]
Directory Rhode Island Libraries
[http://www.dsls.state.ri.us/genref/rilibdir.htm]
Links, Library Associations
[http://www.dsls.state.ri.us/prolib/libassoc.htm]

## Other State Sites

| Brown University | http://www.brown.edu/ |
| --- | --- |

John Hay Library
20 Prospect Street
Providence, RI 02912-9039

Phone   (401) 863-3723
          (401) 863-2148 Archives
E-mail   rock@brownvm.brown.edu

Archives
    [http://www.brown.edu/Facilities/University_Library/general/guides/archives.html]
Genealogy
    [http://www.brown.edu/Facilities/University_Library/general/guides/archives.html#genea]

| University of Rhode Island | http://www.uri.edu/ |
| --- | --- |

University Library
Kingston, RI 02881

Phone   (401) 874-2594

Special Collections Department
    [http://www.library.uri.edu/Web_Files/Library_Services/SpecialCollections.html#TOP]

# SOUTH CAROLINA

## State Home Page

| South Carolina Home Page | http://www.state.sc.us/ |
| --- | --- |

Links, South Carolina Government
    [http://www.state.sc.us/stateage.html]

## State Archives

**South Carolina Department of Archives and History**
    http://www.scdah.sc.edu/homepage.htm

1430 Senate Street
Columbia, SC 29211

Phone   (803) 734-8577
E-mail   sox@history.scdah.sc.edu

Bibliography, Brief
    [http://www.scdah.sc.edu/selected.htm]
South Carolina History
    [http://www.scdah.sc.edu/history.htm]

## State Library

| South Carolina State Library | http://www.state.sc.us/scsl/ |
| --- | --- |

1500 Senate Street
P.O. Box 11469
Columbia, SC 29211-1469

Phone   (803) 734-8666
Fax     (803) 734-8676
E-mail   curtis@leo.scsl.state.sc.us
         reference@leo.scsl.state.sc.us

Bibliographies
    [http://www.state.sc.us/scsl/readmore.html]
County Histories
    [http://www.state.sc.us/scsl/cnties.html]

Links, South Carolina Colleges
    [http://www.citadel.edu/sciway/lib/colindex.html]
Links, South Carolina Libraries
    [http://www.state.sc.us/scsl/colibs1.html]
Links, South Carolina Newspapers, Media
    [http://www.state.sc.us/scsl/newsmed.html]
New Resources, Newsletter
    [http://www.state.sc.us/scsl/newres.html]

## State Historical Society

| South Carolina Historical Society | http://www.historic.com/schs/index.html |
|---|---|

| 100 Meeting Street<br>Charleston, SC 29401-2299 | Phone   (803) 723-3225<br>Fax      (803) 723-8584 |
|---|---|

Links, South Carolina Archives Sites
    [http://www.sciway.net/hist/archives.html]
Links, South Carolina Genealogy Sites
    [http://historic.com/schs/othrsits.html]

## Other State Sites

| University of South Carolina | http://www.sc.edu/ |
|---|---|

| Columbia, SC 29208 | Phone   (803) 777-5183<br>Fax      (803) 777-5747<br>E-mail  cuthrellb@tcl.sc.edu |
|---|---|

South Caroliniana Library
    [http://www.sc.edu/library/socar/]
University South Caroliniana Society
    [http://www.sc.edu/library/socar/uscs/index.html]

# SOUTH DAKOTA

## State Home Page

| South Dakota Home Page | http://www.state.sd.us/ |
|---|---|

Links, South Dakota Government
    [http://www.state.sd.us/]

## State Archives

| South Dakota State Archives | |
|---|---|
| http://www.state.sd.us/state/executive/deca/cultural/archives.htm | |

| 900 Governors Drive<br>Pierre, SD 57501-2217 | Phone   (605) 773-3804<br>Fax      (605) 773-6041<br>E-mail  richardp@chc.state.sd.us |
|---|---|

Collections
    [http://www.state.sd.us/deca/cultural/general.htm]
South Dakota Newspaper Project
    [http://www.state.sd.us/state/executive/deca/cultural/newspap.htm]

Surname Files
  [http://www.state.sd.us/deca/cultural/surname.htm]

## State Library

### South Dakota State Library
  http://www.state.sd.us/state/executive/deca/ST_LIB/st_lib.htm

800 Governor's Drive
Pierre, SD 5750-2294

Phone  (605) 773-3131
       (800) 423-6665
Fax    (605) 773-4950
E-mail refrequest@stlib.state.sd.us

Links, South Dakota Libraries
  [http://www.state.sd.us/state/executive/deca/st_lib/sdlib.htm]
State Documents
  [http://www.state.sd.us/state/executive/deca/st_lib/stinfo3.htm]

## State Historical Society

### South Dakota State Historical Society
  http://www.state.sd.us/state/executive/deca/cultural/sdshs.htm

900 Governor's Drive
Pierre, SD 57501-2217

Phone  (605) 773-3458
E-mail jeffm@chc.state.sd.us

Overview
  [http://www.state.sd.us/state/executive/deca/cultural/sdshs.htm]

# TENNESSEE

## State Home Page

### Tennessee State HomePage          http://www.state.tn.us/

Office of Vital Records
  [http://www.state.tn.us/health/bir/vr0.html]
Tennessee Military Department War Records Division
  [http://www.state.tn.us/military/warec.html]

## State Library and Archives
### *Outstanding Site*

### Tennessee State Library and Archives
  http://www.state.tn.us/other/statelib/tslahome.htm

403 7th Avenue North
Nashville, TN 37243-0312

Phone  (615) 741-2764
Fax    (615) 741-6471
E-mail referenc@mail.state.tn.us

Acts of Tennessee, 1796-1830, Index
  [http://www.state.tn.us/sos/statelib/pubsvs/actindex.htm]
Bibliography
  [http://www.state.tn.us/sos/statelib/pubsvs/bibindex.htm]
Census Holdings
  [http://www.state.tn.us/sos/statelib/pubsvs/microcen.htm]

Census Indexes, 1820-1840
   [http://www.state.tn.us/sos/statelib/pubsvs/cen1820.htm]
Census Indexes, 1850-1870
   [http://www.state.tn.us/sos/statelib/pubsvs/cen1850.htm]
Cherokee Research
   [http://www.state.tn.us/sos/statelib/pubsvs/cherokee.htm]
City Directories
   [http://www.state.tn.us/sos/statelib/pubsvs/cdirect.htm]
Civil War Records
   [http://www.state.tn.us/sos/statelib/pubsvs/civilwar.htm]
County Historians
   [http://www.state.tn.us/sos/statelib/pubsvs/historns.htm]
County Records
   [http://www.state.tn.us/sos/statelib/pubsvs/earlyrec.htm]
County Records, Address List
   [http://www.state.tn.us/sos/statelib/pubsvs/govtarch.htm]
Court Records
   [http://www.state.tn.us/sos/statelib/pubsvs/court.htm]
Genealogical Guide
   [http://www.state.tn.us/sos/statelib/pubsvs/tnsource.htm]
Genealogical Guides, By County
   [http://www.state.tn.us/sos/statelib/pubsvs/countypg.htm]
Maps
   [http://www.state.tn.us/sos/statelib/pubsvs/maps.htm]
Military Records
   [http://www.state.tn.us/sos/statelib/pubsvs/milhis.htm]
Obituary Indexes
   [http://www.state.tn.us/sos/statelib/pubsvs/tn-obits.htm]
Vital Records
   [http://www.state.tn.us/sos/statelib/pubsvs/vital3.htm]

# Other State Sites

## Middle Tennessee State University
   http://frank.mtsu.edu/~kmiddlet/history/women.html

Todd Library                          Phone   (615) 898-2549
Murfreesboro, TN 37132                E-mail  kmiddlet@frank.mtsu.edu

Civil War Resources
   [http://frank.mtsu.edu/~kmiddlet/history/civwar/cwrghome.html]
History Research
   [http://frank.mtsu.edu/~kmiddlet/history/histhom2.html]
Tennessee History Resources
   [http://frank.mtsu.edu/~kmiddlet/history/tenn/tennhist.html]
Women, Bibliographies
   [http://frank.mtsu.edu/~kmiddlet/history/women/wom-bibl.html]
Women, Guide to Sources, by State
   [http://frank.mtsu.edu/~kmiddlet/history/women/wh-state.html]
Women, Listserv's
   [http://frank.mtsu.edu/~kmiddlet/history/women/network.html]
Women, Sources
   [http://frank.mtsu.edu/~kmiddlet/history/women/wombio-todd.html]

## University of Tennessee, Knoxville        http://www.utk.edu/

Knoxville, TN 37996                         E-mail  jlloyd@utk.edu

Library
   [http://www.lib.utk.edu/]
Links, Tennessee
   [http://www.lib.utk.edu/refs/tennessee.html]
Manuscripts Guide
   [http://toltec.lib.utk.edu/~spec_coll/manuscripts/]


# TEXAS

## State Home Page
### *Outstanding Site*

## Texas State HomePage        http://www.state.tx.us/

Texas General Land Office          Phone   (512) 463-5288
1700 North Congress Avenue         E-mail  tgloarc@glo.state.tx.us
Austin, TX  78701-1495


Texas Historical Commission        Phone   (512) 463-6100
P.O. Box 12276                     Fax     (512) 475-4872
Austin, TX 78711-2276              E-mail  thc@nueces.thc.state.tx.us


Bureau of Vital Records
   [http://www.tdh.state.tx.us/hcqs/bvs/bvs.htm]
Bureau of Vital Records, Birth or Death Records
   [http://www.tdh.state.tx.us/hcqs/bvs/registra/certcop.htm]
Bureau of Vital Records, Birth Certificates, Heirloom
   [http://www.tdh.state.tx.us/hcqs/bvs/registra/heirloom.htm]
Bureau of Vital Records, Marriage or Divorce Records
   [http://www.tdh.state.tx.us/hcqs/bvs/registra/marr.htm]
Links, City Government
   [http://www.state.tx.us/cities.html]
Links, County Government
   [http://www.state.tx.us/county/counties.html]
Links, State Government
   [http://link.tsl.state.tx.us/t/txgov.html]
Texas Courthouse Alliance
   [http://www.thc.state.tx.us/courth.html]
Texas Electronic Library
   [http://link.tsl.state.tx.us/]
Texas General Land Office
   [http://www.glo.state.tx.us/]
Texas General Land Office, Archives and Documents
   [http://www.glo.state.tx.us/central/arc/index.html]
Texas General Land Office, Archives, Finding Aids
   [http://www.glo.state.tx.us/central/arc/findaid.html]
Texas General Land Office, Spanish, Mexican Collection
   [http://www.glo.state.tx.us/central/arc/spanmex.html]

Texas Historic Site Atlas
    [http://www.thc.state.tx.us/atltemp/]
Texas Historical Commission
    [thc@nueces.thc.state.tx.us]
Texas Historical Commission, Courthouses in Texas, a History
    [http://www.thc.state.tx.us/history.html]
Texas State Cemetery
    [http://www.thc.state.tx.us/cemetery.html]

# State Library and Archives

| Texas State Library | http://www.tsl.state.tx.us/ |
|---|---|
| Lorenzo de Zavala Building<br>1201 Brazos<br>Austin, TX 78701 | Phone  (512) 463-5460<br>          (512) 463-5463 Genealogy Collection<br>Fax     (512) 463-5436 |
| Mail to:<br>P.O. Box 12927<br>Austin, TX 78711-2927 | E-mail  geninfo@tsl.state.tx.us Genealogy<br>        archinfo@tsl.state.tx.us  Archives |

Birth and Death Indexes
    [http://www.tsl.state.tx.us/lobby/genfirst.htm]
City and Telephone Directories
    [http://link.tsl.state.tx.us/a/aids/.files/citylink.out]
Confederate Pension Records
    [http://link.tsl.state.tx.us/c/compt.html]
County Records; Microfilm Loan Collection
    [http://link.tsl.state.tx.us/.dir/countyrec.dir/]
Finding Aids
    [http://www.tsl.state.tx.us/lobby/findmenu.htm]
Genealogy Collection
    [http://www.tsl.state.tx.us/lobby/genfirst.htm]
Military Records
    [http://www.tsl.state.tx.us/lobby/arcfirst.htm]
Newspapers
    [http://www.tsl.state.tx.us/lobby/genfirst.htm]
State and Local Records Management
    [http://www.tsl.state.tx.us/SLRM/SLRMhome.html]
Local Record, Newsletter
    [http://www.tsl.state.tx.us/SLRM/localrecord.html]
Texas Historical Records Advisory Board
    [http://www.tsl.state.tx.us/lobby/thrab/index.html]
Texas Library Association
    [http://www.txla.org/]
Texas Library Journal, Fulltext
    [http://www.txla.org/pubs/pubs.html]
Texas State Archives
    [http://www.tsl.state.tx.us/lobby/arcfirst.htm]
Vital Records, Birth and Death
    [http://www.tsl.state.tx.us/lobby/genfirst.htm]
Vital Records, Marriage and Divorce
    [http://www.tsl.state.tx.us/lobby/genfirst.htm]

# Other State Sites

## Austin Public Library
http://www.ci.austin.tx.us/library/

Austin History Center
9th and Guadalupe Streets
Austin, TX 78768-2287

Phone (512) 499-7480
E-mail aplmail@library.ci.austin.tx.us

Austin Records Center
211 East Alpine
Austin, TX 78768

Austin Records Center
[http://www.ci.austin.tx.us/library/lbahc.htm]

## Brazoria County Historical Museum
http://www.tgn.net/~bchm/

100 East Cedar
Courthouse Square
Angleton, TX 77515

Phone (409) 849-5711 x1208
E-mail handy@tenet.edu

Bibliography, Texas and Brazoria County
[http://www.tgn.net/~bchm/texbiblg.html]
Genealogy Database
[http://www.tgn.net/~bchm/Genealogy/gene.html]
Links, Texas History
[http://www.tgn.net/~bchm/other.html]

## Catholic Archives of Texas
http://www.onr.com/user/cat/

Diocese of Austin Chancery Building
1600 North Congress Avenue
Austin, TX 78701

Phone (512) 476-4888
E-mail cat@onr.com

Mail to:
P.O. Box 13327, Capitol Station
Austin, TX 78711

Collections
[http://www.onr.com/user/cat/#resources_overview]
Manuscripts
[http://www.onr.com/user/cat/cathol95.html#manuscripts_collection]
Microfilm Records
[http://www.onr.com/user/cat/cathol95.html#personal_papers]
Organizational Records
[http://www.onr.com/user/cat/cathol95.html#corporate_records]
Personal Papers
[http://www.onr.com/user/cat/cathol95.html#personal_papers]

## *Outstanding Site*

## Dallas Genealogical Society
http://www.chrysalis.org/dgs/

P.O. Box 12648
Dallas, TX 75225-0648

Phone (214) 670-7932
Fax (214) 670-7932
E-mail don.raney@chrysalis.org

Dallas Census, 1868
      [http://www.chrysalis.org/dgs/census68.htm]
Links
      [http://www.chrysalis.org/dgs/txgenweb.htm#links]
Links, Texas Genealogical Societies
      [http://www.chrysalis.org/dgs/txgenweb.htm]
Texas GenWeb Project
      [http://www.chrysalis.org/dgs/txgenweb.htm]
Texas GenWeb Project County Index
      [http://www.chrysalis.org/dgs/txgenweb.htm#index]

## Dallas Historical Society          http://www.arlington.net/interact/library.htm

1717 Gano Street                      E-mail  dhs@startext.net
Dallas, TX  75215


Legacies, Journal
      [http://www.arlington.net/interact/table.htm]
Library
      [http://www.arlington.net/interact/library.htm]
Register, Journal. Full Text
      [http://www.arlington.net/interact/register.htm]

## Dallas Public Library              http://205.165.160.15/home.htm

1515 Young Street                     Phone       (214) 670-1400
Dallas, TX 75201                      TDD/TTY   (214) 670-1716

Online Card Catalog
      [http://lib.ci.dallas.tx.us/marion]

## Daughters of the Republic of Texas Library
      http://www.drtl.org/~drtl/index.html

P.O. Box 1401                         Phone  (210) 225-1071
San Antonio, TX 78295-1401            Fax    (210) 212-8514
                                      E-mail drtl@salsa.net
Alamo: An Illustrated Chronology
      [http://www.drtl.org/~drtl/webchro1.html]
Alamo Bibliography
      [http://www.drtl.org/~drtl/alamorev.html]
Collections
      [http://www.drtl.org/~drtl/libcoll.html]
Genealogy Resources
      [http://www.drtl.org/~drtl/genalgy.html]
Links to Texas History Sites
      [http://www.drtl.org/~drtl/links.html]
Manuscripts
      [http://www.drtl.org/~drtl/register.html]
Maps
      [http://www.drtl.org/~drtl/vaultmap.html]
Photograph Collections
      [http://www.drtl.org/~drtl/photopol.html]
Sheet Music Collection
      [http://www.drtl.org/~drtl/music.html]

# Fort Worth Public Library
http://198.215.16.7:443/fortworth/Fwpl/index.htm

300 Taylor Street
Fort Worth, TX  76102

Phone   (817) 871-7701
(817) 871-7740 Genealogy
E-mail  wmaster@amon.pub-lib.ci.fort-worth.tx.us

Archives
[http://198.215.16.7:443/fortworth/FWPL/archive.htm]
Census Holdings
[http://198.215.16.7:443/fortworth/FWPL/census.htm]
Genealogical Resources, Local
[http://198.215.16.7:443/fortworth/FWPL/lgenres.htm]
Genealogy and Local History Section
[http://198.215.16.7:443/fortworth/FWPL/genlhst.htm]
Links, Genealogy
[http://198.215.16.7:443/fortworth/FWPL/genea.htm]

## *Outstanding Site*

# Historical Society of Denton County
http://www.iglobal.net/mayhouse/hsdc.html

P.O. Box 50503
Denton, TX 76206-0503

Phone   (817) 387-0995
E-mail  Mcochran@iglobal.net

African American Resources
[http://www.iglobal.net/mayhouse/Blackhistory.html]
Cemetery Records, Index
[http://www.iglobal.net/mayhouse/cemeterypage.html]
Census, 1850, Index and Abstracts
[http://www.iglobal.net/mayhouse/1850Census.html]
Confederate Pension Abstracts
[http://www.iglobal.net/mayhouse/Confeder@pens.html]
County Records
[http://www.iglobal.net/mayhouse/CountyRecords.html]
History of Denton County
[http://www.iglobal.net/mayhouse/LowryContents.html]
Links, Texas History
[http://www.iglobal.net/mayhouse/Historylinks.html]
Oral Histories
[http://www.iglobal.net/mayhouse/oralhist.html]

## *Outstanding Site*

# Hood County Genealogical Society
http://genealogy.emcee.com:80/~granbury/welcome.html

P.O. Box 1623
Granbury, TX 76048-8623

E-mail  granbury@emcee.com

Antioch Baptist Church Records
[http://www.genealogy.org/~granbury/church/antbapch.htm]
Birth Records, 1903-1928. Index
[http://www.genealogy.org/~granbury/birth/birth.htm]
Cemetery Records, Abstracts
[http://www.genealogy.org/~granbury/index.htm]
Death Records, 1903-1940. Index
[http://www.genealogy.org/~granbury/church/d3-40a-c.htm]

Index of Online Databases
    [http://www.genealogy.org/~granbury/index.htm]
Marriages 1875-1900, Indexes
    [http://genealogy.emcee.com:80/~granbury/mar/title_pg.htm]
Queries
    [http://www.dsenter.com/query//txhood.htm]
School Records
    [http://genealogy.emcee.com:80/~granbury/school/scholast.htm]
Tax Records
    [http://www.genealogy.org/~granbury/tax_pyr.htm]

## *Outstanding Site*

| Houston Public Library | http://sparc.hpl.lib.tx.us/hpl/hplhome.html |
|---|---|

Central Library                          Phone    (713) 236-1313
500 McKinney
Houston, TX 77002

Clayton Library for Genealogical Research        Phone    (713) 524-0101
5300 Caroline
Houston, TX 77004-6896

African-American Records
    [http://sparc.hpl.lib.tx.us/hpl/clmct1.html#AFRO AMER.]
Cemetery Research
    [http://sparc.hpl.lib.tx.us/hpl/cr002.html]
Census, Soundex Guide
    [http://sparc.hpl.lib].tx.us/hpl/soundex.html]
Clayton Library for Genealogical Research
    [http://sparc.hpl.lib.tx.us/hpl/clayton.html]
Collection Guide
    [http://sparc.hpl.lib.tx.us/hpl/clasum.html]
Family Histories Guide
    [http://sparc.hpl.lib.tx.us/hpl/clmcd0.html]
Federal Land Records
    [http://sparc.hpl.lib.tx.us/hpl/lr001.html]
Freedmen's Bureau Records
    [http://sparc.hpl.lib.tx.us/hpl/aa002.html]
French-American Research
    [http://sparc.hpl.lib.tx.us/hpl/ec002.html]
Friends of the Clayton Library
    [http://sparc.hpl.lib.tx.us/hpl/clf.html]
Friends, Newsletter. Fulltext
    [http://sparc.hpl.lib.tx.us/hpl/clf.html#newsletter]
Georgia Research
    [http://sparc.hpl.lib.tx.us/hpl/ga001.html]
Military Records
    [http://sparc.hpl.lib.tx.us/hpl/clmcm0.html]
Native American Records
    [http://sparc.hpl.lib.tx.us/hpl/clmct1.html#NATIVE AMER.]
NUCMC, National Union Catalog of Manuscript Collections
    [http://sparc.hpl.lib.tx.us/hpl/ml005.html]
Passenger Lists
    [http://sparc.hpl.lib.tx.us/hpl/px001.html]

Quaker Records
    [http://sparc.hpl.lib.tx.us/hpl/qk002.html]
Virginia Research
    [http://sparc.hpl.lib.tx.us/hpl/va002.html]
Texas and Local History Department
    [http://sparc.hpl.lib.tx.us/hpl/txr.html]

## *Outstanding Site*

### Lone Star Junction                http://www.lsjunction.com/index.htm

Biography
    [http://www.lsjunction.com/people/people.htm]
Historic Documents
    [http://www.lsjunction.com/docs/docs.htm]
Historic Events
    [http://www.lsjunction.com/events/events.htm]
Historic Places
    [http://www.lsjunction.com/places/ismap2b.htm]
Links
    [http://www.lsjunction.com/weblinks.htm]
Photographs
    [http://www.lsjunction.com/images/images.htm]
Texana Book Reviews
    [http://www.lsjunction.com/cox.htm]
Texas Genealogy Family Register
    [http://www.lsjunction.com/gen.htm]
Texas History Forum, E-mail Exchange
    [http://www.lsjunction.com/forumhst.htm]

## *Outstanding Site*

### Island Multimedia, Virtual Bookshelf
            http://www.islandmm.com/islandmm/cgi-bin/sitemllsw.pl

Dobie, J. Frank. Guide to Life and Literature of the Southwest. Fulltext.
    [http://www.islandmm.com/islandmm/cgi-bin/sitemllsw.pl]
Southwick, Noah. Evolution of a State or Recollections of Old Texas. Fulltext.
    [http://www.islandmm.com/islandmm/cgi-bin/sitemllsw.pl]

### Rice University                http://riceinfo.rice.edu/

Woodson Research Center          Phone   (713) 527-8101 x2586
Fondren Library                  E-mail  boothe@rice.edu
6100 South Main Street
Houston, TX 77251-1892

Journal of Southern History      Fax     (713) 285-5207
P.O. Box 1892                    E-mail  jsh@rice.edu
Houston, TX 77251

Journal of Southern History
    [http://www.ruf.rice.edu/~jsh/]
Journal of Southern History, Contents
    [http://www.ruf.rice.edu/~jsh/content/text.html]
Manuscripts
    [http://riceinfo.rice.edu/Fondren/Woodson/mss.html]

Papers of Jefferson Davis
    [http://www.ruf.rice.edu/~pjdavis/jdp.htm]
Rare Books (Texana Collection)
    [http://riceinfo.rice.edu/Fondren/Woodson/books.html]
Southern Historical Association
    [http://www.ruf.rice.edu/~jsh/sha/info.html]
Special Collections Department
    [http://riceinfo.rice.edu/Fondren/Woodson/]

## San Antonio Public Library    HTTP://WWW.CI.SAT.TX.US/SAPL/

600 Soledad Street        Phone  (512) 299-7790
San Antonio, TX 78205

Genealogy Collection
    [HTTP://WWW.CI.SAT.TX.US/SAPL/html/genealogy.html]
Microfilm Records
    [HTTP://WWW.CI.SAT.TX.US/SAPL/html/saplgen.html]

## Southern Methodist University    http://www.smu.edu/

Fondren Library        Phone  (214) 768-2326
Dallas, TX 75275        Fax    (214) 768-1842
                E-mail  mstark@mail.smu.edu

DeGolyer Library of Special Collections    Phone  (214) 768-2012
P.O. Box 750396        Fax    (214) 768-1565
Dallas, TX 75275-0396    E-mail  dfarmer@mail.smu.edu

DeGolyer Library
    [http://www.smu.edu/~cul/degolyer/index.html]
DeGolyer Collections
    [http://www.smu.edu/~cul/degolyer/collections.html]
Links, Archives and Libraries
    [http://www.smu.edu/~cul/southwest_all.html#archives]
Southwest Studies
    [http://www.smu.edu/~cul/southwest_all.html]

## Southwestern University    http://www.southwestern.edu/home.html

A. Frank Smith, Jr. Library Center    Phone  (512) 863-1311
P.O. Box 770        E-mail  libweb@southwestern.edu
Georgetown, TX 78627- 0770

Special Collections Department    Phone  (512) 863-1568
                E-mail  stallark@southwestern.edu
Library
    [http://www.southwestern.edu/library/library-home.html]
Special Collections
    [http://www.southwestern.edu/library/special-collections.html]

## Stephen F. Austin State University    http://www.sfasu.edu/

The Center for East Texas Studies    Phone  (409) 468-1392
Ferguson Building 340        Fax    (409) 468-2190
P.O. Box 6134 SFA Station    E-mail  CETS@sfasu.edu
Nacogdoches, TX 75962

East Texas Research Center
Steen Library
Box 13055, SFA Station
Nacogdoches, TX 75962-3055

Phone   (409) 468-4100
E-mail   LNicklas@SFALIB.SFASU.EDU

The Center for East Texas Studies
    [http://144.96.211.125/CETS.html]
East Texas Research Center
    [http://www.lib.sfasu.edu/etrc/]

## Texas Catholic Historical Society
    http://www.history.swt.edu/Catholic_Southwest.htm

c/o Texas Catholic Conference
1625 Rutherford Lane, Building D
Austin, TX 78754-5105

E-mail   jd10@swt.edu

Catholic Southwest, A Journal of History and Culture
    [http://www.history.swt.edu/Catholic_Southwest.htm]

## *Outstanding Site*

## Texas State Cemetery
    http://sparky.gsc.state.tx.us/statecemetery/

901 Navasota Street
P.O. Box 13047
Austin, TX 78711-3047

Phone   (512) 463-0605
Fax      (512) 463-3311
E-mail   statecemetery@gsc.state.tx.us

Cemetery History
    [http://sparky.gsc.state.tx.us/statecemetery/h.html]
Confederate Section
    [http://sparky.gsc.state.tx.us/statecemetery/hocs.html]
Data Feedback Form
    [http://sparky.gsc.state.tx.us/statecemetery/dff.html]
Master List of Burials
    [http://sparky.gsc.state.tx.us/statecemetery/mlob.html]

## Texas Women's University
    http://www.twu.edu/

Blagg-Huey Library
Denton, Texas 76204

Phone   (817) 898-3708
Fax      (817) 898-3808
E-mail   s_hepner@twu.edu

Library
    [http://twu.edu/www/twu/library/mnn.html]
Links
    [http://twu.edu/www/twu/library/wfem.html]
Women's History Collection
    [http://twu.edu/www/twu/library/wm.html]

## University of Texas at Arlington
    http://www.uta.edu/library/

UTA Libraries
P.O. Box 19497
Arlington, TX 76019-0497

Phone   (817) 272-3394
             (817) 272-3393 Special Collections
E-mail   www@library.uta.edu

Compass Rose, Newsletter
    [http://www.uta.edu/library/publications/compass/compass_fall94.html]
Special Collections Department
    [http://www.uta.edu/library/SpCo/special_collections.html]

## University of Texas at Austin          http://www.utexas.edu/

| | | |
|---|---|---|
| Benson Latin American Collection | Phone | (512) 495-4520 |
| P.O. Box P | Fax | (512) 495-4568 |
| Austin, TX 78713-8916 | E-mail | blac@lib.utexas.edu |
| | | |
| Center for American History | Phone | (512) 495-4515 |
| (Includes the Texas History Collection, | Fax | (512) 495-4542 |
|    Southern History Collection, etc.) | E-mail | m.norkunas@mail.utexas.edu |
| | | |
| Population Research Center Library | E-mail | draaijer@prc.utexas.edu |
| 1800 Main Building | | |
| Austin, TX 78712 | | |

Benson Latin American Collection
    [http://www.lib.utexas.edu/Libs/Benson/benson.html]
BiblioNoticias
    [http://www.lib.utexas.edu/Libs/Benson/bibnot/bib_noticias_www.html]
Center for American History
    [http://www.lib.utexas.edu/Libs/CAH/cah.html]
Center for Studies in Texas History
    [http://www.dla.utexas.edu/texhist/]
International Census Collection Online Catalog
    [http://www.prc.utexas.edu/lib/icc/icc.html]
Mexican Archives
    [http://www.lib.utexas.edu/Libs/Benson/Mex_Archives/Collection_list.html]

## University of Texas at San Antonio          http://www.utsa.edu/Library/index.html

| | | |
|---|---|---|
| Library | Phone | (210) 458-5505 |
| 6900 North Loop 1604 West | Fax | (210) 458-4571 |
| San Antonio, TX 78249-0651 | E-mail | dguerra@lonestar.utsa.edu |
| | | |
| Archives for Research on Women and Gender | Phone | (210) 458-2385 |
| 801 South Bowie Street | Fax | (210) 458-2386 |
| San Antonio, TX 78205-3296 | | |
| | | |
| Hispanic Research Center, HRC | Phone | (210) 691-515 |
| | E-mail | avaldez@pclan.utsa.edu |
| | | |
| Institute of Texan Cultures | Phone | (210) 458-2228 |
| 801 South Bowie Street | | (800) 776-7651 |
| San Antonio, TX 78205-3296 | Fax | (210) 458-2218 |
| | E-mail | lcatalin@itcpost1.utsa.edu |
| | | sgreen@itcpost1.utsa.edu Library |
| | | dbruce@itcpost1.utsa.edu Photos |

Archives and Manuscripts
    [http://www.utsa.edu/Library/Special_Collections/arch&man.htm]
Archives for Research on Women and Gender, Collections
    [http://www.utsa.edu/Library/Archives/collex.htm]

Archives for Research on Women and Gender, Church Women United, Records
    [http://www.utsa.edu/Library/Archives/church.htm]
Archives for Research on Women and Gender, Links to Women's History
    [http://ww]w.utsa.edu/Library/Archives/links.htm]
Archives for Research on Women and Gender, Woman's Club of San Antonio
    [http://www.utsa.edu/Library/Archives/wcsa.htm]
Hispanic Research Center, Downloadable Databases
    [http://hrcweb.utsa.edu/library.htm]
Hispanic Research Center, Hispanic Research Center
    [http://hrcweb.utsa.edu/index.htm]
Hispanic Research Center, Mexican American Archives Project
    [http://hrcweb.utsa.edu/archives.htm]
Institute of Texan Cultures Library
    [http://www.utsa.edu/itc/library.htm]
Links to Texas Libraries
    [http://link.tsl.state.tx.us/t/texcats.html]
Spanish Texas Microfilm Files
    [http://www.utsa.edu/Library/Special_Collections/spanish.htm]]
Special Collections Department
    [http://www.utsa.edu/Library/Special_Collections/index.htm]
Texas Folklife Festival
    [http://www.utsa.edu/itc/hpfolk.htm]

## West Texas A&M University     http://www.wtamu.edu/wtamu.htm

| | |
|---|---|
| Cornette Library | Phone   (806) 656-2210 |
| 2501 4th Avenue | E-mail   media@wtamu-library.wtamu.edu |
| Canyon, TX 79016-0001 | |
| | |
| Panhandle-Plains Historical Museum | Phone   (806) 656-2244 |
| WTAMU Box 967 | Fax      (806) 656-2250 |
| Canyon, TX 79016 | E-mail   museum@wtamu.edu |

Panhandle-Plains Historical Museum
    [http://www.wtamu.edu/museum/home.html]

# UTAH

## State Home Page

## Utah Home Page                 http://www.state.ut.us/

Links, State Government
    [http://www.state.ut.us/html/agencies.htm]

## State Archives
*Extraordinary Site*

## Utah State Archives            http://www.archives.state.ut.us

| | |
|---|---|
| State Capitol, Archives Building | Phone   (801) 538-3013 |
| Salt Lake City, UT 84114-1021 | Fax      (801) 538-3354 |
| | E-mail   research@email.state.ut.us |

Guide to Archives and Manuscript Collections in Selected Utah Repositories
    [http://www.ce.ex.state.ut.us/history/utahguid.htm]
Links, Archives
    [http://www.archives.state.ut.us/referenc/archive.htm]
Links, Genealogy
    [http://www.archives.state.ut.us/referenc/genealo.htm]
Links, History
    [http://www.archives.state.ut.us/referenc/history.htm]
Links, Legal and Government
    [http://www.archives.state.ut.us/referenc/legal.htm]
Links, Library Catalogs
    [http://www.archives.state.ut.us/referenc/cats.htm]
Links, Links, Links
    [http://www.archives.state.ut.us/referenc/world.htm]
Links, Utah
    [http://www.archives.state.ut.us/referenc/utah.htm]
Reference Services
    [http://www.archives.state.ut.us/referenc/referen.htm]

# State Library

## Utah State Library                    http://www.state.lib.ut.us/

2150 South 300 West, Suite 15        Phone   (801) 468-6777
Salt Lake City, UT 84115             E-mail  dslater@inter.state.lib.us

Library Directory
    [http://www.state.lib.ut.us/pubs/pldirect/aacover.htm]
Links, Utah
    [http://www.state.lib.ut.us/resource/utah.htm]
State Documents Lists
    [http://www.state.lib.ut.us/publicat/publicat.htm]

# State Genealogical Society
*Outstanding Site*

## Genealogical Society of Utah—Family History Library
    http://www.lds.org/
    http://www.fgs.org/~fgs/soc0068.ht

35 North West Temple Street          Phone   (801) 240-2323
Salt Lake City, UT 84150                     (800) 346-6044
                                     Fax     (801) 240-1216

All Family History Centers Listed by State
    [http://www.deseretbook.com/famhis/]
All Local Chapels and Meetinghouses
    [http://www.deseretbook.com/locate/]
The Family: A Proclamation to the World
    [http://www.lds.org/Policy/Family.html]
Family History Library Research Outlines
    [file://hipp.etsu.edu/pub/genealogy/LDStext/]
How Do I Begin?
    [http://www.lds.org/Family_History/How_Do_I_Begin.html]
Welcome to the Family History Center™
    [http://www.lds.org/Welcome_to_FamHist/Welcome_to_FamHist.html]

What Is a Family History Center™?
    [http://www.lds.org/Family_History/What_is.html]
Why Family History?,
    [http://www.lds.org/Family_History/Why_Family_History.html]
Why Family History? by David Mayfield
    [http://reled.byu.edu/jsblab/why.htm]

## Utah Genealogical Association     http://www.infouga.org/

| | |
|---|---|
| P.O. Box 1144 | Phone  (888) 463-6842 |
| Salt Lake City, UT 84110-1144 | E-mail  perkes@mail.utah.uswest.net |

Overview
    [http://www.infouga.org/]

# State Historical Society

## Utah Historical Society     http://www.ce.ex.state.ut.us/history/

| | |
|---|---|
| 300 Rio Grande | Phone  (801) 533-3500 |
| Salt Lake City, UT 84110-1143 | Fax    (801) 533-3503 |
| |         (801) 533-3502 TDD |
| | E-mail  cehistry.ushs@email.state.ut.us |

Collections
    [http://www.ce.ex.state.ut.us/history/COLL.htm]
Manuscripts
    [http://www.ce.ex.state.ut.us/history/COLL.htm#Manuscript collections]
Utah Historical Quarterly, Table of Contents
    [http://www.xmission.com/~drudy/ushs/uhq.html]
Utah History Encyclopedia
    [http://eddy.media.utah.edu/medsol/UCME/UHEindex.html]

# Other State Sites

## Brigham Young University     http://www.byu.edu/newhome.html

| | |
|---|---|
| Utah Valley Regional FHC | Phone  (801) 378-6200 |
| Harold B. Lee Library, 4th floor | E-mail  diane_parkinson@byu.edu |
| Provo, UT 84601 | |

Ancestors, KBYU/PBS Series
    [http://www2.kbyu.byu.edu.ancestors/]
BYU Family History Society
    [http://reled.byu.edu/jsblab/society.htm]
Family History Centers Worldwide
    [http://www.lib.byu.edu/~uvrfhc/states.html]
Family History Technology Lab
    [http://issl.cs.byu.edu/FHiTL/homepage.html]
Utah Valley Regional Family History Center™
    [http://www.lib.byu.edu/~uvrfhc/]

## Mormon Pioneer Trail Home Page     http://www.omahafreenet.org/ofn/trails/

| | |
|---|---|
| | E-mail  dbylund@mail.unmc.edu |

Links, LDS Heritage Sites
    [http://www.omahafreenet.org/ofn/trails/]

## National Society of the Sons of Utah Pioneers　　　http://www.uvol.com/sup/

3301 East 2920 South　　　　　　　　　　　　E-mail　editor@uvol.com
Salt Lake City, UT 84109-4260

Overview
　　[http://www.uvol.com/sup/]

## Tracing Mormon Pioneers　　　http://www.vii.com/~nelsonb/pioneer.htm

Emigration Card Index
　　[http://www.vii.com/~nelsonb/pioneer.htm#europe]
Handcart Companies
　　[http://www.vii.com/~nelsonb/handcart.htm]
Mormon Emigrant Ships
　　[http://www.vii.com/~nelsonb/pioneer.htm#ships]
Pioneer Companies
　　[http://www.vii.com/~nelsonb/company.htm]
Sources for Tracing a Pioneer
　　[http://www.vii.com/~nelsonb/pioneer.htm#sources]

## University of Utah　　　http://www.utah.edu/

Martiott Library　　　　　　　　　　　Phone　(801) 581-8046
Salt Lake City, UT 84112　　　　　　　E-mail　gthompso@alexandria.lib.utah.edu

Manuscripts
　　[http://www.lib.utah.edu/spc/mss/spcmss.html]
Martiott Library
　　[http://www.lib.utah.edu/]
Special Collections Department
　　[http://www.lib.utah.edu/spc/spc.html]
Western Americana
　　[http://www.lib.utah.edu/spc/wam/division.html]

# VERMONT

## State Home Page

### State of Vermont　　　http://www.state.vt.us/

Links, Vermont Government
　　[http://www.state.vt.us/]

## State Archives

### Vermont State Archives　　　http://www.sec.state.vt.us/archives/archives.htm

Office of the Secretary of State　　　Phone　(802) 828-2308
Redstone Building　　　　　　　　　　E-mail　gsanford@sec.state.vt.us
26 Terrace Street
Montpelier, VT 05609

Mail to:
109 State Street
Montpelier, VT 05609-1103

Collections
[http://170.222.200.66/archives/archives.htm]
Notaries Public, Guide
[http://170.222.200.66/tutor/notaries/notary.htm]
Public Records Law
[http://www.sec.state.vt.us/munimo/4596/4596mun2.htm]

## State Library

| Vermont Department of Libraries | http://dol.state.vt.us/ |
|---|---|

109 State Street             Phone   (802) 828-3268
Montpelier, VT 05609-0601

Newsletter
[http://dol.state.vt.us/GOPHER_ROOT5/000000/EXEC_BRANCH_DOCS/
LIBRARIES/NEWS/]
Overview
[http://dol.state.vt.us/WWW_ROOT/000000/HTML/_VALS.HTML]
Vermont Library Directory
[http://dol.state.vt.us/gopher_root5/000000/exec_branch_docs/libraries/dir/directory.txt]

## State Historical Society

| Vermont Historical Society | http://www.cit.state.vt.us:80/vhs/ |
|---|---|

109 State Street             Phone   (802) 828-2291
Montpelier, VT 05609-0901      Fax     (802) 828-3638
                                  E-mail   Vhs@vhs.state.vt.us

Collections Guide
[http://www.cit.state.vt.us:80/vhs/libinfo.htm]
Genealogical Research in Vermont
[http://www.cit.state.vt.us:80/vhs/generes.htm]
Genealogy Researchers in Vermont
[http://www.cit.state.vt.us:80/vhs/genames.htm]
Links, Vermont
[http://www.cit.state.vt.us:80/vhs/links.htm]
Local Historical Societies
[http://www.cit.state.vt.us:80/vhs/lhs/lhsindex.htm]
Manuscripts
[http://www.cit.state.vt.us:80/vhs/msscoll.htm]
Vermont in the Civil War
[http://members.aol.com/vtcw150/vt-cw.htm]

## Other State Sites

| University of Vermont | http://moose.uvm.edu/ |
|---|---|

Special Collections Department     Phone   (802) 656-2138
Bailey Howe Library              Fax     (802) 656-4038
Burlington, VT 05405-40036      E-mail  edow@zoo.uvm.edu

Libraries
[http://sageunix.uvm.edu/]
Overview of Their Collections
[http://sageunix.uvm.edu/~sc/speccol.html]

Special Collections Department
    [http://sageunix.uvm.edu/~sc/]
Wilbur Collection of Electronic Vermontiana
    [http://sageunix.uvm.edu/~sc/vtlinks.html]

# VIRGINIA

## State Home Page

| Virginia Home Page | http://www.state.va.us/ |
|---|---|

Links, Virginia Cities and Counties
    [http://www.state.va.us/home/arolocal.html]
Office of Vital Records
    [http://www.vdh.state.va.us/misc/f_08.htm]
Virginia Institute of Government Service
    [http://www.institute.virginia.edu/]

## State Library
*Outstanding Site*

| Library of Virginia | http://leo.vsla.edu/lva/lva.html |
|---|---|

| 800 East Broad Street | Phone | (804) 692-3777 |
|---|---|---|
| Richmond, VA 23219-3491 | Fax | (804) 692-3556 |
| | E-mail | wwweb@leo.vsla.edu |

| Virginia Colonial Records Project | Phone | (804) 692-3720 |
|---|---|---|
| | E-mail | jkneebon@leo.vsla.edu |

Civil War Records
    [http://leo.vsla.edu/archives/mcivilwar.html]
County Records Guide, Pre 1865
    [http://image.vtls.com/Reel461/]
County Records Guide, Post 1865
    [http://leo.vsla.edu:80/~jgreve/]
Digital Library Initiative
    [http://leo.vsla.edu/lva/digital.html]
Guides and Finding Aids
    [http://leo.vsla.edu/research.html]
Land Office Records
    [http://leo.vsla.edu/archives/landoffice.html]
Libraries, Virginia
    [http://leo.vsla.edu:80/directory/]
Links, Genealogy
    [http://leo.vsla.edu/archives/genie.html]
Newspapers, Virginia
    [http://www.lib.virginia.edu/cataloging/vnp/sort/ind2.htm]
Preserving Family Papers
    [http://leo.vsla.edu:80/preserve/]
Repositories, Virginia
    [http://leo.vsla.edu/reposit/reposit.html]
Research Guides
    [http://leo.vsla.edu/research.html]

Virginia Colonial Records
    [http://image.vtls.com/colonial/]
Virginia Colonial Records Project
    [http://leo.vsla.edu/colonial/vcrp.html]
Virginia History, Listserv
    [http://leo.vsla.edu/listservs/vahist.html]
Virginia Newspaper Project
    [http://www.lib.virginia.edu/cataloging/vnp/home.html]
Virginia Notes, Handouts
    [http://leo.vsla.edu:80/vanotes/]
Virginia Roots, Listserv
    [http://leo.vsla.edu/colonial/vcrp.html]
Vital Records
    [http://leo.vsla.edu/archives/vital.html]

# State Genealogical Society

| Virginia Genealogical Society | http://www.fgs.org/~fgs/soc0197.htm |
|---|---|
| 5001 West Broad Street, #115<br>Richmond, VA 23230-3023 | Phone  (804) 285-8954<br>Fax     (804) 285-8954 |

Overview
    [http://www.fgs.org/~fgs/soc0197.htm]

# State Historical Society

| Virginia Historical Society | http://www.vahistorical.org/ |
|---|---|
| 428 North Boulevard<br>P.O. Box 7311<br>Richmond, VA 23221-0311 | Phone  (804) 342-9676 |

Overview
    [http://www.vahistorical.org/]

# Other State Sites

| College of William and Mary | http://www.wm.edu/ |
|---|---|
| Manuscripts and Rare Books Department<br>College of William and Mary<br>Earl Gregg Swem Library<br>P.O. Box 8794<br>Williamsburg, VA 23187-8794 | Phone  (804) 221-3091<br>E-mail  spcoll@mail.swem.wm.edu |

Special Collections Department
    [http://swem.wm.edu/spcolhp.html]
Swem Library  http://swem.wm.edu/
    [http://swem.wm.edu/]

| George Mason University | http://www.gmu.edu |
|---|---|
| Special Collections Department<br>Fenwick Library<br>Fairfax, VA 22030-4444 | Phone  (703) 993-2220<br>Fax     (703) 993-2200<br>E-mail  speccoll@osf1.gmu.edu |

Archives
[http://www.gmu.edu/library/specialcollections/archives.html]
Civil War, Virginia, Images
[http://www.gmu.edu/library/specialcollections/harper.html]
Collections
[http://www.gmu.edu/library/specialcollections/research.html]
Libraries
[http://fenweb.gmu.edu/lib/index.html]
Special Collections Department
[http://www.gmu.edu/library/specialcollections/]

## *Outstanding Site*

## James Madison University          http://www.jmu.edu/

Special Collections Department       Phone   (540) 568-3612
Carrier Library                      Fax     (540) 568-3405
Harrisonburg, VA 22807               E-mail  bolgiace@jmu.edu

African American History Guide
[http://www.jmu.edu/libliaison/millergw/afrahist.htm]
Carrier Library
[http://www.jmu.edu:80/library/]
Census Guide
[http://www.jmu.edu/libliaison/millergw/histcen.htm]
Civil War Guide
[http://www.jmu.edu/libliaison/millergw/amcivwar.htm]
Diaries Guide
[http://www.jmu.edu/libliaison/millergw/diaries.htm]
Genealogy Guide
[http://www.jmu.edu/libliaison/millergw/genology.htm]
History Guide
[http://www.jmu.edu/libliaison/millergw/histcen.htm]
JMU Bibliography
[http://www.jmu.edu/libliaison/sc/jmubibli.htm]
Manuscripts
[http://www.jmu.edu/libliaison/sc/aboutmss.htm]
Military History Guide
[http://www.jmu.edu/libliaison/millergw/milhist.htm]
Native Americans Guide
[http://www.jmu.edu/libliaison/millergw/amerin.htm]
Special Collections Department
[http://www.jmu.edu/libliaison/sc/aboutsc.htm]
Virginia Guide
[http://www.jmu.edu/libliaison/millergw/virginia.htm]
Women's Studies Guide
[http://www.jmu.edu/libliaison/prestola/wmst/wmstguid.htm]

## Mariner's Museum          http://www.mariner.org/library.html

100 Museum Drive                     Phone   (757) 596-2222
Newport News, VA 23606-3759                  (800) 581-7245
                                     E-mail  tmmlib@infi.net
Collections
[http://www.mariner.org/collections.html]

Library
    [http://www.mariner.org/library.html]

## Museum of the Confederacy       http://www.moc.org/

1201 East Clay Street                    Phone    (804) 649-1861
Richmond, VA 23219                       E-mail   library@moc.org

Collections
    [http://www.moc.org/moc-col.htm]
Newsletter
    [http://www.moc.org/moc-new.htm]

## Old Dominion University       http://www.odu.edu/

Special Collections Department           Phone    (757) 683-4178
Library                                  E-mail   userid@shakespeare.lib.odu.edu
Norfolk, VA 23529

Archives
    [http://www.lib.odu.edu/special.collections/archives/index.html]
Civil War Collection
    [http://www.lib.odu.edu/special.collections/civilwar/index.htm]
Library
    [http://www.lib.odu.edu/index.html]
Library Update, Newsletter
    [http://www.lib.odu.edu/aboutodulib/libupdate.html]
Special Collections Department
    [http://www.lib.odu.edu/special.collections/]
Virginia History
    [http://www.lib.odu.edu/special.collections/tidewater/index.html]

### *Outstanding Site*

## University of Virginia       http://www.virginia.edu/

Special Collections Department           Phone    (804) 924-3143
Alderman Library                         E-mail   mssbks@virginia.edu
Charlottesville, VA 22903-2498

Archives
    [http://www.lib.virginia.edu/speccol/uarch/uarch.html]
Cubic Foot Equivalents
    [http://www.lib.virginia.edu/speccol/uarch/recman/convert.html]
Finding Aids
    [http://www.lib.virginia.edu/speccol/guide_search.html]
McGregor Library of American History
    [http://www.lib.virginia.edu/speccol/colls/mcgregor.html]
Manuscripts Division
    [http://www.lib.virginia.edu/speccol/mss/msshome.html]
Public Records
    [http://www.lib.virginia.edu/speccol/uarch/recman/destroy.html]
Special Collections Department
    [http://www.lib.virginia.edu/speccol/]
Special Collections Digital Center
    [http://www.lib.virginia.edu/speccol/scdc/scdc.html]

# Virginia Commonwealth University Library          http://www.vcu.edu/

Special Collections Department          Phone    (804) 828-1108
James Branch Cabell Library            Fax      (804) 828-0151
901 Park Avenue                        E-mail   bpittman@gems.vcu.edu
P.O. Box 842033
Richmond, VA 23284-2033


Special Collections Department          Phone    (804) 828-9898
Tompkins-McCaw Library                 Fax      (804) 828-6089
509 North 12th Street                  E-mail   jkoste@gems.vcu.edu
P.O. Box 980582
Richmond, VA 23298-0582


African American Resources
    [http://exlibris.uls.vcu.edu/library/jbc/speccoll/vbha/vbha.html]
Black History Archives
    [http://exlibris.uls.vcu.edu/library/jbc/speccoll/vbha/vbharepo.html]
Collections Guide
    [http://exlibris.uls.vcu.edu/library/jbc/speccoll/repo/repointr.html]
Special Collections, Cabell Library
    [http://exlibris.uls.vcu.edu/library/jbc/speccoll/speccoll.html]
Special Collections, Tompkins-McCaw Library
    [http://exlibris.uls.vcu.edu/library/tml/speccoll/hmpge.html]


# Virginia Military Institute          http://www.vmi.edu/

VMI Archives                           Phone    (540) 464-7566
Preston Library                        Fax      (540) 464-7279
Lexington, VA 24450                    E-mail   jacobdb@vax.vmi.edu

Alumni, 19th Century
    [http://www.vmi.edu/~archtml/alumni.html]
Archives Department
    [http://www.vmi.edu/~archtml/index.html]
Civil War, Collection
    [http://www.vmi.edu/~archtml/cwsource.html]
Civil War, Manuscripts
    [http://www.vmi.edu/~archtml/msguide2.html]
Links, Civil War, etc.
    [http://www.vmi.edu/~archtml/cwinet.html]
Photograph Collection
    [http://www.vmi.edu/~archtml/photos.html]
VMI Bibliography
    [http://www.vmi.edu/~archtml/nmsource.html]


# Virginia Polytechnic Institute and State University
    http://www.vt.edu/

University Libraries                    Phone    (540) 231-6308
Virginia Tech                          Fax      (540) 231-9263
Blacksburg, VA 24062-9001              E-mail   gailmac@vt.edu

Appalachian History Collection
   [http://scholar2.lib.vt.edu/spec/appal/apintro.htm]
Blacksburg, Virginia, History
   [http://scholar2.lib.vt.edu/spec/specgen/Bburgguide.htm]
Civil War Collection
   [http://scholar2.lib.vt.edu/spec/civwar/cwhp.htm]
Manuscripts
   [http://scholar2.lib.vt.edu/spec/specgen/msguide/mgintro.htm]
Map Collections
   [http://scholar2.lib.vt.edu/spec/specgen/map/mapintro.htm]
Montgomery County, Virginia History
   [http://scholar2.lib.vt.edu/spec/specgen/mcintro.htm]
Oral History Collections
   [http://scholar2.lib.vt.edu/spec/specgen/oralindx.htm]
Photograph Collections
   [http://scholar2.lib.vt.edu/spec/specgen/photogph.htm]
Railroad History
   [http://scholar2.lib.vt.edu/spec/railroad/rrintro.htm]
Special Collections Department
   [http://scholar2.lib.vt.edu/spec/spechp.htm]
University Libraries
   [http://www.lib.vt.edu/]
Women in Architecture
   [http://scholar2.lib.vt.edu/spec/iawa/iawa.htm]
Women's History Research
   [http://scholar2.lib.vt.edu/spec/women/wmnunidx.htm]

## Virtual Library of Virginia        http://scholar2.lib.vt.edu/spec/viva/viv.htm

E-mail  gailmac@vt.edu

Links, Virginia Special Collections
   [http://scholar2.lib.vt.edu/spec/viva/viv.htm]
Virginia Colonial Records Project
   [http://leo.vsla.edu/colonial/vcrp.html]
Virginia Newspaper Project
   [http://www.lib.virginia.edu/cataloging/vnp/home.html]

# WASHINGTON

## State Home Page

## Home Page Washington        http://www.wa.gov/

Links, Libraries
   [http://www.wa.gov/locinfo.html#lib]
Links, Local Government and Services
   [http://www.wa.gov/locinfo.html]
Links, Washington Public Libraries Online Project
   [http://www.walib.spl.org/home.html]
State Courts
   [http://www.wa.gov/courts/home.htm]
Vital Records, State Department of Health
   [http://198.187.0.42/Topics/chs-cert.html]

# State Archives

## Archives and Records Management Division    http://www.wa.gov/sec/

East Capitol
P.O. Box 40220
Olympia, WA 98504-0220

Phone   (360) 753-5485
Fax      (360) 586-5629
E-mail   secstate@www.wa.gov,

Overview
    [http://www.wa.gov/sec/phones.htm]
Responsibilities
    [http://www.wa.gov/sec/ososdesc.htm]

# State Library

## Washington State Library    http://www.wa.gov/wsl/

415 15th Avenue S.W.
P.O. Box 42460
Olympia, WA 98504-2460

Phone   (360) 753-4024
Fax      (360) 586-2475

Overview of Services
    [http://www.wa.gov/wsl/]

# State Genealogical Society

## Washington State Genealogical Society
    http://www.thurston.com/~rmccoy/wsgshome.htm

P.O. Box 1422
Olympia, WA 98507-1422

E-mail   gmccoy@thurston.com

Overview of the WSGS
    [http://www.thurston.com/~rmccoy/wsgshome.htm]

# State Historical Society

## Washington State Historical Society    http://www.kcts.org/columbia/aboutwsh.htm

Heritage Resource Center
315 North Stadium Way
Tacoma, WA 98403

Phone   (360) 586-0219
        (360) 737-2044   Center for Columbia
                     River History
E-mail   steplile@aol.com

Columbia, Journal
    [http://www.kcts.org/columbia/index.htm]

# Other State Sites

## Clark County Genealogical Society
    http://www.worldaccess.com/NonProfitOrganizations/ccgs/

P.O. Box 2728
Vancouver, WA 98668-2728

E-mail   katschke@worldaccess.com

Overview
    [http://www.worldaccess.com/NonProfitOrganizations/ccgs/]

## Gonzaga University    http://www.gonzaga.edu/

| | |
|---|---|
| Special Collections Department | Phone   (509) 328-4220 ext. 3814 |
| Foley Center Library | Fax     (509) 324-5904 |
| Spokane, WA 99258 | E-mail  edwards@foley.gonzaga.edu |

Jesuit Oregon Province Archives         E-mail  jopa@foley.gonzaga.edu

Jesuit Oregon Province Archives
    [http://www.gonzaga.edu/foley/jopa.html]
Library
    [http://www.gonzaga.edu/foley/index.html]
Special Collections Department
    [http://www.gonzaga.edu/foley/speccoll.html]

## Seattle Municipal Archives
    http://www.pan.ci.seattle.wa.us/seattle/leg/clerk/archhome.htm

| | |
|---|---|
| 600 Fourth Avenue, Room 104 | Phone   (206) 684-8353 |
| Seattle, WA 98104 | Fax     (206) 386-9025 |
| | E-mail  scott.cline@ci.seattle.wa.us |

Archives Guide, Online
    [http://clerk.ci.seattle.wa.us/~public/ARCH1.htm]
Office of the City Clerk
    [http://www.pan.ci.seattle.wa.us/seattle/leg/clerk/clerk.htm]

## Seattle Public Library    http://www.spl.lib.wa.us/contents.html

| | |
|---|---|
| 1000 Fourth Avenue | Phone   (206) 386-4629 |
| Seattle, WA 98104 | E-mail  infospl@spl.lib.wa.us |

Genealogy Collection
    [http://www.spl.lib.wa.us/collec/geneal/genpage.html]
Seattle Collection
    [http://www.spl.lib.wa.us/collec/seattle/searoom.html]

### *Outstanding Site*

## Tacoma Public Library    http://www.tpl.lib.wa.us/

| | |
|---|---|
| 1102 Tacoma Avenue, South | Phone   (206) 591-5622 |
| Tacoma, WA  94802 | |

Genealogy
    [http://www.tpl.lib.wa.us/nwr/tplgene.htm]
Murray's People, Biography
    [http://www.tpl.lib.wa.us/nwr/people/contents.htm]
Newsletter
    [http://www.tpl.lib.wa.us/news/ntouch96.jun/intouch1.htm]
Photography Collection
    [http://www.tpl.lib.wa.us/nwr/nwphoto.htm]
Searchable Databases, Obituaries
    [http://www.tpl.lib.wa.us/nwr/obitscgi.htm]
Searchable Databases, Ships and Shipping
    [http://www.tpl.lib.wa.us/nwr/shipscgi.htm]

Searchable Databases, Unsettling Events
      [http://www.tpl.lib.wa.us/nwr/unsetng.htm]
Searchable Databases, Washington Placenames
      [http://www.tpl.lib.wa.us/nwr/placecgi.htm]
Special Collections Department
      [http://www.tpl.lib.wa.us/nwr/nwhome.htm]

## University of Washington            http://www.washington.edu/

Allen Library                          Phone   (206) 543-1929
P.O. Box 352900                        E-mail  speccoll@u.washington.edu
Seattle, WA 98195-2900

Bibliography, American History
      [http://weber.u.washington.edu/~mudrock/HISTORY/am-bib.html]
Genealogy Links
      [http://weber.u.washington.edu/~mudrock/BI/geneal.html]
History Department, Newsletter
      [http://weber.u.washington.edu/~mudrock/HISTORY/uw.html]
Libraries
      [http://www.lib.washington.edu/]
Special Collections and Preservation
      [http://www.lib.washington.edu/libinfo/libunits/suzzallo/special/]

# WEST VIRGINIA

## State Home Page

### West Virginia Home Page          http://129.71.96.11:80/DEFAULT.HTM

Links, West Virginia
      [http://access.k12.wv.us/~governor/wvlinks.html]

## State Archives

### West Virginia State Archives     http://www.wvlc.wvnet.edu/history/wvsamenu.html

Archives and History Library         Phone   (304) 558-0230
The Cultural Center
1900 Kanawha Boulevard, East
Charleston, WV 25305-0300

Archives
      [http://www.wvlc.wvnet.edu/history/wvsacoll.html]
Resources, by County
      [http://www.wvlc.wvnet.edu/history/guide2.html]
Resources, Outside West Virginia, with West Virginia Content
      [http://www.wvlc.wvnet.edu/history/reposits_not_wv/states.html]
West Virginia History, Journal, Table of Contents
      [http://www.wvlc.wvnet.edu/history/journal_wvh/journal_toc.html]
West Virginia Historical Society Quarterly, Fulltext
      [http://www.wvlc.wvnet.edu/history/wvhssoc.html]

# State Library

## West Virginia Library Commission        http://www.wvlc.wvnet.edu/

Science and Cultural Center
Charleston, WV 25305

Links, West Virginia Libraries
    [http://www.wvlc.wvnet.edu/fam_matters/libxv.html]
West Virginia History Database
    [http://www.wvlc.wvnet.edu/history/historyw.html]

# Other State Sites
*Outstanding Site*

## Allegheny Regional Family History Society
    http://www.swcp.com/~dhickman/arfhs.html

P.O. Box 1804                          E-mail  dhickman@swcp.com
Elkins, WV 26241

ARA Journal, Table of Contents
    [http://www.swcp.com/~dhickman/journal.html]
Cemeteries, Barbour County
    [http://www.swcp.com/~dhickman/bcodes.html]
Cemeteries, Randolph County
    [http://www.swcp.com/~dhickman/randcem.htm]
Census, 1850 Database
    [http://www.swcp.com/~dhickman/census/census.html]
Chenoweth Family
    [http://www.swcp.com/~dhickman/noel/noel.html]
Faded Ages, Appalachia. Fulltext
    [http://www.swcp.com/~dhickman/pubs/fadeages.html]
Hamrick, Eli "Rimfire", West Virginia Mountaineer. Fulltext.
    [http://www.swcp.com/~dhickman/pubs/rimfire.html]
Shay Family
    [http://www.swcp.com/~dhickman/shay.html]

## Marshall University        http://www.marshall.edu/

James E. Morrow Library              Phone   (304) 696-2343
Marshall University                  Fax     (304) 696-5858
Huntington, WV 25755                 E-mail  speccoll@marshall.edu

Bibliography, West Virginia
    [http://www.marshall.edu/speccoll/wv-resource.html]
Blake Library of the History of the Confederacy
    [http://www.marshall.edu/speccoll/blake.html]
Local History and Genealogy
    [http://www.marshall.edu/speccoll/title.html]

## West Virginia University        http://www.wvu.edu/

Library                              Phone   (304) 293-3536
Morgantown, WV 26506-6009            E-mail  u147f@wvnvm.wvnet.edu

Appalachian Collection
    [http://www.wvu.edu/~library/appal.htm]
Archives
    [http://www.wvu.edu/~library/wvarhc.htm#a]
Census Records
    [http://www.wvu.edu/~library/wvarhc.htm#ce]
Church Records
    [http://www.wvu.edu/~library/wvarhc.htm#ch]
County Records
    [http://www.wvu.edu/~library/wvarhc.htm#co]
West Virginia and Regional History Collection
    [http://www.wvu.edu/~library/wvarhc.htm]

# WISCONSIN

## State Home Page
### *Outstanding Site*

| Badger Wisconsin State HomePage | http://badger.state.wi.us/ |
|---|---|

| Veteran's Affairs Department | Phone | (608) 266-1311 |
| 30 West Mifflin Street | | (800) 947-8387 Wisconsin |
| Madison, WI  53707-7843 | E-mail | wdva@mail.state.wi.us |

State Veterans Cemeteries                  E-mail  tgilbert@mail.state.wi.us

Wisconsin Veterans Museum                  Phone  (608) 264-6086
                                           E-mail  museum@mail.state.wi.us

Civil War Database
    [http://badger.state.wi.us/agencies/dva/museum/hist/cwdbhist.html]
Civil War, GAR Posts
    [http://badger.state.wi.us/agencies/dva/museum/hist/garlist.html]
Civil War Regimental Histories
    [http://badger.state.wi.us/agencies/dva/museum/cwregts/reglist.html]
Links, Links, Links
    [http://badger.state.wi.us/agencies/dva/museum/wvmlinks.html]
Links, Wisconsin Cities and Counties
    [http://badger.state.wi.us:80/local.html]
Medal of Honor Recipients
    [http://badger.state.wi.us/agencies/dva/museum/hist/wwwmohbr.html]
State Statutes
    [http://badger.state.wi.us/agencies/wilis/Statutes.html]
State Veterans Cemeteries
    [http://badger.state.wi.us/agencies/dva/services/cemtmain.html]
Wisconsin County Veterans Service Offices
    [http://badger.state.wi.us/agencies/dva/museum/hist/cvsohist.html]
Wisconsin Veterans Museum
    [http://badger.state.wi.us/agencies/dva/museum/wvmmain.html]
WWII
    [http://badger.state.wi.us/agencies/dva/museum/hist/rolemain.html]

# State Archives and Historical Society

## State Historical Society of Wisconsin
http://www.wisc.edu:80/shs-archives/

| | |
|---|---|
| 816 State Street | Phone    (608) 264-6535 (Reference) |
| Madison, WI 53706 | E-mail   Virginia.Fritzsch@ccmail.adp.wisc.edu |
| | Brenda.Burk@ccmail.adp.wisc.edu |

ArCat, Online Archives Catalog
[http://www.wisc.edu:80/shs-archives/arcat.html]
Links, Wisconsin
[http://www.wisc.edu:80/shs-archives/websites.html]
Manuscripts
[http://www.wisc.edu:80/shs-archives/readroom/wiscol.html]
Wisconsin Historical Records Advisory Board
[http://www.wisc.edu:80/shs-archives/whrab/index.html]
Wisconsin State Archives
[http://www.wisc.edu:80/shs-archives/staterec/index.html]
WWII Resources
[http://www.wisc.edu:80/shs-archives/ww2guide/index.html]

# State Library

## Division for Library
http://badger.state.wi.us/agencies/dpi/dlcl/

| | |
|---|---|
| Wisconsin Department of Public Instruction | Phone    (608) 266-2127 |
| 125 South Webster Street | Fax      (608) 267-1052 |
| P.O. Box 7841 | E-mail   bocherf@mail.state.wi.us |
| Madison, WI 53707 | |

Wisconsin Library Directory
[http://badger.state.wi.us/agencies/dpi/dlcl/lib_dir.html]

# State Genealogical Society

## Wisconsin State Genealogical Society
http://www.fgs.org/~fgs/soc0203.htm

2109 Twentieth Avenue
Monroe, WI 53566

Overview
[http://www.fgs.org/~fgs/soc0203.htm]

# Other State Sites

## University of Wisconsin, Eau Claire
http://www.uwec.edu

| | |
|---|---|
| McIntyre Library | Phone    (715) 836-3873 |
| Eau Claire, WI | E-mail   lynchld@uwec.edu |

Archives
[http://www.uwec.edu/Admin/Library/archweb.html]

Local History Collection
[http://www.uwec.edu/Admin/Library/lochist.html]
Special Collections Department
[http://www.uwec.edu/Admin/Library/speccoll.html]

## *Outstanding Site*

| University of Wisconsin, Milwaukee | http://www.uwm.edu/New3/index.html |
|---|---|

| Golda Meir Library | Phone | (414) 229-4659 |
| Milwaukee, WI 53201 | E-mail | html@gml.lib.uwm.edu |

| Milwaukee Urban Archives | Phone | (414) 229-5402 |
| P.O. Box 604 | Fax | (414) 229-3605 |
| Milwaukee, WI 53201-0604 | E-mail | archives@gml.lib.uwm.edu |

African-American Collections
[http://www.uwm.edu:80/Library/arch/blacks.htm]
American Geographical Society Collection
[http://leardo.lib.uwm.edu/]
Birth Records
[http://www.uwm.edu:80/Library/arch/birth.htm]
Cemetery, Church and Synagogue Records
[http://www.uwm.edu:80/Library/arch/church.htm]
Census, Federal, State, Local
[http://www.uwm.edu:80/Library/arch/census.htm]
Change of Name Records
[http://www.uwm.edu:80/Library/arch/names.htm]
Civil War Collections
[http://www.uwm.edu:80/Library/arch/civilwar.htm]
Court, Naturalization Records
[http://www.uwm.edu:80/Library/arch/court.htm]
Death Records
[http://www.uwm.edu:80/Library/arch/death.htm]
Genealogical Records
[http://www.uwm.edu:80/Library/arch/genie.htm]
Genealogical Records, Legal Restrictions
[http://www.uwm.edu:80/Library/arch/special.htm]
German-American Records
[http://www.uwm.edu:80/Library/arch/germans.htm]
Golda Meir Library
[http://www.uwm.edu/Library/index.html]
Jewish Collections
[http://www.uwm.edu:80/Library/arch/jews.htm]
Milwaukee Urban Archives
http://www.uwm.edu:80/Library/arch/]
Waukesha County Collections
[http://www.uwm.edu:80/Library/arch/wauk.htm]
Women's History
[http://www.uwm.edu:80/Library/arch/women.htm]
WWI Collections
[http://www.uwm.edu:80/Library/arch/ww1.htm]
WWII Collections
[http://www.uwm.edu:80/Library/arch/ww2.htm]

# WYOMING

## State Home Page

Wyoming State HomePage                   http://www.state.wy.us/

Wyoming Judiciary System
  [http://courts.state.wy.us/]
Wyoming Judicial System, Overview
  [http://courts.state.wy.us/OVER.HTM]

## State Library

Wyoming State Library                    http://www-wsl.state.wy.us/

2301 Capitol Avenue                      Phone   (307) 777-7281
Cheyenne, WY 82002-0060                  Fax     (307) 777-6289

Coming Attractions, Newsletter
  [http://www-wsl.state.wy.us/slpub/index.html]
Links, Wyoming Libraries
  [http://www-wsl.state.wy.us/wyld/libraries/index.html]
Links, Wyoming Sites
  [http://www.uwyo.edu/Lib/Wyoming/index.html]
Wyoming Bibliographies
  [http://www-wsl.state.wy.us/sis/wybib.html#bib]
Wyoming State Library, Online Catalog
  [http://www-wsl.state.wy.us/wyld/index.html]

## Other State Sites

Casper College                           http://www.cc.whecn.edu/library/welcome.htm

Goodstein Foundation Library             Phone   (307) 268-2680
Casper, WY 82601                         Fax     (307) 268-2682
                                         E-mail  cspcbibman@wyld.state.wy.us

Special Collections Department
  [http://www.cc.whecn.edu/library/sc.htm]
Western Vertical File Subject Headings
  [http://www.cc.whecn.edu/library/wvfhead.htm]

## History of Johnson County
  http://www.buffalo.com/JohnsonCounty/jchist/jchistmn.htm#mainmenu

El 'n Al Enterprises                      E-mail  ASVD@worldnet.att.net
P.O. Box 62
Kaycee, WY 82639-0062

Bibliography
  [http://www.buffalo.com/JohnsonCounty/jchist/bibliog/biblio.htm#biblio]
Episodes
  [http://www.buffalo.com/JohnsonCounty/jchist/invtext.htm#text]

# University of Wyoming          http://www.uwyo.edu

American Heritage Center          Phone    (307) 766-4114
P.O. Box 3924                     Fax      (307) 766-5511
Laramie WY 82071                  E-mail   AHCRef@UWyo.edu

Albany County Historical Society
    [http://www.uwyo.edu/ahc/achs/index.htm]
American Heritage Center
    [http://www.uwyo.edu/ahc/geninfo.htm]

# INTERNATIONAL

# ALBANIA
## Albanian Research List

http://dcn.davis.ca.us/~feefhs/al/alrl.html

Joseph A. Tobia
144 Marine Street, Apartment #1
St. Augustine, FL 32084-5027

E-mail   jtobia@aug.com

Albanian Research List
[http://dcn.davis.ca.us/~feefhs/al/alrl.html]

# ARGENTINA
## National Library

http://www.bibnal.edu.ar/:_home_page.html

Aguero 2502 (1425)

Phone   806-6155

Reference Services
[http://www.bibnal.edu.ar/:_bibliographic_reference_service.html]

# ARMENIA
## Armenian Genealogical Society   http://dcn.davis.ca.us/~feefhs/am/frg-amgs.html

P.O. Box 1383
Provo, UT  84603-1383

E-mail   gfa@itsnet.com

Genealogy for Armenians
[http://dcn.davis.ca.us/~feefhs/am/gfa.html]
Overview
[http://dcn.davis.ca.us/~feefhs/am/frg-amgs.html]

# ASIA
## Council on East Asian Libraries

http://darkwing.uoregon.edu/~felsing/ceal/welcome.html

c/o East Asian Library
1100 East 57th Street
Chicago, IL 60637-1502

Phone   (312) 702-8436
Fax      (312) 702-6623
E-mail  felsing@oregon.uoregon.edu

CEAL Bulletin
[http://darkwing.uoregon.edu/~felsing/ceal/reports.html]
Links, China-Hong Kong
[http://darkwing.uoregon.edu/~felsing/hkstuff/hkshelf.html]
Links, China-Macau
[http://darkwing.uoregon.edu/~felsing/macstuff/macshelf.html]
Links, China-PRC
[http://darkwing.uoregon.edu/~felsing/cstuff/cshelf.html]
Links, China-PRC Libraries
[http://darkwing.uoregon.edu/~felsing/cstuff/clib.html]
Links, China-Taiwan
[http://darkwing.uoregon.edu/~felsing/rocstuff/rocshelf.html]
Links, China-Taiwan Libraries
[http://darkwing.uoregon.edu/~felsing/rocstuff/lib.html]

Links, East Asian Institutes and Programs
[http://darkwing.uoregon.edu/~felsing/ceal/caps.html]
Links, Japan
[http://darkwing.uoregon.edu/~felsing/jstuff/jshelf.html]
Links,  Japan Libraries
[http://darkwing.uoregon.edu/~felsing/jstuff/lib.html]
Links, Korea
[http://darkwing.uoregon.edu/~felsing/kstuff/kshelf.html]
Links, Korea Libraries
[http://darkwing.uoregon.edu/~felsing/kstuff/lib.html]
Member Libraries, Online Library Catalogs
[http://darkwing.uoregon.edu/~felsing/ceal/ceallibs.html]

# AUSTRALIA

## *Outstanding Site*

| Australian Archives | http://www.aa.gov.au/AA_WWW/AA_Home_Page.html |
| --- | --- |

| Mining Industry House | Phone | (011) +61 6 209 3633 |
| 216 Northbourne Avenue | Fax | (011) +61 6 209 3931 |
| Braddon ACT, Australia 2612 | E-mail | archives@aa.gov.au |

P.O. Box 34                          E-mail  libaa@aa.gov.au Library
Dickson ACT, Australia 2602                 ref@aa.gov.au Reference

Fact Sheets
[http://www.aa.gov.au/AA_WWW/FactSheets/FSlist.html]
Finding Aids
[gopher://aa01.aa.gov.au:70/11/Australian%20Government/The%20Australian%20Archives/
Finding%20records%20in%20the%20Australian%20Archives]
Genealogical Records
[http://www.aa.gov.au/AA_WWW/AA_Holdings/AA_Genie/Genie.html]
Genealogy Resources at Canberra
[http://www.aa.gov.au/AA_WWW/FactSheets/FS86.html]
Genealogy Resources, South Australia Office
[http://www.aa.gov.au/AA_WWW/FactSheets/FS87.html]
Holdings
[http://www.aa.gov.au/AA_WWW/AA_Holdings/AA_Holdings.html]
Library
[http://www.aa.gov.au/AA_WWW/AA_Sect_Serv/AA_Library/AA_Library.html]
Links, State and Territorial Archives
[http://www.aa.gov.au/AA_WWW/StateAs.html]
Photograph Collections
[http://www.aa.gov.au/AA_WWW/AA_Holdings/AA_Photos/Photos.html]
WWI Records
[http://www.aa.gov.au/AA_WWW/AA_Sect_Serv/AA_WW1/AA_WW1.html]

## *Outstanding Site*

| Australian Family History Compendium | http://www.cohsoft.com.au/afhc/ |
| --- | --- |

| Coherent Software Australia Pty. Ltd. | Phone | (011) + 61 3 9583 8245 |
| P.O. Box 201 | E-mail | coherent@cohsoft.com.au |
| Southland Centre, Victoria, Australia 3192 | | |

Links, Australia
[http://www.cohsoft.com.au/afhc/netrecs.html]

## Australian Society of Archivists
http://www.aa.gov.au/AA_WWW/ProAssn/ASA/ASA.html

| P.O. Box 83 | E-mail  mshapley@aa.gov.au   ACT Branch |
| O'Connor, ACT, Australia 2601 | greg.coleman@nt.gov.au |
| | Northern Territories Branch |

ACT Branch Newsletter
[http://www.aa.gov.au/AA_WWW/ProAssn/ASA/Newsletters/Newsletters.html]
ASA Listserv
[http://www.aa.gov.au/AA_WWW/ProAssn/ASA/ASAlist.html]
Directory of Australian Archives
[http://www.asap.unimelb.edu.au/asa/directory/asa_dir.htm]
Links, Australian Archives
[http://www.asap.unimelb.edu.au/asa/directory/asa_urls.htm]
Membership
[http://www.aa.gov.au/AA_WWW/ProAssn/ASA/ASA_Structure.html]

### *Outstanding Site*

## National Heritage Foundation Ltd.
http://www.ke.com.au/cgi-bin/texhtml?form=VicGold

| National and Victorian Secretariat | Phone  (011) +61 3 9603-5893 |
| Level 1, 295 Queen Street | Fax    (011) +61 3 9603-5891 |
| Melbourne, Victoria, Australia 3000 | |

# AUSTRALIAN CAPITOL TERRITORY
## Archives
gopher://aa01.aa.gov.au:70/11/State%20and%20Territory/Australian%20Capital%20
Territory%20Archives

| G.P.O. Box 158 | Phone  (011) +61 6 207 5921 |
| Canberra, ACT, Australia 2601 | Fax    (011) +61 6 207 5800 |

Overview
[gopher://aa01.aa.gov.au:70/11/State%20and%20Territory/Australian%20Capital%20
Territory%20Archives]

# NEW SOUTH WALES
## Archival Authority of New South Wales     http://www.records.nsw.gov.au/

| Level 3, 66 Harrington Street | Phone  (011) +61 2 9237 0200 |
| Sydney, NSW, Australia 2000 | Fax    (011) +61 2 9237 0142 |
| | E-mail  ceoaansw@records.nsw.gov.au |

Archives Authority of NSW
[http://www.records.nsw.gov.au/]
Concise Guide to the Archives, 2nd Edition
[http://www.records.nsw.gov.au/cguide/httoc.htm]

For the Record, Newsletter
[http://www.records.nsw.gov.au/ftr.htm]
Links, Australian Sites
[http://www.records.nsw.gov.au/othrlnks.htm]
Regional Repositories
[http://www.records.nsw.gov.au/access.htm#regional]

# NORTHERN TERRITORY
## Northern Territory Archives Service
gopher://aa01.aa.gov.au:70/11/State%20and%20Territory/Northern%20Territory%20
Archives%20Service

| Old Law Faculty Building | Phone | (011) +61 89 895188 |
| Northern Territory University | Fax | (011) +61 89 411458 |
| Myilly Point Campus | | |
| Kahlin Avenue, Darwin | | |

Mail to:
G.P.O. Box 874
Darwin, NT, Australia  0801

Overview
[gopher://aa01.aa.gov.au:70/11/State%20and%20Territory/Northern%20Territory%20
Archives%20Service]

# QUEENSLAND
## Queensland State Archives
gopher://aa01.aa.gov.au:70/11/State%20and%20Territory/Queensland%20State%20Archives

| 435 Compton Road | Phone | (011) +61 7  875 8755 |
| Runcorn, Queensland, Australia 4113 | Fax | (011) +61 7  875 8764 |

Mail to:
P.O. Box 1397
Sunnybank Hills, Queensland, Australia  4109

Reference Services
[gopher://aa01.aa.gov.au:70/00/State%20and%20Territory/Queensland%20State%20
Archives/Reference%20Services]

# TASMANIA
## Archives Office of Tasmania     http://www.tased.edu.au/cultural/archives/archives.htm

| 77 Murray Street | Phone | (011) +61 3  62337488 |
| Hobart, Tasmania, Australia 7000 | E-mail | aot-mail@ecc.tased.edu.au |

Collections
[http://www.tased.edu.au/cultural/archives/refguide.htm]
Finding Aids
[http://www.tased.edu.au/cultural/archives/records.htm]
Indexes
[http://www.tased.edu.au/cultural/archives/refguide.htm#Card Indexes]

# VICTORIA

*Outstanding Site*

| Victoria, Public Records Office | http://www.vicnet.net.au/~provic/ |
|---|---|

| P.O. Box 1156<br>South Melbourne, Victoria, Australia 3205 | Phone   (011) +61 3  9369 3244<br>E-mail  lavpro@vicnet.net.au |
|---|---|

Adoption Records
  [http://www.vicnet.net.au/~provic/2-4-4.htm]
Divorce Records
  [http://www.vicnet.net.au/~provic/2-4-3.htm]
Genealogy Sources
  [http://www.vicnet.net.au/~provic/2-5.htm]
Holdings and Finding Aids
  [http://www.vicnet.net.au/~provic/hold-aid.htm]
Immigration Indexing Project
  [http://www.vicnet.net.au/~provic/6-1.htm]
Immigration Records
  [http://www.vicnet.net.au/~provic/2-4-5.htm]
Indexing Projects Register
  http://www.vicnet.net.au/~provic/6-2.htm]
Newsletters, Fulltext
  [http://www.vicnet.net.au/~provic/nletter.htm]

## Victorian GUM (Genealogists Using Microcomputers) Inc.
  http://www.vicgum.asn.au/

| 252 Swanston Street<br>Melbourne, Victoria, Australia 3000 | Phone   (011) +61 3 9597 0208<br>E-mail  info@vicgum.asn.au |
|---|---|

Newsletter
  [http://www.vicgum.asn.au/gumnews.html]

# WESTERN AUSTRALIA

| Public Records Office | http://www.liswa.wa.gov.au/archives.html |
|---|---|

| LISWA<br>Alexander Library Building<br>Perth Cultural Centre<br>Perth, Western Australia, Australia 6000 | Phone   (011) +61 9 427 3360 |
|---|---|

Reference Services
  [http://www.liswa.wa.gov.au/archref.html]

# AUSTRIA

| Austrian National Library | http://www.onb.ac.at/ |
|---|---|

| Josefsplatz 1<br>Postfach 308<br>A-1015 Vienna, Austria | Phone   (011) +43 1 534 10<br>Fax      (011) +43 1 534 10 x280<br>E-mail  onb@email.onb.ac.at |
|---|---|

Archives
  [http://www.onb.ac.at/hschrs.htm]

# BAHAMAS
## Public Records Office, Bahamas
http://flamingo.bahamas.net.bs/clients/community/archives/

| | |
|---|---|
| P.O. Box SS-6341<br>Nassau, Bahamas | Phone   (809) 393-2175<br>Fax      (809) 393-2855<br>E-mail  archives@bahamas.net.bs |

Overview
[http://flamingo.bahamas.net.bs/clients/community/archives/]

# BELGIUM
## Genealogy in Belgium               http://win-www.uia.ac.be/u/pavp/genbel.html

Belgische Federatie voor Genealogie en Heraldiek and
   the Fédération Généalogique et Héraldique de Belgique
   [http://win-www.uia.ac.be/u/pavp/bfgh.html]
Office Généalogique et Héraldique de Belgique
   [http://win-www.uia.ac.be/u/pavp/oghb.html]
Service de Centralisation des Études Généalogiques et Démographiques de Belgique
   [http://win-www.uia.ac.be/u/pavp/scgd.html]
Vlaamse Vereniging voor Familiekunde
   [http://win-www.uia.ac.be/u/pavp/vvf.html]

## National State Archives
http://arch.arch.be/
http://pucky.uia.ac.be/~janssen/genealogy/arch.html#NAT

| | |
|---|---|
| Ruisbroekstraat 2-10<br>B-1000 Brussels, Belgium | Phone   (011) +32 2 513 76 80<br>Fax      (011) +32 2 513 76  81 |

Archives in Belgium
   [http://arch.arch.be/CONTENTS.HTML]

## Royal Library Albert I Library      http://www.kbr.be/

| | |
|---|---|
| 4 blvd. de l'Empereur<br>1000 Brussels, Belgium | Phone   (011) +32 2 519 57 01<br>Fax      (011) +32 2 519 57 16<br>E-mail  vdpijpen@kbr.be |

Overview
   [http://www.kbr.be/eng/index.html]

# BOLIVIA
## Archives and National Library of Bolivia
http://www.uasb.nch.edu.bo/anb/homepage.html

|  |  |
|---|---|
| | E-mail  director@abnb.nch.edu.bo |

Overview
   [http://www.uasb.nch.edu.bo/anb/homepage.html]

# BOSNIA
BosNet  http://www.bosnet.org/

E-mail  albert@infobahnos.com

Bosnian Ingathering Manuscript Program
[http://www.applicom.com/manu/ingather.htm]


# BRAZIL
## National Archives of Brazil  http://www.mj.gov.br/an/an.htm

R. Azeredo Coutinho, 77          Phone   (011) +55  21 232-4564
Centro                           Fax     (011) +55  21 232-8430
CEP 20.230-170
Rio de Janeiro,  RJ, Brazil

Collection Guides
    [http://www.mj.gov.br/an/anfun.htm]
Databases
    [http://www.mj.gov.br/an/anbases.htm]
Links, Brazilian and World Archives, Libraries
    [http://www.mj.gov.br/an/anoutros.htm]

## National Museum of History  http://www.visualnet.com.br/mhn/mi-home.htm

Praça Marechal Âncora -          Phone   (011) + 55 21 240-2092
    Near to Praça XV             Fax     (011) + 55 21 220-6290
20.021-200                       E-mail  aguedes@visualnet.com.br
Rio de Janeiro, RJ, Brazil

Collections
    [http://www.visualnet.com.br/mhn/mi-m-100.htm]
Library and Archives
    [http://www.visualnet.com.br/mhn/mi-m-1.htm]


# BULGARIA
## St. Cyrill and St. Methodius National Library of Bulgaria
    http://portico.bl.uk/gabriel/en/countries/bulgaria.html#coll

88 Vassil Levski Boulevard       Phone   (011) +359 2 882 811
1504 Sofia, Bulgaria             Fax     (011) +359 2 435 495

Overview
    [http://portico.bl.uk/gabriel/en/countries/bulgaria.html#coll]


# CANADA
## Association of Canadian Archivists  http://www.archives.ca/aca/

P.O. Box 2596, Station D          E-mail  ltardif@magmacom.com
Ottawa, Ontario, Canada K1P 5W6

Archivaria, Journal
      [http://www.archives.ca/aca/Publications/Archivaria/index.html]
Overview
      [http://www.archives.ca/aca/]

## Canadian Council of Archives            http://www.CdnCouncilArchives.ca/

| | |
|---|---|
| 344 Wellington Street | Phone    (613) 996-6445 |
| Ottawa, Ontario, Canada K1A 0N3 | Fax      (613) 947-6662 |
| | E-mail   Webmaster@CdnCouncilArchives.ca |

Canadian Archival Information Network
      [http://www.CdnCouncilArchives.ca/cain.html]
CCA Bulletin , Fulltext
      [http://www.CdnCouncilArchives.ca/news_e.html]
Links, Provincial Archives and Associations
      [http://www.CdnCouncilArchives.ca/councils.html]

*Outstanding Site*

## National Archives of Canada          http://www.archives.ca/index.html

| | |
|---|---|
| Genealogy Unit | Phone    (613) 996-7458 |
| Researcher Services Division | Fax      (613) 995-6274 |
| 395 Wellington Street | |
| Ottawa, Ontario, Canada K1A 0N3 | |

Archives, Quebec
      [http://www.archives.ca/www/sourcesanq.html]
Archives, Provincial
      [http://www.archives.ca/www/OtherSources.html#Provincial/Territorial Archives]
Genealogical Societies
      [http://www.archives.ca/www/OtherSources.html]
Genealogy
      [http://www.archives.ca/www/Genealogy.html]
Genealogy Sources in Canada
      [http://www.archives.ca/www/GenealogicalSources.html]
Immigration Records
      [http://www.archives.ca/www/ImmigrationRecords.html]
Military Records
      [http://www.archives.ca/www/PersonnelRecords.html]
Probate Records
      [http://www.archives.ca/www/WillsEstates.html]
Vital, Civil Registration
      [http://www.archives.ca/www/BMDRecords.html]
WWI, Canadian Expeditionary Force
      [http://www.archives.ca/db/cef/index.html]

## National Library of Canada          http://www.nlc-bnc.ca/ehome.htm

| | |
|---|---|
| 395 Wellington Street | Phone   (613) 996-5278 |
| Ottawa, Ontario, Canada K1A 0N4 | Fax      (613) 943-1112 |
| | E-mail   reference@nlc-bnc.ca |

Canadiana, National Bibliography
      [http://www.nlc-bnc.ca/pubs/cndiana/ecndian1.htm]

Digital Projects
    [http://www.nlc-bnc.ca/digiproj/edigiact.htm]
Genealogy Services
    [http://www.nlc-bnc.ca/services/egnlogy.htm]
Links, Genealogy
    [http://www.nlc-bnc.ca/services/egnlogy.htm#useful sites]
Links, Libraries, Canadian
    [http://www.nlc-bnc.ca/canlib/eindex.htm]
Women's History, Canadian
    [http://www.nlc-bnc.ca/digiproj/women/ewomen4.htm]

## United Church of Canada        http://www.interchange.ubc.ca/bstewart/

| | |
|---|---|
| BC Conference Archives | Phone    (604) 822-9589 |
| 6000 Iona Drive | Fax       (604) 822-9212 |
| Vancouver, BC, Canada V6T 1L4 | E-mail  bstewart@unixg.ubc.ca |

Holdings
    [http://www.interchange.ubc.ca/bstewart/page2.html]
Links, United Church Clergy
    [http://www.kanservu.ca/%7efairchild/united/uccmail/maildir.html#Sindex]
Online Search
    [http://library.ubc.ca/WWW.0.archbc/view+GRoup+code=UCCBC]

# ALBERTA
## Archives Society of Alberta        http://www.glenbow.org/asa/home.htm

| | |
|---|---|
| P.O. Box 21080 | E-mail  glenbow@glenbow.org |
| Dominion Postal Outlet | |
| Calgary, Alberta, Canada T2P 4H5 | |

Archives Network of Alberta Database
    [http://www.glenbow.org/asa/general/database.htm]
Links, Alberta Archives
    [http://www.glenbow.org/asa/general/database.htm]
Links, Archives, Canadian
    [http://www.glenbow.org/asa/general/database.htm]
Newsletter
    [http://www.glenbow.org/asa/newslet/welcome.htm]

# BRITISH COLUMBIA
## Archives Association of British Columbia
    http://www.harbour.com/AABC/index.html

| | |
|---|---|
| P.O. Box 78530 | E-mail  craig_neelands@sfu.ca |
| University Post Office | |
| Vancouver, BC, Canada V6T 1Z4 | |

Guide, British Columbia Archives
    [http://www.harbour.com/AABC/bcguide.html]
Guide, British Columbia Archives, Holdings Union List
    [http://www.harbour.com/AABC/bcaul.html]

Links, British Columbia Archives
[http://www.harbour.com/AABC/archweb.html]
Newsletter
[http://www.harbour.com/AABC/nl-features.html]

## British Columbia Archives    http://www.bcarchives.gov.bc.ca/index.htm

655 Belleville Street                    Phone   (250) 387-1952
Victoria, BC, Canada V8V 1X4             Fax     (250) 387-2072
                                         E-mail  access@www.bcarchives.gov.bc.ca
Mail to:
865 Yates Street
Victoria, BC, Canada V8V 1X4

Archives Directory, British Columbia, Local
[http://www.harbour.com/AABC/bcguide.html]
Guides
[gopher://gopher.bcars.gs.gov.bc.ca/1application/uwi_directory%3b%20item%3d%22
guides%22]
Library Online Catalog
[http://www.bcarchives.gov.bc.ca/library/general/library.htm]
Newspapers
[http://www.bcarchives.gov.bc.ca/library/newspapr/newspapr.htm]
Vital Records, Online Index
[http://www2.bcarchives.gov.bc.ca/textual/governmt/vstats/v_events.htm]

## British Columbia History Internet/World-Wide Web Page
http://www.freenet.victoria.bc.ca/bchistory.html

                                    E-mail   mattison@freenet.victoria.bc.ca

Links, British Columbia and Canadian History Sites
[http://www.freenet.victoria.bc.ca/bchistory.html]

## British Columbia Vital Statistics Agency
http://www.hlth.gov.bc.ca/vs/index.html

818 Fort Street                          Phone   (250) 952-2681
Victoria, BC, Canada V8W 1H8             Fax     (250) 952-2527

Adoption Records
[http://www.hlth.gov.bc.ca/vs/adoption/]
Birth Records
[http://www.hlth.gov.bc.ca/vs/births/]
Death Records
[http://www.hlth.gov.bc.ca/vs/death/]
Marriage Records
[http://www.hlth.gov.bc.ca/vs/marriage/]
Probate Records
[http://www.hlth.gov.bc.ca/vs/wills/]

## Vancouver City Archives
http://www.city.vancouver.bc.ca/ctyclerk/archives/index.html

British Columbia, Canada                 Phone   (604) 736-8561
1150 Chestnut Street                     Fax     (604) 736-0626
Vancouver, BC, Canada V6J 3J9            E-mail  sue_bigelow@city.vancouver.bc.ca

Genealogy Guide
   [http://www.city.vancouver.bc.ca/ctyclerk/archives/g_geneal.html]

## Vancouver Public Library       http://www.vpl.vancouver.bc.ca/home.html

Special Collections, 7th level        Phone   (604) 331-3780
Vancouver Public Library Central Branch   E-mail   webmaster@vpl.vancouver.bc.ca
350 West Georgia Street
Vancouver, BC, Canada V6B 6B1

Collections
   [http://www.vpl.vancouver.bc.ca/branches/LibrarySquare/spe/home.html#Collections]
Indexes
   [http://www.vpl.vancouver.bc.ca/branches/LibrarySquare/spe/home.html#Indexes]
Special Collections Department
   [http://www.vpl.vancouver.bc.ca/branches/LibrarySquare/spe/home.html#Indexes]

## Victoria City Archives       http://www.city.victoria.bc.ca/archives/index.htm

#1 Centennial Square        Phone   (250) 361-0375
Victoria, BC, Canada V8W 1P6    Fax     (250) 361-0394
                            E-mail   careyp@ch.city.victoria.bc.ca

Genealogical Records
   [http://www.city.victoria.bc.ca/archives/genogy.htm]
House Research
   [http://www.city.victoria.bc.ca/archives/house.htm]
Land Records
   [http://www.city.victoria.bc.ca/archives/land.htm]
Photographs
   [http://www.city.victoria.bc.ca/archives/photos.htm]

# MANITOBA
## Association for Manitoba Archives       http://slis6000.slis.uwo.ca/~rlavergn/

P.O. Box 26005              Phone   (204) 942-3491
Westminster Post Office     Fax     (204) 942-3492
Winnipeg, Manitoba, Canada R3C 4K9   E-mail   archsgm@mts.net

Directory, AMA Membership
   [http://slis6000.slis.uwo.ca/~rlavergn/direc.html]

## Provincial Archives of Manitoba       http://www.gov.mb.ca/chc/archives/index.html

200 Vaughan Street          Phone   (204) 945-3971
Winnipeg, Manitoba, Canada R3C 1T5   Fax     (204) 948-2008
                            E-mail   pam@chc.gov.mb.ca

Collection Guides
   [http://www.gov.mb.ca/chc/archives/accessguide/index.html]
The Hudson's Bay Company Archives
   [http://www.gov.mb.ca/chc/archives/hbca/index.html]

# NEW BRUNSWICK

## Council of Archives New Brunswick　　http://moondog.usask.ca/cca/index.html

| P.O. Box 6000 | Phone | (506) 453-2122 |
| Fredericton, NB, Canada E3B 5H | Fax | (506) 453-3288 |

Directory, Membership
[http://moondog.usask.ca/cca/nbmem.html]

## Provincial Archives of New Brunswick
http://www.gov.nb.ca/supply/archives/index.htm

| P.O. Box 6000 | Phone | (506) 453-2122 |
| Fredericton, NB, Canada E3B 5H1 | Fax | (506) 453-3288 |

Climbing Your Family Tree
[http://www.gov.nb.ca/supply/archives/climbing.htm]
Links, Archival
[http://www.gov.nb.ca/supply/archives/links.htm]

# NEWFOUNDLAND AND LABRADOR

## Association of Newfoundland and Labrador Archives
http://www.infonet.st-johns.nf.ca/providers/anla/anlahome.html

| Colonial Building | Phone | (709) 726-2867 |
| Military Road | Fax | (709) 729-2222 |
| St. John's, Newfoundland, Canada A1C 1C4 | | |

Directory, Membership
[http://www.infonet.st-johns.nf.ca/providers/anla/direct.html]

## Newfoundland and Labrador Genealogical Society Inc.
http://www.infonet.st-johns.nf.ca/providers/anla/direct/nfld_gen.html

| Baird Building Room 421 | Phone | (709) 754-9525 |
| 354 Water Street | E-mail | ajackman@ucs.morgan.ucs.mun.ca |
| St. John's, Newfoundland, Canada | | |

Mail to:
Colonial Building
Military Road
St. John's, Newfoundland, Canada A1C 2C9

Overview
[http://www.infonet.st-johns.nf.ca/providers/anla/direct/nfld_gen.html]

## Newfoundland and Labrador Home Page　　http://www.gov.nf.ca/

| Vital Statistics | Phone | (709) 729-3311 |
| P.O. Box 8700 | Fax | (709) 729-0946 |
| St. John's, Newfoundland, Canada A1B 4J6 | | |

Vital Records
   [http://www.gov.nf.ca/health/policy/vitalst.htm]

## Provincial Archives of Newfoundland and Labrador
   http://www.gov.nf.ca/tcr/cultural/archives.htm

| | |
|---|---|
| Colonial Building | Phone (709) 729-3065 |
| Military Road | Fax (709) 729-0578 |
| St. John's, Newfoundland, Canada A1C 2C9 | E-mail INFO@GOV.NF.CA |

Introduction
   [http://www.infonet.st-johns.nf.ca/providers/anla/direct/panl.html]
Overview
   [http://www.gov.nf.ca/tcr/cultural/archives.htm]

# NORTHWEST TERRITORIES
## Northwest Territories Archives          http://tailpipe.learnnet.nt.ca/pwnhc/nwta.htm

| | |
|---|---|
| Prince of Wales Northern Heritage Centre | Phone (403) 873-7698 |
| Yellowknife, Northwest Territories, | E-mail nwtarchives@ece.learnnet.nt.ca |
|    Canada Z1Z 1Z1 | |

Collections
   [http://tailpipe.learnnet.nt.ca/pwnhc/collect.htm]

# NOVA SCOTIA
## Council of Nova Scotia Archives          http://fox.nstn.ca/~cnsa

| | |
|---|---|
| 6016 University Avenue | Phone (902) 424-7093 |
| Halifax, Nova Scotia, Canada 3H 1W4 | Fax (902) 424-0628 |
| | E-mail cnsa@fox.nstn.ca |

Links and Membership Directory
   [http://Fox.nstn.ca:80/~cnsa/director.html]
Links, Archival, Canada & Beyond
   [http://Fox.nstn.ca:80/~cnsa/councils.html]
Newsletter. Fulltext
   [http://Fox.nstn.ca:80/~cnsa/newslett.html]
Overview
   [http://Fox.nstn.ca:80/~cnsa/]

# ONTARIO
## Archives Association of Ontario          http://www.fis.utoronto.ca/groups/aao/

| | |
|---|---|
| 444 Yonge Street | Phone (905) 792-1173 |
| P.O. Box 46009 | Fax (905) 792-2530 |
| College Park Post Office | E-mail dubeau@fis.utoronto.ca |
| Toronto, Ontario, Canada M5B 2L8 | teeple@fis.utoronto.ca |

Overview
   [http://www.fis.utoronto.ca/groups/aao/whowhat.htm]

## Ontario Government Website    http://www.gov.on.ca/MBS/english/index.html

| Archives of Ontario | Phone | (416) 327-1582 |
| 77 Grenville Street, Unit 300 | Fax | (416) 327-1999 |
| Toronto, Ontario, Canada M5S 1B3 | E-mail | sommerc@archives.gov.on.ca |

| Office of the Registrar General | Phone | (807) 343-7420 |
| 189 Red River Road | | (800) 461-2156 in Ontario |
| P.O. Box 4600 | | |
| Thunder Bay, Ontario, Canada   P7B 6L8 | | |

Archives of Ontario
   [http://www.gov.on.ca/MCZCR/archives/index.html]
Genealogy Holdings
   [http://www.gov.on.ca/MCZCR/archives/english/genmajor.htm]
Native Peoples
   [http://www.gov.on.ca/MCZCR/archives/aborige/aborige.htm]
Ontario Library Service
   [http://www.library.on.ca/index.html]
Registrar General
   [http://www.gov.on.ca/MBS/english/faq/CCR0935.html]
Vital, Civil Registration
   [http://www.gov.on.ca/MBS/english/programs/CCR0451.html]
Vital Records
   [http://www.gov.on.ca/MCZCR/archives/english/vsbule.htm]
Vital Records, Indexes
   [http://www.gov.on.ca/MCZCR/archives/english/rg80expe.htm]

# PRINCE EDWARD ISLAND
## The Island Register          http://www.isn.net/~dhunter/index.html

E-mail  dhunter@isn.net

Links, Prince Edward Island Genealogy
   [http://www.isn.net/~dhunter/index.html]
Prince Edward Island Genealogical Society
   [http://www.isn.net/~dhunter/peigs.html]

## Prince Edward Island Provincial Archives
   http://www.gov.pe.ca/educ/archives/archives_index.html

| Hon. George Coles Building | Phone | (902) 368-4290 |
| Box 1000, Richmond Street | Fax | (902) 368-4227 |
| Charlottetown, PEI, Canada C1A 7N4 | E-mail | genealogy@gov.pe.ca |

Genealogical Records
   [http://www.gov.pe.ca/educ/archives/research/research.html]
Tracing Your Family Tree on Prince Edward Island
   [http://www.gov.pe.ca/educ/archives/fam_history/fam_history.html]
Vital Records
   [http://www.gov.pe.ca/educ/archives/research/births.html]

## Provincial Library of Prince Edward Island
http://www.gov.pe.ca/educ/library/index.html

| | |
|---|---|
| P.O. Box 7500 | Phone   (902) 368-4631 |
| Charlottetown, PEI Canada C1A 8T8 | |

Directory, PEI Libraries
[http://www.gov.pe.ca/educ/library/index.html]

# QUEBEC
## Federation of Quebec Genealogical Societies
http://www.gouv.qc.ca/francais/minorg/mccq/dpm/organis/fqsg/fqsg.htm

| | |
|---|---|
| C.P. 9454 | Phone   (418) 653-3940 |
| Sainte-Foy, Québec, Canada G1V 4B8 | |

Directory of Member Societies
[http://www.gouv.qc.ca/francais/minorg/mccq/dpm/organis/fqsg/fqsg4.htm]

## French Speaking Archives                http://tornade.ERE.UMontreal.CA:80/~boughidk/

E-mail  boughidk@ere.umontreal.ca

Links, Genealogical and Historical for French Speaking Canada
[http://tornade.ERE.UMontreal.CA:80/~boughidk/nat_prov.htm]

## Quebec Association of Archivists          http://www.archives.ca/AAQ/

| | |
|---|---|
| C.P. 423 | Phone   (418) 652-2357 |
| Sillery, Québec, Canada G1T 2R8 | Fax     (418) 646-0868 |
| | E-mail  aaq@microtec.net |

Overview
[http://www.archives.ca/AAQ/]

## Quebec National Archives              http://www.cgocable.ca/archives/index.htm

| | |
|---|---|
| 3930, rue Louis-Pinard suite 201 | Phone   (819) 691-2597 |
| Trois-Rivières, Québec, Canada G9A 2G7 | Fax     (819) 691-2597 |
| | E-mail  anq@mccq.gouv.qc.ca |

Collections
[http://www.cgocable.ca/archives/fonds.htm]
Directory
[http://www.cgocable.ca/archives/centres.htm]

# SASKATCHEWAN
## Saskatchewan Council on Archives       http://www.usask.ca/archives/sca.html

P.O. Box 22041
Regina, Saskatchewan, Canada S4S 7G7

Directory, Membership
[http://www.usask.ca/archives/memb.html]

## University of Saskatchewan                http://www.usask.ca

301 Murray Building                          Phone    (306) 966 6028
3 Campus Drive                               Fax      (306) 966 6040
Saskatoon, Saskatchewan, Canada S7N 5A4      E-mail   archref@sklib.usask.ca

Archives
    [http://www.usask.ca/archives/]
Archives, Database
    [http://www.usask.ca/archives/uskarch.html]
Links, Canadian Archival Resources
    [http://www.usask.ca/archives/menu.html]
Photograph Collections
    [http://www.usask.ca/archives/photo.html]

# YUKON
## Yukon Council of Archives        http://moondog.usask.ca/cca/yuk1.html

P.O. Box 6053
Whitehorse, Yukon, Canada Y1A 5L7

Overview
    [http://moondog.usask.ca/cca/yuk1.html]

# CARIBBEAN
## Caribbean Genealogy and History    http://members.aol.com/GHCaraibe/index.html

Pavillon 23, 12 Avenue Charles de Gaulle     E-mail   GHCaraibe@aol.com
78230 La Pecq, France

Guadeloupe
    [http://members.aol.com/GHCaraibe/geo/geoguad1.html]
Guyane
    [http://members.aol.com/GHCaraibe/geo/geoguya1.html]
Martinique
    [http://members.aol.com/GHCaraibe/geo/geomart1.html]
Publications
    [http://members.aol.com/GHCaraibe/pub/pubbula.html]
Saint-Pierre et Miquelon
    [http://members.aol.com/GHCaraibe/geo/geospmi1.html]

# CHILE
## National Archives of Chile        http://www.dibam.renib.cl/isc145.html

Miraflores # 50                              Phone    (011) +562 633 89 57 x258
Santiago, Chile                              E-mail   egonzale@oris.renib.cl

Archivo Siglo XX                             Phone    (011) +562 681 79 79
Agustinas # 3250
Santiago, Chile

Collections
[http://www.dibam.renib.cl:80/ISC366]

## National Library of Chile        http://www.dibam.renib.cl:80/ISC137

Av. Bernardo OíHiggins 651          Phone  (011) +562  633 89 57 x227
Santiago, Chile                     E-mail  egonzale@oris.renib.cl

Libraries
[http://www.renib.cl:80/miembros.html]
Links, Public Libraries
[http://www.dibam.renib.cl:80/ISC146]

# CHINA
## CALA, Chinese American Librarians Association

Diana Shih, CALA                    Phone  (212) 769-5413
American Museum of Natural History
Central Park West at 79th Street
New York, NY 10024-5192

Chapters
[http://www.lib.siu.edu/swen/cala/calachap.htm]

## Chinese Historical Society of America
http://www.sirius.com/~tedwong/CHSA/chsa_p1.html

650 Commercial Street               Phone  (415) 391-1188
San Francisco, CA 94111

Chinese America: History and Perspectives, Journal, Table of Contents, Volume 1- .
[http://www.sirius.com/~tedwong/CHSA/research_sources/CAHPp2.html]
Early Chinese Emigrants
[http://www.sirius.com/~tedwong/CHSA/research_sources/syllabus/syllabus_contents_1.html]
History of the Chinese in California: A Syllabus
[http://www.sirius.com/~tedwong/CHSA/research_sources/syllabus.html]
Resources
[http://www.sirius.com/~tedwong/CHSA/research_sources.html]

## Council on East Asian Libraries
http://darkwing.uoregon.edu/~felsing/ceal/welcome.html

c/o East Asian Library              Phone  (312) 702-8436
1100 East 57th Street               Fax    (312) 702-6623
Chicago, IL 60637-1502              E-mail  felsing@oregon.uoregon.edu

CEAL Bulletin
[http://darkwing.uoregon.edu/~felsing/ceal/reports.html]
Links, China-Hong Kong
[http://darkwing.uoregon.edu/~felsing/hkstuff/hkshelf.html]
Links, China-Macau
[http://darkwing.uoregon.edu/~felsing/macstuff/macshelf.html]
Links, China-PRC
[http://darkwing.uoregon.edu/~felsing/cstuff/cshelf.html]

Links, China-PRC Libraries
　　[http://darkwing.uoregon.edu/~felsing/cstuff/clib.html]
Links, China-Taiwan
　　[http://darkwing.uoregon.edu/~felsing/rocstuff/rocshelf.html]
Links, China-Taiwan Libraries
　　[http://darkwing.uoregon.edu/~felsing/rocstuff/lib.html]
Links, East Asian Institutes and Programs
　　[http://darkwing.uoregon.edu/~felsing/ceal/caps.html]
Member Libraries, Online Library Catalogs
　　[http://darkwing.uoregon.edu/~felsing/ceal/ceallibs.html]
Non-Western Name Conventions
　　[gopher://liberty.uc.wlu.edu/00/library/human/eashum/nameconv]

## Hong Kong Library Association
http://www.hk.super.net/~hkla/

P.O. Box 10095　　　　　　　　　　　　E-mail　prehkla@hk.super.net
General Post Office
Hong Kong, China

Newsletter
　　[http://www.hk.super.net/~hkla/news0297.html]

## Internet Chinese Librarians Club
http://www.lib.siu.edu/swen/iclc/index.htm

E-mail　shwen@siu.edu

Chinese Librarianship, an International Electronic Journal
　　[http://www.lib.siu.edu/swen/iclc/clej.htm]
Library and Information Science Research, Online Journal
　　[http://www.lib.siu.edu/swen/iclc/lisr.htm]
Links, China, Online Library Catalogs
　　[http://www.lib.siu.edu/swen/iclc/libcat.htm]
Reference Services
　　[http://www.lib.siu.edu/swen/iclc/chinref.htm]

# CROATIA

## Croatia Genealogy Home Page
http://dcn.davis.ca.us/~feefhs/cro/frg-hr.html

P.O. Box 4327　　　　　　　　　　　　E-mail　feefhs@feefhs.org
Davis, CA 95617-4327

Croatian Place Names
　　[http://dcn.davis.ca.us/~feefhs/cro/crotowns.html]
Croatian Research at the FHL by Thomas K. Edlund
　　[http://dcn.davis.ca.us/~feefhs/frl/cro/edlund1.html]

## Croatian Genealogical and Historical Society
http://dcn.davis.ca.us/~feefhs/cro/frg-cghs.html

2527 San Carlos Avenue　　　　　　　Phone　(415) 592-1190
San Carlos, CA 94070-1747　　　　　　E-mail　croatians@aol.com

Guide to Croatian Genealogy
　　[http://dcn.davis.ca.us/~feefhs/cro/cghs-gcg.html]

# CUBA
## Cuban Genealogical Resources
http://ourworld.compuserve.com/homepages/ee/

E-mail  ee@acm.org

Cuban Genealogical Society, Revista. Index
[http://ourworld.compuserve.com/homepages/ee/Revista.htm]
Index to "Historia de Familias Cubanas"
[http://ourworld.compuserve.com/homepages/ee/Jaruco.htm]
Links, Hispanic Genealogy
[http://ourworld.compuserve.com/homepages/Alfred_Sosa/]

# CZECH

## The Czech, Bohemian, and Moravian Genealogical Research Page
http://www.iarelative.com/czech/

E-mail  Czeching@iarelative.com t

Czeching Out Our Ancestors, Online Discussion Group
[http://www.iarelative.com/czech/search.htm]
Czechoslovak Genealogical Society International
[http://members.aol.com/cgsi/index.html]
Links, Links, Links to Czech Genealogy Sites
[http://www.iarelative.com/czech/]

### *Outstanding Site*

### Czech National Library
http://www.nkp.cz/

Klementinum 190
CZ 110 01 Prague 1 Czech

Phone  (011) +42 2 24229500
Fax    (011) +42 2 24227796
E-mail  sekret.ur@nkp.cz

Overview
[http://www.nkp.cz/]

# DENMARK
### *Outstanding Site*

### Danish Data Archives
http://www.sa.dk/dda/dda_gb.htm

Islandsgade 10
DK-5000 Odense C, Denmark

Phone  (011) +45 66 11 30 10
Fax    (011) +45 66 11 30 60
E-mail  mailbox@dda.dk

Danish Demographic Database
[http://ddd.sa.dk/ddd2.htm]
Danish Demographic Database, Background
[http://ddd.sa.dk/kip/uk/sources.htm#tekst]
Danish Demographic Database, Source Records
[http://ddd.sa.dk/kip/uk/the_source_entry_project.htm]
Overview
[http://www.sa.dk/dda/introgb.html]

## *Outstanding Site*

### Danish Emigration Archives
http://users.cybercity.dk/~ccc13656/

Arkivstrœde 1
P.O. Box 1731
DK - 9100 Aalborg, Denmark

Phone  (011) +45  98125793
Fax    (011) +45  98102248
E-mail  emiarch@vip.cybercity.dk

Archives Database, Search
    [http://users.cybercity.dk/~ccc13656/uk/archives/archives.htm]
Introduction
    [http://users.cybercity.dk/~ccc13656/uk/info/info.htm]

### Danish State Archives
http://www.sa.dk/default.htm

Rigsdagsgarden
9 DK 1218
Copenhagen, Denmark

Phone  (011) +45  33 12 33 10
Fax    (011) +45  33 15 33 39
E-mail  mailbox@sa.dk

Overview
    [http://www.sa.dk/sa/saintro.htm]

### National Library of Denmark
http://www.kb.bib.dk/

P.O. Box  2149
1016 Copenhagen K
Denmark

Phone  (011) +45  33 93 01 11
Fax    (011) +45  33 32 98 46
Telex  15009
E-mail  kb@kb.bib.dk

Collections
    [http://www.kb.bib.dk/kb/geninfo/index-en.htm]

# ENGLAND, WALES, AND CHANNEL ISLANDS
## Association of Commonwealth Archivists and Records Managers

28 Russell Square
London, England WC1B 5DS

Phone  (011) +44 171 580 5876
Fax    (011) +44 171 580 6827
E-mail  a.thurston@sas.ac.uk

Directory, Archival Associations
    [http://www.comnet.mt/acarm/asscdir.html]
Directory, Commonwealth Archives
    [http://www.comnet.mt/acarm/arcdir.html]
Overview
    [http://www.comnet.mt/acarm/index.html#acarm]

### Berkshire Record Office
http://www.earl.org.uk/earl/members/berkshire/archive.htm

Shire Hall
Shinfield Park
Reading, England  RG2 9XD

Phone  (011) +44 (0) 1734 233182
Fax    (011) +44 (0) 1734 233203

Family History Resources
    [http://www.earl.org.uk/earl/members/berkshire/family.htm]
Overview
    [http://www.earl.org.uk/earl/members/berkshire/ro.htm]

## The British Library                http://portico.bl.uk/

Newspaper Library              Phone   (011) +44  171 412 7353
Colindale Avenue               Fax     (011) +44 171 412 7379
London, England NW9 5HE

Oriental and India Office Collections    Phone   (011) +44 171 412 7873
197 Blackfriars Road                     Fax     (011) +44 171 412 7641
London, England SE1 8NG                   E-mail  oioc-enquiries@bl.uk

Gabriel, Gateway European National Libraries
    [http://portico.bl.uk/gabriel/en/welcome.html]
Gabriel, Links European National Libraries
    [http://portico.bl.uk/gabriel/en/eurocoun.html]
India Office Records
    [http://portico.bl.uk/oioc/records/overview.html]
India Office Records, Family History Guide
    [http://portico.bl.uk/oioc/records/iorfamhi.html]
Links, British and World
    [http://portico.bl.uk/otherwww.html#ukgov]
Newspaper Library
    [http://portico.bl.uk/newspaper/]
Oriental and India Office Collection
    [http://portico.bl.uk/oioc/]

## Channel Islands Family History Society
    http://user.itl.net/~glen/AbouttheChannelIslandsFHS.html

P.O. Box 507
St. Helier, Jersey, Channel Islands JE4 5TN UK

Overview
    [http://user.itl.net/~glen/AbouttheChannelIslandsFHS.html]

## Cheshire Record Office               http://www.u-net.com/cheshire/recoff/home.htm

Duke Street                    Phone   (011) +44 (0) 1244 602574
Chester, England CH1 1RL       Fax     (011) +44 (0) 1244 603812
                                E-mail  peplerj@cheshire-cc.btx400.co.uk

Family History Society of Cheshire
    [http://www.users.zetnet.co.uk/blangston/fhsc/]

## Corporation of London Records Office
    http://pitcairn.lib.uci.edu/largo/clr/clr_hold/clr_hold.html#scope

P.O. Box 270                   Phone   (011) +44 (0) 171 332 1251
Guildhall
London, England EC2P 2EJ

Collections
    [http://pitcairn.lib.uci.edu/largo/clr/clr_hold/clr_hold.html#scope]

## Devon Record Office
    http://www.devon-cc.gov.uk/dcc/services/dro/homepage.html

Castle Street                  Phone   (011) +44 (0)  384253
Exeter, England EX4 3PU

Newsletter
[http://www.devon-cc.gov.uk/dcc/services/dro/novnew96.html]
Overview
http://www.devon-cc.gov.uk/dcc/services/dro/homepage.html]

## East Sussex Record Office
http://www.eastsussexcc.gov.uk/council/services/general/archives/main.htm

Phone    (011) +44 (0) 1273) 482349
Civil Registration Offices
[http://www.eastsussexcc.gov.uk/council/services/reg/offices/main.htm]

## *Outstanding Site*

## GENUKI, Genealogy, United Kingdom and Ireland
http://sentinel.mcc.ac.uk/genuki/mindex.html

E-mail   genukiwww@mcc.ac.uk
Link,  soc.genealogy.uk+ireland
[http://midas.ac.uk/genuki/org/email.html]
Links, UK and Ireland Sites
[http://sentinel.mcc.ac.uk/genuki/mindex.html]

## *Outstanding Site*

## Greater Manchester County Record Office
http://www.personal.u-net.com/~gmcro/home.htm

| 56 Marshall Street | Phone   (011) +44 (0) 161 832 5284 |
| New Cross | Fax     (011) +44 (0) 161 839 3808 |
| Manchester, England M4 5FU | E-mail  archives@gmcro.u-net.com |

Business Records as a Genealogical Resource
[http://www.personal.u-net.com/~gmcro/business.htm]
Guide to the Records Office
[http://www.personal.u-net.com/~gmcro/guide.htm]
Probate Records
[http://www.personal.u-net.com/~gmcro/wills.htm]
Record Society of Lancashire and Cheshire
[http://www.personal.u-net.com/~gmcro/leaflet.htm]
Repositories Guide, Area
[http://www.personal.u-net.com/~gmcro/purple1.htm]
Vital Records
[http://www.personal.u-net.com/~gmcro/st_caths.htm]

## Guernsey Archives Service          http://user.itl.net/~glen/archgsy.html

| 29 Victoria Road | Phone   (011) +44 (0) 1481 724512 |
| St. Peter Port, Guernsey, Channel Islands | Fax     (011) +44 (0) 1481 715814 |
| GY1 1UG  UK | |

Constables Records of St. Peter Port
[http://user.itl.net/~glen/constables.html]
Overview
[http://user.itl.net/~glen/archgsy.html]

Priaulx Library
   [http://user.itl.net/~glen/priaulx.html]
Surname Research List
   [ftp://members.aol.com/johnf14246/ci/surnames.txt]

## Hampshire Record Office
http://www.hants.gov.uk/sadexn/i24.html

Sussex Street
Winchester, England SO23 8TH

Phone   (011) +44 (0) 1962 870500
E-mail   sadeax@hants.gov.uk

Genealogy Sources
   [http://www.hants.gov.uk/sadexn/c59.html]
Overview
   [http://www.hants.gov.uk/sadexn/c10.html]
Vital Records
   [http://www.hants.gov.uk/sadexn/c63.html]

## Hereford and Worcester County Record Office
http://www.open.gov.uk/hereford/pages/h&w_cc/h&w_rec1.htm

County Hall
Spetchley Road
Worcester, England WR5 2NP

Phone   (011) +44 (0) 1905 766351

Collections
   [http://www.open.gov.uk/hereford/pages/h&w_cc/h&w_rec1.htm#r3]
Genealogy
   [http://www.open.gov.uk/hereford/pages/h&w_cc/h&w_rec1.htm#dr2]
Local History
   [http://www.open.gov.uk/hereford/pages/h&w_cc/h&w_rec1.htm#dr1]

## Institute of Historical Research
http://ihr.sas.ac.uk/

University of London
Senate House
London, England WC1E 7HU

Phone   (011) +44 (0) 171-6360272
Fax      (011) +44 (0) 171-436 2183

Links, Historians in Europe
   [http://ihr.sas.ac.uk/ihr/oleu.html]
Links, Historians in London
   [http://ihr.sas.ac.uk/ihr/source.lon.html]
Links, Historians in UK
   [http://ihr.sas.ac.uk/ihr/online.uk.html]
Victoria County History Project
   [http://ihr.sas.ac.uk/vch/vchnew.asc.html]

## Jersey Archives Service
http://www.jersey.gov.uk/heritage/archives/jasweb.html

The Weighbridge
St. Helier, Jersey, Channel Islands
   JE2 3NF  UK

Phone   (011) +44 (0) 1534  617441
Fax      (011) +44 (0) 1534  66085

Overview
   [http://www.jersey.gov.uk/heritage/archives/jasweb.html]
Surname Research List
   [ftp://members.aol.com/johnf14246/ci/surnames.txt]

## Lincolnshire Archives

http://www.demon.co.uk/lincs-archives/la_ndx.htm

St. Rumbold Street
Lincoln, England LN2 5AB

Phone   (011) +44 (0) 1522 526204
Fax       (011) +44 (0) 1522 530047
E-mail  100743.3645@CompuServe.com

Australian Convict Records, Searchable
    [http://www.demon.co.uk/lincs-archives/convicts.htm]
Genealogy Services
    [http://www.demon.co.uk/lincs-archives/fam.htm]

## Liverpool Central Library

http://www.liverpool.gov.uk/public/council_info/direct-info/leisure/libraries/central.html

Record Office and Local Studies
William Brown Street
Liverpool, England L3 8EW

Phone   (011) +44 (0) 151 225 5417
Fax       (011) +44 (0) 151 207 1342

Record Office and Local Studies
    [http://www.liverpool.gov.uk/public/council_info/direct-info/leisure/libraries/ro.html]

## Nottinghamshire Archives

http://www.nottscc.gov.uk/cc/00000533.htm

County House
Castle Meadow Road
Nottingham, England NG2 1AG

Phone   (011) +44 (0) 115 958 1634

Collections
    [http://www.nottscc.gov.uk/cc/idx_iac.htm]

## Office for National Statistics

http://www.emap.co.uk/ons/welcome.htm

General Register Office
Overseas Registration Section
Trafalgar Road
Southport, England PR8 2HH

Phone   (011) +44 151 471 4801

Adoption Records
    [http://www.emap.co.uk/ons/public/reg.shtml]
Family Records Office
    [http://www.emap.co.uk/ons/public/pnp.shtml]
Links, Worldwide
    [http://www.emap.com/ons/links.htm]
Popular First Names
    [http://www.emap.co.uk/ons/public/names.shtml]
St. Catherine's Marriage Index
    [http://boulmer.ncl.ac.uk/genuki/StCathsTranscriptions/]
Vital Records, Overseas Requests
    [http://www.emap.co.uk/ons/public/overseas.shtml]

## Public Record Office

http://www.open.gov.uk/pro/prohome.htm

Ruskin Avenue
Kew, Surrey, England TW9 4DU

Phone   (011) +44 (0) 181 392 5200
Fax       (011) +44 (0) 181 878 8905
E-mail  enquiry.pro.rsd.kew@gtnet.gov.uk

Family Records Centre, FRC
Office For National Statistics
(Formerly Housed at St. Catherine's House)
1 Myddelton Street
London, England EC1R 1UW

Phone    (011) +44 (0) 181 392 5300
Fax      (011) +44 (0) 181 392 5307
E-mail   enquiry.pro.rsd.kew@gtnet.gov.uk

Family Records Centre
    [http://www.open.gov.uk/pro/clbu.htm]
Family Records Centre Newsletter
    [http://www.open.gov.uk/pro/frcnews.htm]
Guides
    [http://www.open.gov.uk/pro/books.htm]

## *Outstanding Site*

## Royal Commission on Historical Manuscripts      http://www.hmc.gov.uk/

Quality House
Quality Court
Chancery Lane
London, England WC2A 1HP

Phone    (011) +44 (0) 171 242 1198
Fax      (011) +44 (0) 171 831 3550
E-mail   nra@hmc.gov.uk

Archives and Internet Group
    [http://www.hmc.gov.uk/network/ai.html]
Genealogy Sources
    [http://www.hmc.gov.uk/sheets/geneal6.html]
Guide Sheets
    [http://www.hmc.gov.uk/sheets/sheets.html]
Links, Archives
    [http://www.hmc.gov.uk/network/links.html]
Manorial Documents Register
    [http://www.hmc.gov.uk/mdr/mdr.html]
Military Records Sources
    [http://www.hmc.gov.uk/sheets/army8.html]
National Registry of Archives
    [http://www.hmc.gov.uk/nra/nra.html]

## Shropshire Records and Research Centre
    http://www.shropshire-cc.gov.uk/librr.htm

Castle Gates
Shrewsbury, England SY1 2AQ

Phone    (011) +44 (0) 1743 255350
Fax      (011) +44 (0) 1743 255355

Overview
    [http://www.shropshire-cc.gov.uk/librr.htm]

## Society of Genealogists      http://www.cs.ncl.ac.uk/genuki/SoG/

14 Charterhouse Buildings
Goswell Road
London, England EC1M 7BA

Phone    (011) +44 (0) 171 251 8799

Using the Library of the Society
    [http://www.cs.ncl.ac.uk/genuki/SoG/SoGtext.html]

## Somerset Archive and Record Service        http://www.somerset.gov.uk/archives/

| | |
|---|---|
| Obridge Road | Phone   (011) +44 (0) 1 823 337 600 |
| Taunton, Somerset, England TA2 4BU | Fax     (011) +44 (0) 1 823 325 402 |
| | E-mail  100064.2776@compuserve.com |

Collection Guides
[Http://www.somerset.gov.uk/archives/genguide.htm]
Genealogy Resources
[Http://www.somerset.gov.uk/archives/yosomfam.htm]
Indexes
[Http://www.somerset.gov.uk/archives/indexes.htm]
Parish Records Holdings
[Http://www.somerset.gov.uk/archives/parindex.htm]

## Suffolk Record Office      http://www.suffolkcc.gov.uk/libraries_and_heritage/sro/index.html

| | |
|---|---|
| Bury St. Edmunds | Phone   (011) +44 (0) 1284 352352 |
| 77 Raingate Street | Fax     (011) +44 (0) 1284 352355 |
| Bury St. Edmunds, Suffolk, England IP33 2AR | |
| | |
| Ipswich Office | Phone   (011) +44 (0) 1473 584541 |
| Gatacre Road | Fax     (011) +44 (0) 1473 584533 |
| Ipswich, Suffolk, England IP1 2LQ | |
| | |
| Lowestoft Office | Phone   (011) +44 (0) 1502 405357 |
| Clapham Road South | Fax     (011) +44 (0) 1502 405350 |
| Lowestoft, Suffolk, England NR32 1DR | E-mail  webmaster@suffolkcc.gov.uk |

Collections
[http://www.suffolkcc.gov.uk/libraries_and_heritage/sro/sro_collections.html]
County Archive Research Network
[http://www.suffolkcc.gov.uk/libraries_and_heritage/sro/carn.html]
Newsletter
[http://www.suffolkcc.gov.uk/libraries_and_heritage/sro/whats_new.html]

### *Outstanding Site*

## Surrey History Service        http://www.surreycc.gov.uk/scc/shs/shs.html

| | |
|---|---|
| Surrey Record Office | Phone   (011) +44 (0) 181 541 9065 |
| County Hall | Fax     (011) +44 (0) 181 541 9606 |
| Penrhyn Road | E-mail  shs@dial.pipex.com |
| Kingston upon Thames, England KT1 2DN UK | |

Genealogy Notes
[http://www.surreycc.gov.uk/scc/shs/famhist.html]
Library
[http://www.surreycc.gov.uk/scc/shs/inf2.html]
Nonconformist Church Records
[http://www.surreycc.gov.uk/scc/shs/nonconf.html]

## Warwickshire County Record Office
http://lirn.viscount.org.uk/earl/members/warwickshire/countyro.htm

| | |
|---|---|
| Priory Park | Phone   (011) +44 (0) 1926 412735 |
| Cape Road | Fax     (011) +44 (0) 1926 412509 |
| Warwick, England  CV34 4JS | |

Overview
[http://lirn.viscount.org.uk/earl/members/warwickshire/countyro.htm]

# ESTONIA

## National Library of Estonia          http://portico.bl.uk/gabriel/en/countries/estonia.html

Tonismagi 2                         Phone   (011) +372 6307 611
Tallinn EE 0100                     Fax     (011) +372 6 311 410
Estonia                             E-mail  nlib@venus.nlib

Libraries, Estonia
[http://portico.bl.uk/gabriel/en/countries/estonia.html]

# EUROPE

### *Outstanding Site*

## Federation of East European Family History Societies
http://dcn.davis.ca.us/~feefhs/

P.O. Box 51089
Salt Lake City, UT 84151-0898

FEEFHS Membership Directory and Links
[http://dcn.davis.ca.us/~feefhs/]
FEEFHS Membership by Location
[http://dcn.davis.ca.us/~feefhs/location.html]
Public Libraries of Europe
[http://dspace.dial.pipex.com/town/square/ac940/eurolib.html]

# FINLAND

## National Library of Finland          http://linnea.helsinki.fi/hyk/index.html

P.O. Box 15                         Phone   (011) +358 9 1912 2740
FIN-00014 University of Helsinki    Fax     (011) +358 9 1912 2719
Finland                             Telex   121 538 hyk sf
                                    E-mail  HYK_TIETO@Helsinki.FI

Library
[http://www.helsinki.fi/]
Online Catalogs
[http://portico.bl.uk/gabriel/en/countries/finland-www-en.html]

# FRANCE

## French National Archives          http://www.culture.fr/culture/sedocum/caran.htm

60, rue des Francs-Bourgeois        Phone   (011) +33 (0)1 40 27 64 19
75141 Paris Cedex 03, France        Fax     (011) +33 (0)1 40 27 66 28

Overview
[http://www.culture.fr/culture/sedocum/caran.htm]

## FYI France

http://www.fyifrance.com/indexa.html

E-mail   kessler@well.sf.ca.us

Links, Everything French
 [http://www.fyifrance.com/indexa.html]

## National Library of France

http://www.bnf.fr/bnfgb.htm

| | |
|---|---|
| 58, rue de Richelieu | Phone   (011) +33 1 47 03 81 26 |
| 75 084 Paris Cedex 02, France | Fax      (011) +33 1 42 96 84 47 |
| | Telex    212 614 |
| | E-mail  webmaster@bnf.fr |

Collections
 [http://www.bnf.fr/institution/anglais/collecgb.htm]
Libraries in France
 [http://www.bnf.fr/institution/anglais/bibpolgb.htm]
Online Catalog
 [http://www.bnf.fr/web-bnf/catalog/opalegb.htm]

# GERMANY

*Outstanding Site*

## German Genealogy Home Page

http://www.genealogy.com/

Czech Archives
 [http://www.genealogy.com/gene/reg/SUD/sudet_crarch_en.html]
German Genealogical Societies
 [http://www.genealogy.com/gene/www/ghlp/verbaende.html]
Links, Regional Research
 [http://www.genealogy.com/gene/reg/regio.htm]
Sample Letter, Croatian, Archive
 [http://www.genealogy.com/gene/ghlp/let-arc.html#croatian]
Sample Letter, Croatian, Church
 [http://www.genealogy.com/gene/ghlp/let-pas.html#croatian]
Sample Letter, Czech
 [http://www.genealogy.com/gene/ghlp/let-arc.html#czech]
Sample Letter, French, Archives
 [http://www.genealogy.com/gene/ghlp/let-arc.html#french]
Sample Letter, French, Church
 [http://www.genealogy.com/gene/ghlp/let-pas.html#french]
Sample Letter, German, Archives
 [http://www.genealogy.com/gene/ghlp/let-arc.html#german]
Sample Letter, German, Church
 [http://www.genealogy.com/gene/ghlp/let-pas.html#german]
Sample Letter, German, Civil Registrar
 [http://www.genealogy.com/gene/www/ghlp/muster.html#off]
Sample Letter, German, Join a German Genealogical Society
 [http://www.genealogy.com/gene/www/ghlp/muster.html#org]
Sample Letter, Hungarian, Archive
 [http://www.genealogy.com/gene/ghlp/let-arc.html#hungarian]
Sample Letter, Hungarian, Church
 [http://www.genealogy.com/gene/ghlp/let-pas.html#hungarian]

Sample Letter, Romanian, Archives
    [http://www.genealogy.com/gene/ghlp/let-arc.html#romanian]
Sample Letter, Romanian, Church
    [http://www.genealogy.com/gene/ghlp/let-pas.html#romanian]
Sample Letter, Serbian, Archives
    [http://www.genealogy.com/gene/ghlp/let-arc.html#serbian]
Sample Letter, Serbian, Church
    [http://www.genealogy.com/gene/ghlp/let-pas.html#serbian]
Telephone, Australia
    [http://www.genealogy.com/gene/misc/phone.html#austr]
Telephone, Austria
    [http://www.genealogy.com/gene/misc/phone.html#oestr]
Telephone, Canada
    [http://www.genealogy.com/gene/misc/phone.html#canad]
Telephone, Switzerland
    [http://www.genealogy.com/gene/misc/phone.html#switz]

## National Library of Germany     http://www.ddb.de/welcome.htm

Adickesallee 1                        Phone   (011) +49 69 7566 1
60322 Frankfurt am Main               Fax     (011) +49 69 7566 x476
Germany                               E-mail  info@dbf.ddb.de

Overview
    [http://www.ddb.de/]·

# GREECE
## National Library of Greece
    http://portico.bl.uk/gabriel/en/countries/greece.html

32 Panepistimiou Avenue               Phone   (011) +30 1 361 44 13
106 79 Athens, Greece                 Fax     (011) +30 1 360 84 95

Overview
    [http://portico.bl.uk/gabriel/en/countries/greece.html]

# HUNGARY
## National Széchényi Library     http://portico.bl.uk/gabriel/en/countries/hungary.html

Budavári Palota F épület               Phone   (011) +36 1 155 6169
H-1827, Budapest, Hungary             Fax     (011) +36 1 202 0804
                                       E-mail  poprady@oszk.hu
National Bibliography
    [http://portico.bl.uk/gabriel/en/countries/hungary-ikb-en.html]

# ICELAND
## The National and University Library of Iceland     http://bok.hi.is/

Arngrimsgata 3                         Phone   (011) +354 563 5600
IS 107 Reykjavik, Iceland             Fax     (011) +354 563 5615
                                       E-mail  lbs@bok.hi.is
                                               upplys@bok.hi.is Reference

Overview
    [http://portico.bl.uk/gabriel/en/countries/iceland.html]

# IRELAND and NORTHERN IRELAND

## *Outstanding Site*

### National Archives of Ireland          http://www.kst.dit.ie/nat-arch/

Bishop Street                        Phone   (011) + 353 1 478 3711
Dublin 8, Ireland                    Fax     (011) + 353 1 478 3650

Census Records
    [http://www.kst.dit.ie/nat-arch/genealogy.html#census]
Genealogy Sources
    [http://www.kst.dit.ie/nat-arch/genealogy.html]
Great Famine, 1845-1850
    [http://www.kst.dit.ie/nat-arch/famine.html]
Ordnance Survey, Archives
    [http://www.kst.dit.ie/nat-arch/os.html]
Ordnance Survey, Parish Index
    [http://www.kst.dit.ie/cgi-bin/naigenform02?index=OS+Parish+List]
Probate Records
    [http://www.kst.dit.ie/nat-arch/genealogy.html#wills]
Sources for Women's History
    [http://www.kst.dit.ie/nat-arch/women.html]
Tithe applotment books and Primary Valuation
    [http://www.kst.dit.ie/nat-arch/genealogy.html#tithe]
Transportation of Irish Convicts to Australia
    [http://www.kst.dit.ie/nat-arch/transp1.html]
Vital Records
    [http://www.kst.dit.ie/nat-arch/genealogy.html#births]

### National Library of Ireland          http://gopher.hea.ie/natlib/homepage.html

Kildare Street                       Phone   (011) +353-1-6618811
Dublin 2, Ireland                    Fax     (011) +353-1-6766690

Services
    [http://gopher.hea.ie/natlib/services.html]

## *Outstanding Site*

### North of Ireland Family History Society      http://www.os.qub.ac.uk/nifhs/

c/o School of Education
The Queen's University of Belfast
69 University Street
Belfast BT7 1HL
Northern Ireland

Antrim, 1851 Census Online Index
    [http://www.os.qub.ac.uk/nifhs/census/]
Irish Genealogical Journals
    [http://www.os.qub.ac.uk/nifhs/journals.html]

Library, Book List
   [http://www.os.qub.ac.uk/nifhs/library.html]
Member's Research Interests
   [http://www.os.qub.ac.uk/nifhs/interests.html]
North Irish Roots, Newsletter, Index
   [http://www.os.qub.ac.uk/nifhs/journal_index.html]

## Public Record Office of Northern Ireland
   http://proni.nics.gov.uk/pro_home.htm

| | |
|---|---|
| Balmoral Avenue | Phone   (011) +44 0232 6611621 |
| Belfast, Northern Ireland | E-mail  proni@nics.gov.uk |

Cemetery Records
   [http://proni.nics.gov.uk/family/family21.htm]
Collection Strengths
   [http://proni.nics.gov.uk/major.htm]
Collections
   [http://proni.nics.gov.uk/exhibition/index.htm]
Genealogy Fact Sheets
   [http://proni.nics.gov.uk/family.htm]
Local History Fact Sheets
   [http://proni.nics.gov.uk/local.htm]

## TIARA—The Irish Ancestral Research Association
   http://world.std.com/~ahern/TIARA.html

| | |
|---|---|
| P.O. Box 619 | E-mail  ahern@world.std.com |
| Sudbury, MA 01776 | |

Links, Online Irish Newspapers
   [http://world.std.com/~ahern/books.html#news]

## Ulster Historical Foundation   http://www.mayo-ireland.ie/Geneal/AntmDown.htm

| | |
|---|---|
| 12 College Square East | Phone   (011) +44 1232 332288 |
| Belfast, Northern Ireland BT1 6DD | Fax     (011) +44 1232 239885 |
| | E-mail  napierj@uhf.dnet.co.uk |

Overview
   [http://www.mayo-ireland.ie/Geneal/AntmDown.htm]

# COUNTY ARMAGH
## County Armagh Genealogy—Armagh Ancestry
   http://www.mayo-ireland.ie/Geneal/Armagh.htm

| | |
|---|---|
| 42 English Street | Phone   (011) +44 1861 521802 |
| Armagh, Co. Armagh BT61 7BA | Fax     (011) +44 1861 510033 |
|    Northern Ireland | |

Overview
   [http://www.mayo-ireland.ie/Geneal/Armagh.htm]

# COUNTY CAVAN
CavanNet                                    http://www.cavannet.ie/

E-mail   kevins@iol.ie

Genealogical Forum, Online Exchange
   [http://www.cavannet.ie/history/families/geo-help.htm]
Tracing Your Cavan Roots
   [http://www.cavannet.ie/history/families/roots.htm]

## Cavan Research Centre          http://www.mayo-ireland.ie/Geneal/Cavan.htm

Cana House                      Phone   (011) +353 (0) 49 61094
Farnham Street                  Fax     (011) +353 (0) 49 61094
Cavan, Co. Cavan, Ireland

Overview
   [http://www.mayo-ireland.ie/Geneal/Cavan.htm]

# COUNTY CLARE
Clare Heritage and Genealogical Centre
   http://www.mayo-ireland.ie/Geneal/Clare.htm

Church Street                   Phone   (011) +353 65 37955
Corofin, Co. Clare, Ireland

Overview
   [http://www.mayo-ireland.ie/Geneal/Clare.htm]

# COUNTY CORK
Mallow Heritage Centre          http://www.mayo-ireland.ie/Geneal/Cork.htm

County Cork, Ireland            Phone   (011) +353 22 21778
27/28 Bank Place
Mallow, Co. Cork, Ireland

Overview
   [http://www.mayo-ireland.ie/Geneal/Cork.htm]

# COUNTY DERRY
County Derry or Londonderry Genealogy Centre
   http://www.mayo-ireland.ie/Geneal/Derry.htm

4-22 Butcher Street             Phone   (011) +44 1504 373177
Londonderry BT48 6HL            Fax     (011) +44 1504 374818
Northern Ireland

Overview
   [http://www.mayo-ireland.ie/Geneal/Derry.htm]

# COUNTY DONEGAL
## Donegal Ancestry in County Donegal
http://www.mayo-ireland.ie/Geneal/Donegal.htm

| | |
|---|---|
| Old Meeting House | Phone (011) +353 74 51266 |
| Back Lane | Fax (011) +353 74 51266 |
| Ramelton, Co. Donegal, Ireland | |

Overview
[http://www.mayo-ireland.ie/Geneal/Donegal.htm]

# COUNTY FERMANAGH
## Families of Fermanagh-Monaghan     http://expo.nua.ie/dagda/families/

E-mail  web@nua.ie

Cassidy Family
[http://expo.nua.ie/dagda/families/cassidy.html]
McMahon Family
[http://expo.nua.ie/dagda/families/mcmahon.html]
Maguire/McGuire Family
[http://expo.nua.ie/dagda/families/maguire.html]
Rooney - O'Rooney Family
[http://expo.nua.ie/dagda/families/rooney.html]

# COUNTY GALWAY
## East Galway Family History Society
http://www.mayo-ireland.ie/Geneal/EtGalway.htm

| | |
|---|---|
| Woodford | Phone (011) +353 509 49309 |
| Loughrea, Co. Galway, Ireland | Fax (011) +353 509 49309 |

Overview
[http://www.mayo-ireland.ie/Geneal/EtGalway.htm]

## West Galway Family History Society
http://www.mayo-ireland.ie/Geneal/WtGalway.htm

| | |
|---|---|
| Research Unit | Phone (011) +353 91 756737 |
| Venture Centre | |
| Liosbaun Estate | |
| Tuam Road | |
| Galway, Co. Galway, Ireland | |

Overview
[http://www.mayo-ireland.ie/Geneal/WtGalway.htm]

# COUNTY KERRY
## Killarney Genealogical Centre     http://www.mayo-ireland.ie/Geneal/Kerry.htm

| | |
|---|---|
| Cathedral Walk | Phone (011) +353 64 35946 |
| Killarney, Co. Kerry, Ireland | |

Overview
[http://www.mayo-ireland.ie/Geneal/Kerry.htm]

# COUNTY KILDARE
## Kildare Heritage and Genealogy Company
http://www.mayo-ireland.ie/Geneal/Kildare.htm

c/o Kildare County Library                    Phone    (011) +353 45 431486
Newbridge, Co. Kildare, Ireland

Overview
[http://www.mayo-ireland.ie/Geneal/Kildare.htm]

## Kilkenny Ancestry                http://www.mayo-ireland.ie/Geneal/Kilknny.htm

Rothe House                           Phone    (011) +353 (0) 56 22893
16 Parliament Street                  Fax      (011) +353 (0) 56 22893
Kilkenny City, Ireland

Overview
[http://www.mayo-ireland.ie/Geneal/Kilknny.htm]

# COUNTY LAOIS and OFFALY
## Laois and Offaly Family History Research Centre
http://www.mayo-ireland.ie/Geneal/LaoisOff.htm

Bury Quay                             Phone    (011) +353 506 21421
Tullamore, Co. Offaly, Ireland·      Fax      (011) +353 506 21421
                                      E-mail   ohas@iol.ie
Overview
[http://www.mayo-ireland.ie/Geneal/LaoisOff.htm]

# COUNTY LEITRIM
## Leitrim Genealogy Centre        http://www.mayo-ireland.ie/Geneal/Leitrim.htm

County Library                        Phone    (011) +353 78 44012
Ballinamore,  Co. Leitrim,  Ireland   Fax      (011) +353 78 44425

Overview
[http://www.mayo-ireland.ie/Geneal/Leitrim.htm]

# COUNTY LIMERICK
## Limerick Regional Archives      http://www.mayo-ireland.ie/Geneal/Limerick.htm

The Granary                           Phone    (011) +353 61 410777
Michael Street
Limerick City, Co. Limerick, Ireland

Overview
[http://www.mayo-ireland.ie/Geneal/Limerick.htm]

# COUNTY LONGFORD
## Longford Research Centre    http://www.mayo-ireland.ie/Geneal/Longford.htm

Longford Roots                          Phone   (011) +353 (0) 4341235
1 Church Street
Longford, Co. Longford, Ireland

Overview
   [http://www.mayo-ireland.ie/Geneal/Longford.htm]

# COUNTY MAYO
## North Mayo Family Research Centre
   http://www.mayo-ireland.ie/Geneal/NrthMayo.htm

Enniscoe                         Phone   (011) +353 96 31809
Castlehill                       Fax     (011) +353 96 31885
Ballina, Co. Mayo,  Ireland

Overview
   [http://www.mayo-ireland.ie/Geneal/NrthMayo.htm]

## South Mayo Family Research Centre
   http://www.mayo-ireland.ie/Geneal/SouMayo.htm

Main Street                      Phone   (011) +353 92 41214
Ballinrobe, Co. Mayo, Ireland    Fax     (011) +353 92 41214
                                 E-mail  soumayo@iol.ie

Overview
   [http://www.mayo-ireland.ie/Geneal/SouMayo.htm]

# COUNTY MEATH
## Meath Family Research Centre   http://www.mayo-ireland.ie/Geneal/Meath.htm

Mill Street                      Phone   (011) +353 46 36633
Trim, Co. Meath, Ireland         Fax     (011) +353 46 37502

Overview
   [http://www.mayo-ireland.ie/Geneal/Meath.htm]

# COUNTY MONAGHAN
## Families of Fermanagh-Monaghan    http://expo.nua.ie/dagda/families/

                                 E-mail  web@nua.ie

Cassidy Family
   [http://expo.nua.ie/dagda/families/cassidy.html]
McMahon Family
   [http://expo.nua.ie/dagda/families/mcmahon.html]
Maguire/McGuire Family
   [http://expo.nua.ie/dagda/families/maguire.html]
Rooney - O'Rooney Family
   [http://expo.nua.ie/dagda/families/rooney.html]

## Monaghan Research Centre    http://www.mayo-ireland.ie/Geneal/Monaghan.htm

Monaghan Ancestry               Phone   (011) +353 (0) 47 82304
Clogher Historical Society
6, Tully Street
Monaghan,  Co. Monaghan,  Ireland

Overview
    [http://www.mayo-ireland.ie/Geneal/Monaghan.htm]

# COUNTY ROSCOMMON
## County Roscommon Heritage and Genealogy Society
    http://www.mayo-ireland.ie/Geneal/Roscmmn.htm

Church Street                   Phone   (011) +353 78 33380
Strokestown, Co. Roscommon, Ireland

Overview
    [http://www.mayo-ireland.ie/Geneal/Roscmmn.htm]

# COUNTY SLIGO
## County Sligo Heritage and Genealogy Centre
    http://www.mayo-ireland.ie/Geneal/Sligo.htm

Aras Reddan                     Phone   (011) +353 71 43728
Temple Street
Sligo City,  Co. Sligo, Ireland

Overview
    [http://www.mayo-ireland.ie/Geneal/Sligo.htm]

# COUNTY TIPPERARY
## Bru Boru Heritage Centre, Tipperary
    http://www.mayo-ireland.ie/Geneal/STipp.htm

Rock of Cashel                  Phone   (011) +353 62 61122
Co. Tipperary, Ireland          Fax     (011) +353 62 62700

Overview
    [http://www.mayo-ireland.ie/Geneal/STipp.htm]

## Tipperary North Family Research Centre
    http://www.mayo-ireland.ie/Geneal/NTipp.htm

The Gatehouse                   Phone   (011) +353 67 33850
Kickham Street                  Fax     (011) +353 67 33586
Nenagh, Co. Tipperary,  Ireland

Overview
    [http://www.mayo-ireland.ie/Geneal/NTipp.htm]

# COUNTY WATERFORD

## Dun na Si Heritage Centre
http://www.mayo-ireland.ie/Geneal/Wstmeath.htm

| | |
|---|---|
| County Westmeath<br>Knockdanney<br>Co. Westmeath, Ireland | Phone (011) +353 902 81183<br>Fax (011) +353 902 81661 |

Overview
[http://www.mayo-ireland.ie/Geneal/Wstmeath.htm]

## Waterford Research Centre
http://www.mayo-ireland.ie/Geneal/Waterfrd.htm

| | |
|---|---|
| St Patrick's Church<br>Jenkin's Lane<br>Waterford City, Co.Waterford, Ireland | Phone (011) +353 (0) 51 76123<br>Fax (011) +353 (0) 51 50645<br>E-mail mnoc@iol.ie |

Overview
[http://www.mayo-ireland.ie/Geneal/Waterfrd.htm]

## Wexford Genealogy Centre
http://www.mayo-ireland.ie/Geneal/Wexford.htm

| | |
|---|---|
| Yola Farmstead<br>Tagoat, Co. Wexford, Ireland | Phone (011) +353 53 31177<br>Fax (011) +353 53 31177 |

Overview
[http://www.mayo-ireland.ie/Geneal/Wexford.htm]

# ISRAEL

## World Zionist Organization
http://www.wzo.org.il/index.htm

| | |
|---|---|
| Central Zionist Archives<br>P.O. Box 92<br>Zalman Shazar 4<br>Jerusalem 91920, Israel | Phone (011) +972 02 6526 155<br>Fax (011) +972 02 6527 029<br>E-mail cza@wzo.org.il |

Central Zionist Archives
[http://www.wzo.org.il/cza/]
Collection Guide
[http://www.wzo.org.il/cza/record.htm]

## Yad Vashem—Holocaust Martyrs' and Heroes' Remembrance Authority
http://www.yad-vashem.org.il/AA_INDEX.HTM

| | |
|---|---|
| P.O. Box 3477<br>Jerusalem 91034, Israel | Phone (011) +972-2-6751-611<br>Fax (011) +972-2-6433-511<br>E-mail archive@yad-vashem.org.il Archives<br>library@yad-vashem.org.il Library<br>names@yad-vashem.org.il Hall of Names |

Archives
[http://www.yad-vashem.org.il/ARCHIVE.HTM]
Hall of Names
[http://www.yad-vashem.org.il/HALL_O_N.HTM]
Library
[http://www.yad-vashem.org.il/LIBRARY.HTM]

# ITALY
## Italian Genealogy HomePage     http://www.italgen.com/

Edmondo Tardio
Sinnigvelderstraat 395
1382 GB Weesp Netherlands

Genealogy Tips
   [http://www.italgen.com/advise.htm]
Italian Genealogical and Heraldic Institute
   [http://www.italgen.com/ighi.htm]
Links, Italy
   [http://www.italgen.com/m_other.htm]
Links, Surname
   [http://www.italgen.com/fampages.htm]
Surnames Database
   [http://www.italgen.com/surnames.htm]
Vital Records
   [http://www.italgen.com/crri.htm]

# JAPAN
## Council on East Asian Libraries
   http://darkwing.uoregon.edu/~felsing/ceal/welcome.html

| c/o East Asian Library | Phone | (312) 702-8436 |
| 1100 East 57th Street | Fax | (312) 702-6623 |
| Chicago, IL 60637-1502 | E-mail | felsing@oregon.uoregon.edu |

CEAL Bulletin
   [http://darkwing.uoregon.edu/~felsing/ceal/reports.html]
Links, East Asian Institutes and Programs
   [http://darkwing.uoregon.edu/~felsing/ceal/caps.html]
Links, Japan
   [http://darkwing.uoregon.edu/~felsing/jstuff/jshelf.html]
Links, Japan Libraries
   [http://darkwing.uoregon.edu/~felsing/jstuff/lib.html]
Member Libraries, Online Library Catalogs
   [http://darkwing.uoregon.edu/~felsing/ceal/ceallibs.html]

# KOREA
## Council on East Asian Libraries
   http://darkwing.uoregon.edu/~felsing/ceal/welcome.html

| c/o East Asian Library | Phone | (312) 702-8436 |
| 1100 East 57th Street | Fax | (312) 702-6623 |
| Chicago, IL 60637-1502 | E-mail | felsing@oregon.uoregon.edu |

CEAL Bulletin
   [http://darkwing.uoregon.edu/~felsing/ceal/reports.html]
Links, East Asian Institutes and Programs
   [http://darkwing.uoregon.edu/~felsing/ceal/caps.html]

Links, Korea
[http://darkwing.uoregon.edu/~felsing/kstuff/kshelf.html]
Links, Korea Libraries
[http://darkwing.uoregon.edu/~felsing/kstuff/lib.html]
Member Libraries, Online Library Catalogs
[http://darkwing.uoregon.edu/~felsing/ceal/ceallibs.html]

# LATVIA
## Latvian National Library      http://portico.bl.uk/gabriel/en/countries/latvia.html

| K. Barona iela 14 | Phone | (011) +371 2 225626 |
| Riga, LV-1423 | Fax | (011) +371 2 283216 |
| Latvia | Telex | 161277 ANNA |

Overview
[http://portico.bl.uk/gabriel/en/countries/latvia.html]

# LIECHTENSTEIN
## Liechtenstein National Library      http://portico.bl.uk/gabriel/de/countries/liechten.html

| Gerberweg 5 | Phone | (011) +41 75 236 63 62 |
| Postfact 385 | Fax | (011) +41 75 233 14 19 |
| FL-9490 Vaduz, Liechtenstein | | |

Overview
[http://portico.bl.uk/gabriel/de/countries/liechten.html]

# LITHUANIA
## Lithuanian American Genealogical Society
http://dcn.davis.ca.us/~feefhs/frg-lags.html

Balzekas Museum of Lithuanian Culture
6500 Pulaski Road
Chicago, IL 60629-5136

Overview
[http://dcn.davis.ca.us/~feefhs/frg-lags.html]

## Martynas Mazvydas National Library of Lithuania
http://lnb.lrs.lt/index.html

| Gedimino pr. 51 | Phone | (011) +370 2 629 023 |
| 2635 Vilnius, Lithuania | Fax | (011) +307 2 627 129 |
| | E-mail | biblio@lnb.lrs.lt |
| | | jolita@lnb.lrs.lt Manuscripts |

Departments
[http://lnb.lrs.lt/angl/struct/lnbstr.html]
Overview
[http://portico.bl.uk/gabriel/en/countries/lithuan.html]

# LUXEMBOURG

## National Library of Luxembourg

http://portico.bl.uk/gabriel/fr/countries/lux.html

37, boulevard F.D. Roosevelt
L-2450 Luxembourg

Phone   (011) +352 22 97 55-1
Fax     (011) +352 47 56 72

Overview
[http://portico.bl.uk/gabriel/fr/countries/lux.html]

# MALAYSIA

## National Archives of Malaysia

http://arkib.gov.my/

Ministry of Culture, Arts and Tourism
50568 Kuala Lumpur, Malaysia

Phone   (011) +03-651 0688
Fax     (011) +03-651 5679
E-mail  habibah@arkib.gov.my

Overview
[http://arkib.gov.my/]

# MALTA

## National Library of Malta

http://portico.bl.uk/gabriel/en/countries/malta.html

36 Old Treasury Street
Valletta, Malta

Phone   (011) +356 23 65 86
Fax     (011) +356 23 59 92

Overview
[http://portico.bl.uk/gabriel/en/countries/malta.html]

# NAMIBIA

## *Outstanding Site*

### National Archives of Namibia

http://witbooi.natarch.mec.gov.na/

Private Bag 13250
4 Luederitz Street
Windhoeck, Namibia

E-mail  renatem@windhoek.alt.na

Guides to Collections; Searchable Indexes
[http://witbooi.natarch.mec.gov.na/search.html]

# NETHERLANDS

## The Holland Page

http://ourworld.compuserve.com/homepages/paulvanv/homepage.htm

Archives
[http://ourworld.compuserve.com/homepages/paulvanv/dutcharc.htm]
Central Bureau for Genealogy, The Hague
[http://ourworld.compuserve.com/homepages/paulvanv/surncbg.htm]
Dutch Surname Lists
[http://ourworld.compuserve.com/homepages/paulvanv/surnlist.htm]
Links
[http://ourworld.compuserve.com/homepages/paulvanv/dutchweb.htm]

Royal Dutch Society for Ancestry
    [http://ourworld.compuserve.com/homepages/paulvanv/gegenoot.htm]
Van Voorthuijsen Genealogy
    [http://ourworld.compuserve.com/homepages/paulvanv/vvsurn.htm]
Women, Maiden Name Online Index
    [http://www.itsnet.com/~pauld/cgi-bin/ksh_search]

## National Library of the Netherlands     http://www.konbib.nl/home-en.html

Prins Willem-Alexanderhof 5          Phone   (011) +31  070-3140911
2595 BE                              Fax     (011) +31  070-3140450
The Hague, Netherlands               Telex   34402 KB NL
                                     E-mail  info@konbib.nl

Mail to:
P.O. Box 90407
2509 LK
The Hague, Netherlands

Collections and Services
    [http://www.konbib.nl/kb/sbo/bdi-en.html]
Links, Archives in The Netherlands
    [http://www.konbib.nl/ing/nlmenu/archiefe.htm]
Links, Libraries in The Netherlands
    [http://www.konbib.nl/kb/sbo/bdi-en.html#netherlands]

# NEW ZEALAND

## National Archives of New Zealand

10 Mulgrave Street                   Phone   (011) +64-4 499-5595
Thorndon,Wellington                  Fax     (011) +64-4 495 6210
                                     E-mail  national.archives@dia.govt.nz

Mail to:
P.O. Box 12-050
Wellington, New Zealand

Genealogy Guides
    [http://www.archives.dia.govt.nz/publictt.htm #Family History]
Records Centres
    [http://www.archives.dia.govt.nz/recordt.htm]
Services
    [http://www.archives.dia.govt.nz/servicet.htm]

## New Zealand National Library

P.O. Box 1467                        Phone   (011) +64-4 4743-000
Wellington, New Zealalnd             Fax     (011) +64-4 474-3035
                                     E-mail  atl@natlib.govt.nz

Index New Zealand
    [http://www.natlib.govt.nz/docher/innz/]
Manuscripts and Archives
    [http://www.natlib.govt.nz/public/virtual_tour/rarebook.html]
New Zealand National Bibliography
    [http://www.natlib.govt.nz/docher/nznb.htm]

New Zealand/Pacific Collection
  [http://www.natlib.govt.nz/public/virtual_tour/]
Oral History
  [http://www.natlib.govt.nz/public/virtual_tour/oral_history.html]

# NORWAY
## The National Library of Norway          http://www.nbr.no/e_index.html

| | |
|---|---|
| Postboks 2674 Solli | Phone   (011) +47 22 55 33 70 |
| N-0203 Oslo, Norway | Fax      (011) +47 22 55 38 95 |
| | E-mail   nb@nbr.no |

Online Periodicals
  [http://rosa.nbr.no/etids/eltids.html]
Services
  [http://www.nbr.no/tjen/e_index.html]
Teleslekt, Digital 1865, 1900  Census, etc.
  [http://www.nbr.no/nbrana/teleslekt/e_index.html]

## Norwegian American Historical Society
  http://www.stolaf.edu/stolaf/other/naha/naha.html

| | |
|---|---|
| 1510 Street Olaf Avenue | Fax      (507) 646-3734 |
| Northfield, MN 55057-1097 | E-mail   naha@stolaf.edu |

## State Archives of Norway          http://www.riksarkivet.no/national.html

| | |
|---|---|
| Folke Bernadottes vei 21 | Phone   (011) +47 22 02 26 00 |
| Postboks 4013 Ulleväl Hageby | Fax      (011) +47 22 23 74 89 |
| N-0806 Oslo, Norway | E-mail   ra@riksarkivet.dep.telemax.no |

Directory, Archives in Norway
  [http://www.riksarkivet.no/adresses.html]
Genealogy
  [http://www.riksarkivet.no/access.html]

# POLAND
## National Library of Poland          http://portico.bl.uk/gabriel/en/countries/poland.html

| | |
|---|---|
| Al. Niepodleglosci 213 | Phone  (011) +48-22 608-2999 |
| P.O. Box  36 | Fax      (011) +48-22 255-251 |
| 00973 Warszawa 22, Poland | E-mail   biblnar@biblnar.bn.org..pl |

Overview
  [http://portico.bl.uk/gabriel/en/countries/poland.html]

# PORTUGAL
## Association of Portugese Librarians, Archivists and Records Managers
  http://www.sdum.uminho.pt/bad/defaulte.htm

| | |
|---|---|
| R. Morais Soares, 43C-1° dto | Phone  (011) +351 1 8154479 |
| 1900 Lisbon, Portugal | Fax      (011) +351 1 8154508 |
| | E-mail   badbn@mail.telepac.pt |

Links, Portugese Archives and Libraries
[http://www.sdum.uminho.pt/bad/bibpte.htm]

## National Library of Portugal http://www.ibl.pt/ibl/homep0i.html

Campo Grande 83 - 1751
Lisbon, Codex, Portugal

Phone  (011) +351 (1) 7950130
Fax     (011) +351 (1) 7933607
E-mail  spires@ibl.pt

Collections
[http://portico.bl.uk/gabriel/en/countries/portugal.html]
Overview
[http://www.ibl.pt/ibl/homebni.html]

# PUERTO RICO
## Puerto Rican /Hispanic Genealogical Society http://linkdirect.com/hispsoc/

25 Ralph Avenue
Brentwood, NY 11717-2424

E-mail  latinoblue@aol.com

Marriage Records
[http://linkdirect.com/hispsoc/parish.htm]

# ROMANIA
## National Library of Romania http://portico.bl.uk/gabriel/en/countries/romania.html

Strada Ion Ghica 4, sector 3, cod 79708
Bucuresti, Romania

Phone  (011) +40 1 614 24 34
Fax     (011) +40 1 312 33 81

Overview
[http://portico.bl.uk/gabriel/en/countries/romania.html]

# SAN MARINO
## State Library http://portico.bl.uk/gabriel/en/countries/marino.html

San Marino
Contrada Omerelli 13
Palazzo Valloni
47031 San Marino
Republic of San Marino

Phone  (011) +378 88 22 48
Fax     (011) +378 88 22 95

Overview
[http://portico.bl.uk/gabriel/en/countries/marino.html]

# SCANDINAVIA
## Nordic Libraries Information Servers
http://www.ub2.lu.se/resbyloc/Nordic_lib.html#den

Denmark
[http://www.ub2.lu.se/resbyloc/Nordic_lib.html#den]

Estonia
    [http://www.ub2.lu.se/resbyloc/Nordic_lib.html#est]
Faroe Islands
    [http://www.ub2.lu.se/resbyloc/Nordic_lib.html#far]
Finland
    [http://www.ub2.lu.se/resbyloc/Nordic_lib.html#fin]
Iceland
    [http://www.ub2.lu.se/resbyloc/Nordic_lib.html#ice]
Latvia
    [http://www.ub2.lu.se/resbyloc/Nordic_lib.html#lat]
Links, International
    [http://www.ub2.lu.se/resbyloc/Nordic_lib.html#int]
Lithuania
    [http://www.ub2.lu.se/resbyloc/Nordic_lib.html#lit]
Norway
    [http://www.ub2.lu.se/resbyloc/Nordic_lib.html#norw]
Sweden
    [http://www.ub2.lu.se/resbyloc/Nordic_lib.html#swe]

## Scandinavian Genealogy Pages                http://www.algonet.se/~floyd/scandgen/

E-mail   floyd@algonet.se

Links to Site and Guides
    [http://www.algonet.se/~floyd/scandgen/]


# SCOTLAND

## *Outstanding Site*

### General Register Office for Scotland          http://www.open.gov.uk/gros/groshome.htm

New Register House                          Phone    (011) +44 (0) 131 314 0380
Edinburgh, Scotland EH1 3YT                 Fax      (011) +44 (0) 131 314 4400
                                            E-mail   gros@gtnet.gov.uk
Census Records, 1801-1991
    [http://www.open.gov.uk/gros/histcens.htm]
Civil Registration
    [http://www.open.gov.uk/gros/regscot.htm]
First Names, Most Popular
    [http://www.open.gov.uk/gros/names.htm]
Surnames, Most Common
    [http://www.open.gov.uk/gros/surnames.htm]

## Glasgow City Archives
    http://users.colloquium.co.uk/~glw_archives/src001.htm

The Mitchell Library                        Phone    (011) +44  0141 287 2910
North Street                                Fax      (011) +44 0141 226 8452
Glasgow, Scotland G3 7DN                    E-mail   glw_archives@cqm.co.uk

Genealogy Sources
    [http://users.colloquium.co.uk/~glw_archives/src005.htm]
Services
    [http://users.colloquium.co.uk/~glw_archives/src004.htm]

## Link O Mania Scotland on the Web        http://link-o-mania.com/scotgen.htm

E-mail   webmaster@link-o-mania.com

Links
    [http://link-o-mania.com/scotgen.htm]

## National Library of Scotland        http://www.nls.uk/

George IV Bridge                  Phone   (011) +44 (0) 131-226-4531
Edinburgh, Scotland EH1 1EW       Fax     (011) +44 (0) 131-459-4532
                                  E-mail  webmaster@nls.uk
                                          enquiries@nls.uk Special Collections

Bibliography of Scotland
    [http://www.nls.uk/online/bos_srch.htm]
Manuscripts
    [http://www.nls.uk/collect/msscoll.htm]

## Registers of Scotland Executive Agency
    http://www.open.gov.uk/ros/roshome.htm

Meadowbank House                  Phone   (011) +44 (0) 131-659-6111 ext. 3083
153 London Road                   Fax     (011) +44 (0) 131-479-3688
Edinburgh, Scotland EH8 7AU       E-mail  keeper@ros2.ros.btx400.co.uk

Chancery and Judicial Registers
    [http://www.open.gov.uk/ros/roshome.htm#Chancery]
Land Register of Scotland
    [http://www.open.gov.uk/ros/roshome.htm#LandRegister]
Searching the Land and Sasine Registers
    [http://www.open.gov.uk/ros/roshome.htm#Searching]

## Scottish Association of Family History Societies
    http://www.taynet.co.uk/users/scotgensoc/

51/3 Mortonhall Road
Edinburgh, Scotland EH9 2HN

Overview
    [http://www.taynet.co.uk/users/scotgensoc/]

## Scottish Genealogy Society        http://www.taynet.co.uk/users/scotgensoc/

15 Victoria Terrace               Phone   (011) +44 (0) 131 220 3677
Edinburgh, Scotland EH1 2JL       Fax     (011) +44 (0) 131 220 3677
                                  E-mail  scotgensoc@sol.co.uk

Overview
    [http://www.taynet.co.uk/users/scotgensoc/]

# SINGAPORE
## National Archives of Singapore        http://www.museum.org.sg/nas/nasprofile.html

140 Hill Street                   Phone   (011) +65 375-2510
Hill Street Building              Fax     (011) +65 339-3583
Singapore 179369                  E-mail  joeann_lee@nhb.gov.sg

Oral History Collection
  [http://www.museum.org.sg/nas/ohr.html]
Public Records
  [http://www.museum.org.sg/nas/public/public.html]

# SLOVAKIA

## *Outstanding Site*

### Slovak and Carpatho-Rusyn Genealogy Research Pages
  http://www.iarelative.com/slovakia.htm

| | |
|---|---|
| 2233 Keeven Lane | Phone (314) 831-9482 |
| Florissant, MO 63031 | E-mail Greg@iarelative.com |

Searching in Slovakia, E-mail Discussion Group
  [http://www.iarelative.com/search.htm]

### Slovak National Library in Matica slovenská
  http://www.matica.sk/

| | |
|---|---|
| Novomeského 32 | Phone (011) +42 842 31371 |
| 036 52 Martin, Slovakia | Fax (011) +42 842 331 60 |
| | E-mail snk@esix.matica.sk |

Collections
  [http://www.matica.sk/snk/eng/snk-a.html]
Libraries and Information, Newsletter, Fulltext
  [http://www.matica.sk/snk/ki/uvodki.html]
National Bibliography
  [http://www.matica.sk/snk/bibl.html]

# SLOVENIA

### Archives of the Republic of Slovenia
  http://www.sigov.si/cgi-bin/spl/ars/1.htm?language=slo

| | |
|---|---|
| Zvezdarska 1, p.p. 70 | Phone (011) +386-61/125.12.22 |
| 1000 Ljubljana, Slovenia | Fax (011) +386-61/216.551 |
| | E-mail ars@ars.sigov.mail.si |

Overview
  [http://www.sigov.si/cgi-bin/spl/ars/3.htm?language=slo]

## *Outstanding Site*

| Slovene Archives | http://www.pokarh-mb.si/home.html |
|---|---|
| Zvezdarska 1, p.p. 70 | Phone (011) +386-61/125.12.22 |
| 1000 Ljubljana, Slovenia | Fax (011) +386-61/216.551 |
| | E-mail ars@ars.sigov.mail.si |

Development of Archives in Slovenia
  [http://www.pokarh-mb.si/develop.html]
Genealogy Research in Slovenia
  [http://genealogy.ijp.si/]
Genealogy Sources
  [http://www.pokarh-mb.si/menua.html]

Links, Slovene Archives
    [http://www.pokarh-mb.si/today.html]
Slovene Archives Society
    [http://www.pokarh-mb.si/drustvo.html]


# SPAIN
## Buber's Basque Page                    http://weber.u.washington.edu/~buber/basque.html

E-mail  buber@u.washington.edu

Basque Genealogy Tips
    [http://weber.u.washington.edu/~buber/Basque/search.html]
Généalogie en Pays Basque et Béarn
    [http://www.worldnet.fr/~agenphi/ge64home.html]
Surnames
    [http://weber.u.washington.edu/~buber/Basque/surname.html]


## National Library of Spain               http://www.bne.es/

Paseo de Recoletos 20-22               Phone   (011) +34-1-580-78-23
28071, Madrid, Spain                   E-mail  info@bne.es

Collections
    [http://www.bne.es/men-int1.html]


# SWEDEN
## National Archives of Sweden             http://sunsite.kth.se/DDS/ra/RIKSARK.HTM

Box 12541                              Phone   (011) +46  08-737 63 50
102 29 Stockholm, Sweden               Fax     (011) +46  08-737 64 74

Archives Database, ARKIS
    [http://sunsite.kth.se/DDS/ra/DATABAS/ARKIS.HTM]
Collections
    [http://sunsite.kth.se/DDS/ra/BESTANDS.HTM]
Directory, Archives in Sweden
    [http://sunsite.kth.se/DDS/ra/FSERVICE.HTM]
Directory, Landsarkiven
    [http://sunsite.kth.se/DDS/ra/LANDSARK.HTM]
Heraldry
    [http://sunsite.kth.se/DDS/ra/DEPO/HERALDIK.HTM]
Library
    [http://sunsite.kth.se/DDS/ra/BIBLIOTE.HTM]


## National Library of Sweden              http://www.kb.se/eng/kbstart.htm

Box 5039                               Phone   (011) +46 08 463 40 00
S-102 41 Stockholm, Sweden             Fax     (011) +46 08 463 40 04
                                       E-mail  kungl.biblioteket@kb.se

Links
    [http://www.kb.se/eng/utlankar.html]
Overview
    [http://www.kb.se/sekt.htm]

# SWITZERLAND
## Swiss Federal Archives                    http://www.admin.ch/bar/

Archivstrasse 24                          E-mail  Chistoph.Graf@mbox.bar.admin.ch
CH-3003 Bern, Switzerland

Database Projects
    [http://www.admin.ch/bar/de/b2/bar24.htm]
Inventories
    [http://www.admin.ch/bar/de/b2/bar22.htm]

## Swiss National Library                    http://www.snl.ch/

Hallwylstraße 15                    Phone   (011) +41 31 322 89 01
CH-3003 Bern, Switzerland           Fax     (011) +41 31 322 84 63
                                    Telex   912691
                                    E-mail  jauslin@clients.switch.ch
Overview
    [http://portico.bl.uk/gabriel/en/countries/swiss.html]

# TRINIDAD AND TOBAGO
## National Library and Information System of Trinidad and Tobago
    http://www.trinidad.net/library/

Knox Street and Pembroke Streets    Phone   (809) 623 6124 Heritage Library
Port of Spain, Trinidad and Tobago          (809) 624 1130 Public Library
                                    E-mail  heritage@trinidad.net Heritage Library
                                            nalis@trinidad.net Public Library
Heritage Library
    [http://www.trinidad.net/library/newperl.htm#her]
Public Libraries
    [http://www.trinidad.net/library/newperl.htm#pub]

# TURKEY
## National Library of Turkey               http://www.mkutup.gov.tr/

Bahçelievler 06490                  Phone   (011) +90 312 2126 200 / 339
Ankara, Turkey                      E-mail  altinay@www.mkutup.gov.tr
                                            davut@mkutup.gov.tr
Overview
    [http://portico.bl.uk/gabriel/en/countries/turkey.html]

# UKRAINE
## Ukrainian Genealogy and Heritage Page          http://ic.net/~ggressa/ukr.html

Directory of Archives in Ukraine
    [http://ic.net/~ggressa/ukrarc.html]
Queries

[http://ic.net/~ggressa/ukrsname.html]
Surnames, Origin and Meaning of Ukranian
    [http://ic.net/~ggressa/names.html]
Ukranian Information Page
    [http://soma.crl.mcmaster.ca/ukes/ua-links/ukraine.html]

# VENEZUELA
## National Library of Venezuela

Edificio Nueva Sede Foro Libertador      Phone    (011) (582) 564.20.55 Archives
Final Avenida Panteón      Fax      (011) (582) 564.36.69
Caracas, Venezuela

Manuscripts and Archives
    [http://www.bnv.bib.ve/MANUS.HTM]
Public Libraries
    [http://www.bnv.bib.ve/biblio.htm]
Rare Books and Manuscripts
    [http://www.bnv.bib.ve/librora.htm]
Reference Services
    [http://www.bnv.bib.ve/refer.htm]
Venezuelan Collection
    [http://www.bnv.bib.ve/liraro.htm]

# FAMILY ASSOCIATIONS

## Abercrombe Family Association

http://www.america.net/~ka4wujga/

305 8th Street South
Cordele, GA 31015

E-mail   ka4wujga@sowega.net

Overview
[http://www.america.net/~ka4wujga/]

## Acuff Archives Home Page

http://www.public.usit.net/mcnamara/archives.htm

P.O. Box 6764
Knoxville, TN 37919-0764

Phone   (423) 397-6939
E-mail   acuff@rmgate.pop.indiana.edu
mcnamara@usit.net

Overview
[http://www.public.usit.net/mcnamara/archives.htm]

## Clan Agnew

http://www.tartans.com/clans/Agnew/agnew.html

1920 Highland Avenue
Irwin, PA 15642

Phone   (412) 864-5625
Fax      (412) 864-9358
E-mail   70617.2421@compuserve.com

Overview
[http://www.tartans.com/clans/Agnew/agnew.html]

## Albert Family

http://www.humboldt1.com/~cealbert/index.html

E-mail   cealbert@humboldt1.com
vonda@nauticom.net

Lists
[http://www.humboldt1.com/~cealbert/index.html]

## Alden Kindred of America, Inc.

http://members.aol.com/calebj/alden_kindred.html

E-mail   ACWCrane@aol.com

Alicia C. Williams
Alden Kindred Genealogist
18 Martin's Cove Road
Hingham, MA 02043

John Alden Data
[http://members.aol.com/calebj/alden.html]

## Alford American Family Association

http://www.alford.com/alford/aafa/homepage.html

P.O. Box 1586
Florissant, MO 63031-1586

Phone   (314) 831-8648
E-mail   72154.1610@compuserve.com

## Allison Family Clan

http://home1.gte.net/als/index.htm

E-mail   allison@gte.net

Family History
[http://home1.gte.net/als/index.htm]

## Alton-Allton-Aulton Family Association
http://members.aol.com/altonnews/aaaafn.htm

| | |
|---|---|
| 15510 Laurel Ridge Road<br>Dumfries, VA 22026-1019 | Phone  (703) 670-4842<br>E-mail  CCAlton@aol.com |

Overview
[http://members.aol.com/altonnews/aaaafn.htm]

## Clan Anderson
http://www.tartans.com/clans/Anderson/anderson.html

1947 Kensington High Street
Lilburn, GA 30247

Overview
[http://www.tartans.com/clans/Anderson/anderson.html]

## Anderson Table of Contents
http://www.qni.com/~anderson/AndersonTOC.html

E-mail  anderson@qni.com

Overview
[http://www.qni.com/~anderson/AndersonTOC.html]

## Applegate Genealogy Web Site
http://www2.vcn.com/~applegatej/

E-mail  applegatej@vcn.com

Overview
[http://www2.vcn.com/~applegatej/]

## Arduini Family Home Page
http://homepage.interaccess.com/~arduinif/

E-mail  arduinif@interaccess.com

Overview
[http://homepage.interaccess.com/~arduinif/]

## Arledge/Aldridge Family Homepage
http://www.tx3.com/~arledge/

E-mail  mtngoat@flash.net

## Clan Armstrong
http://www.tartans.com/clans/Armstrong/armstrong.html

102 Yorkshire Drive
Pittsburgh, PA 15238
      E-mail  ClanArmstrong@ClanMember.Org

Discussion Group
[http://www.discribe.ca/cgi-bin/net.Thread.pl/message/4/1/4]

### *Outstanding Site*

## Armstrong Genealogy and History Center
http://www.gendex.com/~guest/martin/enigma/index.htm

E-mail  ClanArmstrong@ClanMember.Org

Overview
[http://www.gendex.com/~guest/martin/enigma/index.htm]

## Arnold Family

http://members.aol.com/chukarnold/index.htm
http://members.aol.com/kinseeker6/arnold.html

E-mail  Kinseeker6@aol.com

Overview
[http://members.aol.com/chukarnold/index.htm]

## Arsenault Web Page

http://www.rbmulti.nb.ca/acadie/familles/arsenaul/arseno.htm

59, rue Arran
Campbellton, New Brunswick,
E3N 1L3, Canada

Phone  (506) 857-0908
Fax     (506) 383-7440
E-mail  djsavard@nbnet.nb.ca

Dictionnaire des ARSENAULT d'Amérique du Nord
[http://www.rbmulti.nb.ca/acadie/familles/arsenaul/arseno.htm#Diction]

### Outstanding Site

## Arthur Family Register

http://ourworld.compuserve.com/homepages/David_Ramsdale/text.htm

E-mail  100421.3433@compuserve.com

## Asbill Family

http://arapaho.nsuok.edu/~asbill/asbillpg.htm

E-mail  asbill@cherokee.nsuok.edu

Rt. 2, Box 261
Sallisaw, OK 74955

## Ascolani Family Page

http://www.geocities.com/Heartland/2999/ascolani.htm

E-mail  d-ascolani@geocities.com

Ascolani Families in the United States
[http://www.geocities.com/Heartland/2999/f-us.htm]

## Attwood Family

http://www.bhm.tis.net/~datwood/index.htm

E-mail  datwood@traveller.com

Overview
[http://www.bhm.tis.net/~datwood/index.htm]

## Austill-Austell Family Genealogy Page

http://members.aol.com/elzyaust/index.htm

E-mail  deaustill@aol.com

Biography Index
[http://members.aol.com/elzyaust/bioindex.htm]

## Austin Families Association of America

http://www.rahul.net/afaoa/

E-mail    afaoa@rahul.net

1 Shorter Circle
Rome, GA 30165-0432

Some Descendants of Daniel Austin and Mary Brackett of Maine, 1772
[http://www.rahul.net/afaoa/daniel1.htm]
Some Descendants of Richard Austin of Charlestown, Massachusetts, 1638
[http://www.rahul.net/afaoa/richard1.htm]

Some Descendants of Samuel Austin of Massachusetts, 1669
    [http://www.rahul.net/afaoa/samuel1.htm]

## Autry Genealogy and History    http://www.genealogy.org/~heck/AUTRY.html

17570 Alabama Highway 10                E-mail  ed.autry@truman.nara.gov
Thomasville, AL 36784                           autry@stlouis.sgi.com

Autry Bulletin, Journal
    [http://www.genealogy.org/~heck/afabulletin.html]

## The Clan Baillie    http://www.tartans.com/clans/Baillie/baillie.html

Discussion Group
    [http://www.discribe.ca/cgi-bin/net.Thread.pl/message/4/1/5]

## The Clan Baird    http://www.tartans.com/clans/Baird/baird.html

2708 South Hooker Street
Denver, CO 80236-2508

Discussion Group
    [http://www.discribe.ca/cgi-bin/net.Thread.pl/message/4/1/6]

## Bard Family Genealogy Web Page
    http://www.localnet.com/~cbard/Bard_Gen_Page/Bard_Cool_Gen_index.html

5876 Woodlee Court                      Phone   (716) 648-7180
Orchard Park, NY 14127                  E-mail  cbard@localnet.com

Overview
    [http://www.localnet.com/~cbard/Bard_Gen_Page/Bard_Cool_Gen_index.html]

## Barkley One-Name Study    http://www.mediasoft.net/ScottC/bons.htm

2509 Placid Place                       Phone   (757) 468-5829
Virginia Beach, VA 23456-3743           Fax     (757) 468-8210
                                        E-mail  clbarkle@leo.vsla.edu
Overview
    [http://www.mediasoft.net/ScottC/bons.htm]

### *Outstanding Site*

## Barney Family Historical Association    http://www.gossamer-web.com/barney/

                                        E-mail  bfha@aol.com

Listserv Discussion Group
    To subscribe, just enter SUB BARNEY in the message area
    [majordomo@bolis.com]

## Descendants of Robert Bartlett Society
    http://members.aol.com/calebj/society_bartlett.html

David T. Robertson                      E-mail  FQAN23A@prodigy.com
P.O. Box 309
Quincy Center, MA  02269-0309

Overview
    [http://members.aol.com/calebj/society_bartlett.html]

## Baumgartner Genealogy Page and Family Tree
http://www.feist.com/~slvwng/baum.html

| Heritage Images | Fax | (316) 284-0068 |
| Newton, KS 67114 | E-mail | slvwng@feist.com |

Overview
[http://www.feist.com/~slvwng/baum.html]

## Belknap Family History Page
http://home.earthlink.net/~cwtram/belknap.html

E-mail cwtram@earthlink.net

Belknap Searchers
[http://home.earthlink.net/~cwtram/b-search.html]

## Belknap-Belnap Home Page
http://www.belknap.net/011596a.htm

E-mail alan@belknap.net

Overview
[http://www.belknap.net/011596a.htm]

## Berry Family Genealogy
http://ourworld.compuserve.com/homepages/JOHNBERRY/homepage.htm

E-mail 73023.525@compuserve.com
john_berry@msn.com

Overview
[http://ourworld.compuserve.com/homepages/JOHNBERRY/homepage.htm]

## Beverly Family Newsletter
http://ourworld.compuserve.com/homepages/rbeverly/bfamnews.htm

E-mail 76517.734@compuserve.com

Lists
[http://ourworld.compuserve.com/homepages/rbeverly/bfamnews.htm]

## The Family Bible
http://www.geocities.com/Heartland/2252/

E-mail bascs@wizard.com

Listserv Discussion Group
To subscribe, just enter SUB BIBLE in the message area
[MAISER@rmgate.pop.indiana.edu]

## World-wide Bickerstaff Home Page
http://www.meetoz.com.au/g_day/bickfam.html

E-mail jbstaff@nerak.companet.net

Sources
[http://www.meetoz.com.au/g_day/bickfam.html]

## Bickham Family Home Page
http://www.geocities.com/Heartland/5126/

E-mail rebick@bigfoot.com

Genealogy
[http://www.geocities.com/Heartland/5126/]

## Bigelow Society

http://www.slic.com/bigelow/bigsoc1.htm

8 Prospect Circle
Massena, NY 13662-1702

E-mail  bigelow@slic.com

Lists
[http://www.slic.com/bigelow/bigsoc1.htm]

## Birley Family

http://ourworld.compuserve.com/homepages/David_Birley_/

1022 North Main Street
Tulsa, OK 74106-5171

Phone  (918) 599-7680

Links
[http://ourworld.compuserve.com/homepages/David_Birley_/]

## Official Blackburn Genealogy Home Page

http://members.aol.com/srwings/blackburn/home.htm

E-mail  srwings@aol.com

Genealogy
[http://members.aol.com/srwings/blackburn/home.htm]

## Blackwell Genealogy Study Group Online Web Notebook

http://oasys.drc.com/~blackwell/

72 Center Street
Groveland, MA 01834-1016

Phone  (508) 373-2358
E-mail  dblackwell@S1.DRC.COM

Genealogy
[http://oasys.drc.com/~blackwell/]

## Blair's of the World

http://home.sprynet.com/sprynet/srblair/

E-mail  sblair@sprynet.com

Links
[http://home.sprynet.com/sprynet/srblair/]

## Bonjour Family Genealogy

http://www.geocities.com/Heartland/2700/index.html

E-mail  BonjourF@ix.netcom.com

Overview
[http://www.geocities.com/Heartland/2700/index.html]

## L'Association Des Boutin D'amérique Inc.

http://www.lookup.com/homepages/85950/boutin.html

P.O. Box 6700
Sillery Québec, Canada G1T 2W2

E-mail  bboutin@quebectel.com

Genealogy
[http://www.lookup.com/homepages/85950/boutin.html]

## The Clan Boyd
http://www.tartans.com/clans/Boyd/boyd.html

5 Little Creek Lane
Fredericksburg, VA 22405-3643

Online Discussion List
[http://www.discribe.ca/cgi-bin/net.Thread.pl/message/4/1/7]

## Boyd Family Pages
http://www.swgroup.com/Boyd/

E-mail  webmaster@swgroup.com
sam.boyd@hub.ima.infomail.com

Boyd-L, Mailing List
[http://www.swgroup.com/Boyd/boyd-l/list.html]

## Governor William Bradford Compact
http://members.aol.com/calebj/society_bradford.html

Mrs. L.W. Pogue, Historian  Phone  (301) 654-7233
5204 Kenwood Avenue
Chevy Chase, MD 20815-6604

William Bradford Data
[http://members.aol.com/calebj/bradford.html]

## Bradlee Genealogical Society Homepage
http://www.bradlee.org/

P.O. Box 268  Phone  (614) 777-5900
Hilliard, OH 43026-0268  E-mail  BOB@BRADLEE.ORG

Lists
[http://www.bradlee.org/]

## Brady Family
http://www.cavannet.ie/history/families/brady.htm

Sources
[http://www.cavannet.ie/history/families/brady.htm]

## Branscombe Home Page
http://www.geocities.com/Athens/2155/home.html

Holywell  E-mail  branscombe@globalnet.co.uk
Northumberland, England

Family Data
[http://www.geocities.com/Athens/2155/home.html]

## Brasswell Family Page
http://www.pbmo.net/suburb/braswell/

2192 Penny Street  E-mail  braswell@pbmo.net
Poplar Bluff, MO 63901-2542

Genealogy
[http://www.pbmo.net/suburb/braswell/]

## *Outstanding Site*

# Bratton, Britton, Brayton, Bratten, Brattan, Brattin, Brittin and Brattain Worldwide Clan
http://grampa.GenDex.COM/~guest/69751/BrattonHomePage/

E-mail  sbratton@borderlessworld.com

Data
[http://grampa.GenDex.COM/~guest/69751/BrattonHomePage/]

# Elder William Brewster Society
http://members.aol.com/calebj/society_brewster.html

William Brewster Data
[http://members.aol.com/calebj/brewster.html]

## *Outstanding Site*

# Brink Family USA                http://www.geocities.com/~brinkfamily/

E-mail  john@vegetarians.com

Genealogy
[http://www.geocities.com/~brinkfamily/]

# Brown Family Genealogical Society        http://www.brownfamily.org/index.html

19 Terrace Street                     Phone    (603) 357-3742
Keene, NH 03431-3210                  E-mail   hbrown@top.monad.ne

Links
[http://www.brownfamily.org/genlinks.html]
Newsletter
[http://www.brownfamily.org/sample.html]

# The Clan Bruce              http://www.tartans.com/clans/Bruce/bruce.html

Online Discussion Group
[http://www.discribe.ca/cgi-bin/net.Thread.pl/message/4/1/8]

# The Clan Buchanan           http://www.tartans.com/clans/Buchanan/buchanan.html

Clan Buchanan Society
P.O. Box 1110
Moutrie, GA 31776-1110

Clan Finder, Find Your Clan
[http://www.tartans.com/genalogy.htm]

# Bump Family                http://medgen.iupui.edu/~rebecca/bump.html

E-mail  rebecca@medgen.iupui.edu

Bump Family E-mail Discussion List
[http://medgen.iupui.edu/~rebecca/Bump/bumptalk.html]
Family Queries
[http://medgen.iupui.edu/~rebecca/Bump/bumpqueries.html]

## The Clan Butter                    http://www.tartans.com/clans/Butter/butter.html

E-mail Discussion Group
    [http://www.discribe.ca/cgi-bin/net.Thread.pl/message/4/1/10]


## Callaway Family Association    http://www.lgc.peachnet.edu/callaway/cfa1.htm

P.O. Box 23                                E-mail  kaye@mentor.lgc.peachnet.edu
Waverly, MO 64096

Callaway Journal
    [http://www.lgc.peachnet.edu/callaway/cfa5.htm]
Census Records
    [http://www.lgc.peachnet.edu/callaway/cfa4.htm]


## The Clan Cameron        http://www.tartans.com/clans/Cameron/cameron.html

4876 Thomas Boulevard
Geneva, OH 44041

E-mail Discussion Group
    [http://www.discribe.ca/cgi-bin/net.Thread.pl/message/4/1/11]


## Camp Family Association
    http://www.new-jerusalem.com/genealogy/barbara/camp.htm

4200 Oak Knoll Drive           E-mail  Tfarris268@aol.com
Carmichael, CA 95608

Camp Family Newsletter
    [http://www.new-jerusalem.com/genealogy/barbara/NEWSLETT.HTM]
Census, 1850, Camp Data
    [http://www.new-jerusalem.com/genealogy/barbara/CENSUS.HTM]


## Campbell Database              http://www.csihq.com/campbell/

                                   E-mail  djohnson@csihq.com
Census Records
    [http://www.csihq.com/campbell/censussel.html]
Marriage Records
    [http://www.csihq.com/campbell/marriage_state.html]
Social Security Death Index
    [http://www.csihq.com/campbell/ssn_select.html]


### *Outstanding Site*

## Clan Campbell Society of North America    http://www.ccsna.org/

6412 Newcastle Road            Phone   (910)864-4231
Fayetteville, NC 28303-2137    E-mail  WJC FAYNC@aol.com

Online Forums, Discussion Groups
    [http://www.best.com/~hyle/ccsna/forums/]

## Cannon Family Home Page

http://www.geocities.com/Heartland/3952/canhp.htm

E-mail  auntjean@rapidramp.com

Online Discussion List
[http://www.geocities.com/Heartland/3952/canhp.htm#mail]
Queries
[http://www.geocities.com/Heartland/3952/canhp.htm#query]

## Carroll Cables

http://members.aol.com/kinseeker6/carroll.html

E-mail  Kinseeker6@aol.com

Carroll Research Room
[http://www.kudonet.com/~scarroll/menu.html]
Carroll Surname Page
[http://www.kudonet.com/~scarroll/carrollpage.html]
Queries
[http://members.aol.com/KinSeeker6/carrollquery.html]

## Cato Family Home Page

E-mail  bpalmer@BIHS.net

Data by State
[http://www.webkeeper.com/cato/c.html]

## Cerruti Family

http://cerrutiusa.com/gene.html

1876 Muttontown Road
Muttontown, NY 11791

E-mail  leo@cerrutiusa.com

Meaning of Cerruti Surname
[http://cerrutiusa.com/gene.html#anchor5282275]

## Chamberlain Chain

http://www.cet.com/~weidnerc/

2206 West Borden Road
Spokane, WA 99224-9263

E-mail  weidnerc@cet.com

Overview and Links to Related Sites
[http://www.cet.com/~weidnerc/]

## World Chamberlain Genealogical Society
http://www.livingonline.com/~welmar/wcs.html

E-mail  welmar@livingonline.com

Chamberlain Member Links
[http://www.livingonline.com/~welmar/bureau.html]

## Chapman Family Association

http://ourworld.compuserve.com/homepages/sonfield/

Overview
[http://ourworld.compuserve.com/homepages/sonfield/]

## Pierre Chastain Family Association

http://www.kopower.com/%7Ejimchstn/

8555 South Lewis, Cottage 21-A
Tulsa, OK 74137

E-mail  gerreok@aol.com

Publications
    [http://www.kopower.com/%7Ejimchstn/#Publication Information]
Queries
    [http://www.kopower.com/%7Ejimchstn/query.htm]

## The Clan Chattan      http://www.tartans.com/clans/Chattan/chattan.html

P.O. Box 14070            E-mail  fiona.m3@ukonline.co.uk
Edinburgh, Scotland, EH10 7YD

Online Discussion Group
    [http://www.discribe.ca/cgi-bin/net.Thread.pl/message/4/1/13]

## Chenoweth Family Site      http://www.accessone.com/~jegge/chenweth.htm

Site Menu, 125 Topics
    [http://www.accessone.com/~jegge/chenmenu.htm]

## Cheyne Home Page      http://www.gensource.com/family/Cheyne/

                    E-mail  cheyne@goodnet.net

Overview
    [http://www.gensource.com/family/Cheyne/]

## Chou Clansmen Association of America
    http://www.lookup.com/Homepages/76274/home.html

P.O. Box 4604          E-mail  ex964@cleveland.freenet.edu
Honolulu, HI 96812-4604          lchow@idis.com

ChouOnline 1997
    [http://www.idis.com/ChouOnline/]

## Chrisman Family      http://www.cs.cmu.edu/~chrisman/genealogy/

                    E-mail  ldc+@cs.cmu.edu

Overview
    [http://www.cs.cmu.edu/~chrisman/genealogy/]

## Churchill Family History Page      http://www.geocities.com/Heartland/Plains/4460/

                    E-mail  SCChurchill@worldnet.att.net
Churchill Family in America and England
    [http://www.geocities.com/Heartland/Plains/4460/]

## The Clan Cockburn      http://www.tartans.com/clans/Cockburn/cockburn.html

Online Discussion Group
    [http://www.discribe.ca/cgi-bin/net.Thread.pl/message/4/1/14]

## The Clan Comyn-Cumming      http://www.tartans.com/clans/Comyn/comyn.html

1477 Holly Oaks Lake Road, West    E-mail  davec@jax-inter.net
Jacksonville, FL 32225

Online Discussion Group
    [http://www.discribe.ca/cgi-bin/net.Thread.pl/message/4/1/15]

## Crandall Family Association
http://pages.prodigy.com/NY/cranfamassoc/index.html

P.O. Box 1234
Hudson, NY 12534-0308

E-mail  eperry@capital.net

Overview
   [http://pages.prodigy.com/NY/cranfamassoc/intro.html]

## Cree Family History Society
   http://ourworld.compuserve.com/homepages/Mike_Spathaky/creefhs.htm

11009 Country Knoll
Austin, TX 78750

E-mail  74312.2637@compuserve.com

Cree Family Newsletter
   [http://ourworld.compuserve.com/homepages/Mike_Spathaky/cn8a.htm]

## The Clan Currie
http://www.tartans.com/clans/Currie/currie.html

P.O. Box 541
Summit, NJ  07902-0541

Phone   (908) 273-3509

Online Discussion Group
   [http://www.discribe.ca/cgi-bin/net.Thread.pl/message/4/1/16]

## Curtain Family Home Page
http://www.datadepot.com/~dcurtin/

E-mail  dcurtin@earthlink.net

Overview
   [http://www.datadepot.com/~dcurtin/]

## The Clan Davidson
http://www.tartans.com/clans/Davidson/davidson.html

Online Discussion Group
   [http://www.discribe.ca/cgi-bin/net.Thread.pl/message/4/1/17]

## Deng Clan Genealogy
http://www.geocities.com/Tokyo/3998/deng.htm

E-mail  thien@alfred.med.monash.edu.au

Descendants of Deng Man Ji
   [http://www.geocities.com/Tokyo/3998/deng.htm]

## Dennett Family History Page
http://members.aol.com/cdennett/genealogy/index.html

52 Black Walnut Drive
Rochester, NY 14615-1259

Phone   (716) 865-7012
E-mail  dennett@juno.com

Surname List
   [http://members.aol.com/cdennett/genealogy/SURNAMES.html]

## Doane Family Association, Inc.
http://www.doane.edu/dfa/dfa2.htm

7375 S.W. 172nd Street
Aloha, OR 97007

Phone   (703) 430-2255
FAX     (703) 430-2474
E-mail  kblairh@aol.com

Lists
   [http://www.doane.edu/dfa/dfa2.htm ]

## The Clan Donald                       http://www.tartans.com/clans/MacDonald/donald.html

22 Lincoln Street                        E-mail  Mllasalle@aol.com
Downers Grove, IL 60515

Online Discussion Group
      [http://www.discribe.ca/cgi-bin/net.Thread.pl/message/4/1/38]

## The Clan Donnachaidh
      http://www.tartans.com/clans/Donnachaidh/robertson.html

P.O. Box 742
Edinburgh, Scotland EH4 3UP

Online Discussion Group
      [http://www.tartans.com/clans/Donnachaidh/robertson.html]

## Pilgrim Edward Doty Society          http://members.aol.com/calebj/society_doty.html

Mary Lee Merill                          E-mail  tr917@mail.idt.net
HCR 69 Box 666
Friendship, ME 04547

Edward Doty Data
      [http://members.aol.com/calebj/doty.html]

## Clan Douglas Society                  http://www.hom.net/~jdarbyd/
                                         http://www.tartans.com/clans/Douglas/douglas.html

701 Montgomery Highway, Suite 209        Phone   (205) 822-9670
Birmingham, AL 35216-1833                E-mail  jdarbyd@hom.net

Online Discussion Group
      [http://www.discribe.ca/cgi-bin/net.Thread.pl/message/4/1/19]

## The Clan Dunbar                       http://www.tartans.com/clans/Dunbar/dunbar.html

                                         E-mail  dtracy@nortel.ca

Lion and Thistle, Newsletter
      [http://www.tartans.com/clans/Dunbar/WebStuff/Lion_Thistle.html]
Online Discussion Group
      [http://www.discribe.ca/cgi-bin/net.Thread.pl/message/4/1/20]

## Francis Eaton Society                 http://members.aol.com/calebj/eaton.html

60 Sheridan Street
Brockton, MA 02402-2852

Francis Eaton Data
      [http://members.aol.com/calebj/eaton.html]

## The Clan Elliott Society              http://www.tartans.com/clans/Eliott/eliott.html

Rt. 1, Box 229                           Phone   (812) 597-5996
Morgantown, IN 46160                     E-mail  jelliot@scican.net

Clan Elliott Society of Canada
    [http://www.spots.ab.ca/~selliott/ECSintro.html]
Online Discussion Group
    [http://www.discribe.ca/cgi-bin/net.Thread.pl/message/4/1/21]

# The Clan Erskine

http://www.tartans.com/clans/Erskine/erskine.html
http://www.clan.com/tp/clan/erskine/
http://www.almac.co.uk/es/webclans/dtog/erskine.html

Online Discussion Group
    [http://www.discribe.ca/cgi-bin/net.Thread.pl/message/4/1/22]

# The Clan Farquharson

http://www.tartans.com/clans/Farquharson/farquharson.html

1510 Dora Lane
St. Paul, MN  55106

E-mail  FinlaAer@aol.com

Online Discussion Group
    [http://www.discribe.ca/cgi-bin/net.Thread.pl/message/4/1/23]

# Clan Ferguson

http://www.tartans.com/clans/Fergusson/fergusson.html

3061 O'Brien Drive
Tallahassee, FL 32308

Discussion Group
    [http://www.discribe.ca/cgi-bin/net.Thread.pl/message/4/1/24]

# Flynn Forum

http://pages.prodigy.com/GPGJ41A/flynn.htm

366 Baldwin Road
Patterson, NY 12563

E-mail  charlie_flynn@prodigy.com

Flynn Clan of America
    [http://pages.prodigy.com/GPGJ41A/clan.htm]
Flynn Links
    [http://pages.prodigy.com/GPGJ41A/links.htm]
Online Newsletter
    [http://pages.prodigy.com/GPGJ41A/newslet.htm]

# Folsom Family Association of America

http://www.isp-inter.net/folsom/#sn

13501 S.W. 128th Street, Suite 207
Miami, FL 33186

Phone   (305) 233-4334
E-mail  miamibig@isp-inter.net

# The Clan Forbes

http://www.tartans.com/clans/Forbes/forbes.html

P.O. Box 1118
Alexandria, VA  22313

Online Discussion Group
    [http://www.discribe.ca/cgi-bin/net.Thread.pl/message/4/1/25]

## The Clan Fraser

http://www.tartans.com/clans/Fraser/fraser.html
http://mh102.infi.net/~leathrwd/

P.O. Box 1526
Chico, CA 95927

Phone   (916) 896-0329
E-mail   bdhood01@wiley.butte.cc.ca.us

Online Discussion Group
   [http://www.discribe.ca/cgi-bin/net.Thread.pl/message/4/1/26]

## Fuller Society

http://members.aol.com/calebj/society_fuller.html

Mary Lee Merill
HCR 69 Box 666
Friendship, ME 04547

Edward Fuller Data
   [http://members.aol.com/calebj/efuller.html]
Samuel Fuller Data
   [http://members.aol.com/calebj/sfuller.html]

## Pierre Garcelon Family

http://www.lib.usf.edu/spccoll/guide/g/garcelon/page1.html

Mon Adieu À Mes Chers Enfans
   [http://www.lib.usf.edu/spccoll/guide/g/garcelon/page1.html]

## Gauer Family Home Page

http://users.uniserve.com/~morbeus/

E-mail   morbeus@uniserve.com

GAUER's who came to North America
   [http://users.uniserve.com/~morbeus/immgr.html]

## GEEnealogy, Gee Family

http://www.infogo.com/homepage/mgee/genealo.html

960 Columbia 15
Magnolia, AR 71753

E-mail   mgee@infogo.com

Descendants of Charles and Hannah Gee
   [http://www.infogo.com/homepage/mgee/geefam.html]

## The Clan Gordon

http://www.tartans.com/clans/Gordon/gordon.html

101 Sunset Drive
Newberg, OR  97132

Phone   (503) 538-1216

Online Discussion Group
   [http://www.discribe.ca/cgi-bin/net.Thread.pl/message/4/1/27]

## Gore Family Connection

http://www.yucca.net/jglocke/

P.O. Box 474
Portales, NM 88130-0474

E-mail   jglocke@yucca.net

Overview
   [http://www.yucca.net/jglocke/]

## The Clan Graham Society

http://www.tartans.com/clans/Graham/graham.html

128 Kensington Drive
High Point, NC 27262-7316

E-mail  71116.702@CompuServe.COM

Online Discussion Group
   [http://www.discribe.ca/cgi-bin/net.Thread.pl/message/4/1/28]

## The Clan Grant Society

http://www.tartans.com/clans/Grant/grant.html

372 Churchtown Road
Narvin, PA  17555

Clan Grant Centre
Duthil
Strathspey, Scotland PH23 3ND

Online Discussion Group
   [http://www.discribe.ca/cgi-bin/net.Thread.pl/message/4/1/29]

## Graves Family Association

http://www.andrews.edu/~calkins/gravesfa.html

261 South Street
Wrentham, MA 02093-1504

E-mail  kgraves239@aol.com
          dfrh81a@prodigy.com

Links
   [http://www.andrews.edu/~calkins/gravesfa.html ]

## The Clan Gregor Center

http://lionach.org/cgc/

8 Greenhill Place
Edinburgh, Scotland EH10 4BR

E-mail  gregors@emplus.demon.co.uk

Online Discussion Group
   [http://www.discribe.ca/cgi-bin/net.Thread.pl/message/4/1/41]

## The Clan Gunn

http://www.tartans.com/clans/Gunn/gunn.html

3034 Swiss Drive
Santa Clara, UT 84765

Online Discussion Group
   [http://www.discribe.ca/cgi-bin/net.Thread.pl/message/4/1/30]

## Highland Clan Gunn History and Genealogy
   http://pw1.netcom.com/~jolin/index.html

E-mail  jolin@ix.netcom.com

Genealogy
   [http://pw1.netcom.com/~jolin/index.html]

## The Clan Hamilton

http://www.tartans.com/clans/Hamilton/hamilton.html
http://fox.nstn.ca/~hamlet/

P.O. Box 71881
Charleston, SC 29415

Online Discussion Group
   [http://www.discribe.ca/cgi-bin/net.Thread.pl/message/4/1/31]

## Harris Family Genealogy

http://www.radiks.net/nrharris/genea.html

E-mail  nrharris@radiks.net

Data
[http://www.radiks.net/nrharris/genea.html]

## Harvey Genealogist

http://www.geocities.com/Heartland/6575/

P.O. Box 307
Watertown, MN 55388

Phone   (612) 955-3701
E-mail  thg@geocities.com

Newsletter
[http://www.geocities.com/Heartland/6575/]

## The Clan Henderson Society of the U.S. and Canada

http://www.tartans.com/clans/Henderson/henderson.html
http://www.pe.net/~kenet/ClanHenderson/

711 - 136th Street East
Bradenton, FL 34202-9684

Online Discussion Group
[http://www.discribe.ca/cgi-bin/net.Thread.pl/message/4/1/32]

## Hinshaw Family Association

http://www.blueneptune.com/~hinshaw/

15227 Quito Road
Saratoga, CA 95070

E-mail  hinshaw@blueneptune.com

Data
[http://www.blueneptune.com/~hinshaw/]

## Holden Genealogy Page

http://www.flash.net/~robinl/holden.html

E-mail  robinl@flash.net

Holden Genealogy
[http://www.flash.net/~robinl/holdeng1.html]

## Honeywell Family Association

http://members.aol.com/parkshoney/hfa.html

785 Island Way
Clearwater, FL 34630

E-mail  ParksHoney@aol.com

Family History
[http://members.aol.com/parkshoney/hfa.html]

### *Outstanding Site*

## Houston Family Association

http://clanhuston.com/huston.htm

4413 West Oakland
Broken Arrow, OK 74012-9123

E-mail  hoefling@ix.netcom.com

Overview
[http://clanhuston.com/huston.htm]

## Pilgrim John Howland Society    http://members.aol.com/calebj/society_howland.html

Mrs. Bernard J. Elfring
65 North Street
Tarmouth, ME 04096

John Howland Data
   [http://members.aol.com/calebj/howland.html]

## Hurlbut/Hurlburt Genealogy    http://www.idsonline.com/userweb/hurlburt/

5325 Beech Road
Marlow Heights, MD 20748

Phone   (301) 899-1705
Fax     (301) 899-8624
E-mail  jhurlburt@ids2.idsonline.com

Records
   [http://www.idsonline.com/userweb/hurlburt/]

## Ingersoll Family Research    http://www.geocities.com/Heartland/1163/inger.htm

P.O. Box 8255
Kodiak, AK 99615-8255

Phone   (907) 486-3250
E-mail  Ingersoll@Techie.Com

Overview
   [http://www.geocities.com/Heartland/1163/inger.htm]

## James Family Surname Web    http://members.aol.com/daisy467/james.htm

E-mail  hen1@mail.idt.net

James Family Online Discussion List
   [http://members.aol.com/daisy467/james.htm]

### *Outstanding Site*

## Jarvis Family    http://www.erols.com/fmoran/

E-mail  fmoran@erols.com
        chlamy@acpub.duke.edu

Data
   [http://www.erols.com/fmoran/]

## Johnson Family Tree    http://jspweb.com/johnson/

E-mail  ft@ix.netcom.com

Genealogy
   [http://jspweb.com/johnson/]

## The Clan Johnstone    http://www.tartans.com/clans/Johnstone/johnstone.html

4 Dale Avenue
Shelby, OH 44875

Phone   (419) 347-3337
E-mail  bshuler@awod.com

Online Discussion Group
   [http://www.discribe.ca/cgi-bin/net.Thread.pl/message/4/1/33]

## Jordan Genealogy Website    http://jordan.digital.net/

E-mail  jordan@jordan.digital.net

Civil War Data
   [http://jordan.digital.net/civil_war/civilwar.html]

Jordan Bibliography
    [http://jordan.digital.net/reference/books.html]
Jordan Family Association
    [http://jordan.digital.net/reference/websites.html]
Jordan Online Discussion List
    [http://jordan.digital.net/reference/websites.html]
Revolutionary War Data
    [http://jordan.digital.net/rev_war/revwar.html]

## Judson Connection            http://www.geocities.com/TheTropics/1926/judson.html

E-mail  jdolby@airmail.net

Links
    [http://www.geocities.com/TheTropics/1926/judson.html]

## The Clan Keith            http://www.tartans.com/clans/Keith/keith.html

Online Discussion Group
    [http://www.discribe.ca/cgi-bin/net.Thread.pl/message/4/1/34]

## Kelton Family Home Page            http://rampages.onramp.net/~ekelton/index.html

E-mail  ekelton@onramp.net.

Kelton Links
    [http://rampages.onramp.net/~ekelton/other.html]
Surname Index
    [http://rampages.onramp.net/~ekelton/name.html]

### *Outstanding Site*

## Kemp Family Association            http://www.geocities.com/TheTropics/1926/

E-mail  XDJN57A@prodigy.com

Links Worldwide
    [http://www.geocities.com/TheTropics/1926/]

## The Clan Kennedy            http://www.tartans.com/clans/Kennedy/kennedy.html

520 Harrison Avenue
Cambridge, OH  43725

Online Discussion Group
    [http://www.discribe.ca/cgi-bin/net.Thread.pl/message/4/1/35]

## Clan Kerr            http://www.tartans.com/clans/Kerr/kerr.html

Online Discussion Group
    [http://www.discribe.ca/cgi-bin/net.Thread.pl/message/4/1/71?user=&email=&dept
    h=4&detail=description&lastread=7]

## The Clan Kincaid            http://www.tartans.com/clans/Kincaid/kincaid.html

2864 Baylis Court
Ann Arbor, MI  48108

Online Discussion Group
    [http://www.discribe.ca/cgi-bin/net.Thread.pl/message/4/1/36]

## Kinsella Home Page
http://home.eznet.net/~kinsella/kinsella.htm

E-mail Jimmkin@aol.com

Kinsella Genealogy
[http://home.eznet.net/~kinsella/kinsella.htm]

## Genealogy of the Kinsellas
http://home.eznet.net/~kinsella/genealogy/geneal.htm

Links
[http://home.eznet.net/~kinsella/genealogy/geneal.htm]

## Kirk Society
http://www.kennet.demon.co.uk/kirksoc.htm

E-mail 106314.1235@compuserve.com

Overview
[http://www.kennet.demon.co.uk/kirkinfo.htm]

### Outstanding Site

## Lacy Family
http://www.polaris.net/~legend/

E-mail stlacy@freenet.fsu.edu

E-mail Discussion Group
[http://www.polaris.net/~legend/wwwboard/]

## Clan Lamont Society of North America
http://www.e-gram.com/~websites/lamont/lamont.htm
http://www.tartans.com/clans/Lamont/lamont.html

P.O. Box 29221
Columbus, OH 43229

E-mail ogdenj@msn.com

Online Discussion Group
[http://www.discribe.ca/cgi-bin/net.Thread.pl/message/4/1/76]

### Outstanding Site

## Laprath - One Family in America
http://www.accessone.com/~jegge/laprath.htm

P.O. Box 1188
Woodinville, WA 98072

E-mail jegge@accessone.com

Overview
[http://www.accessone.com/~jegge/laprath.htm]

## Clan Leslie
http://www.mindspring.com/~jdleslie/index.html
http://www.tartans.com/clans/Leslie/leslie.html

1824 Village Road
Glenshaw, PA 15116-2111

E-mail jdleslie@mindspring.com

Leslie Castle
[http://www.regionlink.com/grampian/tartan/members/leslie.html]

## Clan Lindsay
http://www.tartans.com/clans/Lindsay/lindsay.html

Online Discussion Group
   [http://www.discribe.ca/cgi-bin/net.Thread.pl/message/4/1/88]

## Clan Little Society of Scotland
http://www.nwrain.net/~little/
http://www.tartans.com/clans/Little/little.html

2600 Mason Lake Drive West
Grapeview, WA 98546

Phone   (360) 427-8994
E-mail   irlkwl@nwrain.com

Genealogy
   [http://www.nwrain.com/~little/ancestry.htm]
Online Discussion Group
   [http://www.discribe.ca/cgi-bin/net.Thread.pl/message/4/1/69?user=&email=&dept
   h=4&detail=description&lastread=7]

## The Clan MacArthur
http://www.tartans.com/clans/MacArthur/macarthur.html

24479 Audubon Drive
Brooksville, FL 34601

E-mail   rcmcartor@erols.com.

Online Discussion Group
   [http://www.discribe.ca/cgi-bin/net.Thread.pl/message/4/1/37]

## Clan MacCallum/Malcolm Society
http://www.sni.net/~dougm/ClanMacCallum/

E-mail   dougm@csn.net
         majordomo@lists.csn.net

Clan Listserv
   Subscribe clan-mccallum

## McDonald/MacDonald Links
http://www.erie.net/~fti/mcdonald.html

E-mail   fti@erie.net

Heritage
   [http://www.erie.net/~fti/mcdonald.html#heritage]

## The Clan MacDougall
http://www.tartans.com/clans/MacDougall/macdougall.html

901 Woodlawn Drive
Lexington, NC 27292

Online Discussion Group
   [http://www.discribe.ca/cgi-bin/net.Thread.pl/message/4/1/39]

## Clan MacDuff Society of America
http://www.crimson.com/scots_austin/macduff.htm

3524 Slade Boulevard
Fort Worth, TX 76116

E-mail   targe5436@aol.com

## The Clan MacFarlane Society of North America
http://www.tartans.com/clans/MacFarlane/macfarln.htm

207A Brian Drive
Ardmore, AL 35739

E-mail   macfarland@glis.net

Genealogy Database
[http://www.deosil.com/macfarlane/database.html]
Online Discussion Group
[http://www.discribe.ca/cgi-bin/net.Thread.pl/message/4/1/65]

# The Clan MacGillivray
http://www.tartans.com/clans/MacGillivray/macgillivray.html

---

7233 North Denver Avenue                      Phone   (503) 286-8740
Portland, OR 97217

Online Discussion Group
[http://www.discribe.ca/cgi-bin/net.Thread.pl/message/4/1/40]

# McGovern Family                    http://www.cavannet.ie/history/families/mcgovern.htm

---

Cavan, Ireland Line
[http://www.cavannet.ie/history/families/mcgovern.htm]

# The Clan MacGregor
http://www.tartans.com/clans/MacGregor/macgregor.html
http://lionach.org/cgc/

---

The Clan Gregor Center                      E-mail  gregors@emplus.demon.co.uk
8 Greenhill Place
Edinburgh, Scotland,  EH10 4BR

Online Discussion Group
[http://www.discribe.ca/cgi-bin/net.Thread.pl/message/4/1/41]

# Clan McIntosh Home Page          http://www.applink.net/tmcint01/genmcint/index.htm

---

                                            E-mail  01@applelink.net
McIntosh Links
[http://www.applink.net/tmcint01/genmcint/index.htm]

# The Clan MacIntyre
http://www.tartans.com/clans/MacIntyre/macintyre.html

---

Online Discussion Group
[http://www.discribe.ca/cgi-bin/net.Thread.pl/message/4/1/74]

# The Clan MacKay                    http://www.tartans.com/clans/MacKay/mackay.html

---

Online Discussion Group
[http://www.tartans.com/clans/MacKay/mackay.html]

# The Clan MacKenzie
http://www.tartans.com/clans/MacKenzie/mackenzie.html

---

580 Rebecca Street
Oakville, Ontario, Canada L6K 3N9

Online Discussion Group
[http://www.discribe.ca/cgi-bin/net.Thread.pl/message/4/1/42]

## The Clan MacKinnon Society of North America, Inc.
http://www.tartans.com/clans/MacKinnon/mackinnon.html

4012 Tyndale Drive
Jacksonville, FL 32210

E-mail  Wolfdanser@aol.com

Online Discussion Group
[http://www.discribe.ca/cgi-bin/net.Thread.pl/message/4/1/43]

## The Clan MacKintosh
http://www.tartans.com/clans/MacKintosh/mackintosh.html

46715 Lynnhaven Square
Sterling, VA 20165-6478

Online Discussion Group
[http://www.discribe.ca/cgi-bin/net.Thread.pl/message/4/1/44]

## McKusick Family Association Home Page
http://www.metrolink.net/~mckusick/

345 Sheridan Avenue
Satellite Beach, FL 32937-3045

Phone  (407) 773-8698
E-mail  wd4bts@metrolink.net

## The Clan MacLachlan
http://www.tartans.com/clans/MacLachlan/maclachlan.html

1475 Beringer
San Jacinto, CA 92583

E-mail  jacobite@shirenet.com

CMANA Constitution
[http://www.tartans.com/clans/MacLachlan/society/mission.html]
CMANA History
[http://www.tartans.com/clans/MacLachlan/society/society.html]
Online Discussion Group
[http://www.discribe.ca/cgi-bin/net.Thread.pl/message/4/1/45]

## Clan MacLachlan Worldwide        http://www.ShireNet.com/MacLachlan/

119 Wrightwood Place
Sterling, VA 20164

## The Clan MacLaine        http://www.tartans.com/clans/MacLaine/maclaine.html

6909 Raspberry Plain Place
Springfield, VA 22153

E-mail  lorne@nn.independent.co.za

Online Discussion Group
[http://www.discribe.ca/cgi-bin/net.Thread.pl/message/4/1/46]

## The Clan MacLannan
http://www.tartans.com/clans/MacLennan/maclennan.html

8100 West Crestline Avenue
Littleton, CO 80123

Phone  (303) 932-2939
E-mail  winthescot@aol.com

Online Discussion Group
   [http://www.discribe.ca/cgi-bin/net.Thread.pl/message/4/1/48]
Upcoming Events
   [http://www.tartans.com/clans/MacLennan/society/visit.html]

# Clan MacLaren Society of North America
   http://members.aol.com/Rapmack/maclaren.html
   http://people.delphi.com/salsoft/maclaren.html

3632 Lakeside Drive
Louisville, TN 37777

Phone   (423) 970-2926
E-mail   rapmack@aol.com

Newsletter
   [http://people.delphi.com/salsoft/MacStand.html]

# The Clan Maclean
http://www.tartans.com/clans/MacLean/maclean.html

Online Discussion Group
   [http://www.discribe.ca/cgi-bin/net.Thread.pl/message/4/1/53]

# McLean.net
http://www.mclean.net/

E-mail   FreePage@McLean.net

Family History and Links
   [http://www.mclean.net/]

# The Clan MacLellan
   http://www.tartans.com/clans/MacLellan/maclellan.html

1947 West 153rd Street
Gardena, CA 90249

E-mail   sirrob@juno.com

Online Discussion Group
   [http://www.discribe.ca/cgi-bin/net.Thread.pl/message/4/1/47]

# The Clan MacLeod
http://www.tartans.com/clans/MacLeod/macleod.html

Online Discussion Group
   [http://www.discribe.ca/cgi-bin/net.Thread.pl/message/4/1/49]

# The Clan MacMillan
   http://www.tartans.com/clans/MacMillan/macmillan.html

36752 Berkshire Drive
Madera, CA  93638

Phone   (209) 645 6979

Online Discussion Group
   [http://www.discribe.ca/cgi-bin/net.Thread.pl/message/4/1/73]

# The Clan MacNeil
http://www.tartans.com/clans/MacNeil/macneil.html
http://acm.org/~davidhsmith/clanmacn.html

1824 Stoneyridge Drive
Charlotte, NC 28214-8341

Phone   (704) 399-1134
E-mail   RMcne9487@aol.com

Annual Gathering
   [http://acm.org/~davidhsmith/CLANMACN.HTM#GFMHMeet]

Online Discussion Group
[http://www.discribe.ca/cgi-bin/net.Thread.pl/message/4/1/50]
Septs
[http://acm.org/~davidhsmith/MORECLAN.HTM#MoreSepts]

## The Clan MacNicol    http://www.tartans.com/clans/MacNicol/macnicol.html

E-mail  bnicol@cnsnet.net

Online Discussion Group
[http://www.discribe.ca/cgi-bin/net.Thread.pl/message/4/1/51]

## *Outstanding Site*

## Clan Macpherson Association
http://www.clan-macpherson.org/
http://www.tartans.com/clans/MacPherson/macpherson.html

1910 Collier Drive          Phone  (800) 362-6579
Fern Park, FL 32730         E-mail  mhuirich@getnet.com

Homelands, Scotland
[http://www.clan-macpherson.org/clan5.html]
Museum
[http://www.clan-macpherson.org/clan4.html]
Online Discussion Group
[http://www.discribe.ca/cgi-bin/net.Thread.pl/message/4/1/70?user=&email=&dept
h=4&detail=description&lastread=7]
Urlar, Newsletter, Fulltext
[http://www.clan-macpherson.org/publctns.html]

## McReynolds Family Research Center   http://www.midtown.net/~clanman/

E-mail  redshank@mail.europa.com

Family History and Links
[http://www.midtown.net/~clanman/]

## The Clan MacTavish
http://www.tartans.com/clans/MacTavish/mactavish.html

E-mail  dunardry@istar.ca

Online Discussion Group
[http://www.discribe.ca/cgi-bin/net.Thread.pl/message/4/1/52]

## The Clan Maxwell    http://www.tartans.com/clans/Maxwell/maxwell.html

282 Shamrock Court
Oshawa, Ontario, Canada L1J 6X9

Online Discussion Group
[http://www.discribe.ca/cgi-bin/net.Thread.pl/message/4/1/55]

## The Clan Moffat    http://www.tartans.com/clans/Moffat/moffat.html

412 Windstream Drive        Phone  (770) 438-7402
Marietta, GA 30060-7380     Fax    (770) 438-6151
                            E-mail  74044.610@compuserve.com

Online Discussion Group
[http://www.discribe.ca/cgi-bin/net.Thread.pl/message/4/1/56]

## Clan Montgomery Society International
http://www3.sk.sympatico.ca/monta/cmsi/

E-mail   monta@sk.sympatico.ca

Searchable Databases
[http://www.gendex.com/users/monty/cmsi/cmsi/data/]

## The Clan Mowatt                    http://www.tartans.com/clans/Mowat/mowat.html

P.O. Box 3002                          Phone   (813) 422-6252
Haines City, FL 33845-3002             Fax     (813) 421-2818
                                       E-mail  chef@sentex.net
Online Discussion Group
[http://www.discribe.ca/cgi-bin/net.Thread.pl/message/4/1/57]

## The Clan Murray Society            http://www.tartans.com/clans/Murray/murray.html

803 Evergreen Drive                    E-mail   Murrayrw@aol.com
Wyomissing, PA 19610

Online Discussion Group
[http://www.discribe.ca/cgi-bin/net.Thread.pl/message/4/1/68?user=&email=&dept
h=4&detail=description&lastread=7]

## The Clan Napier                     http://www.tartans.com/clans/Napier/napier.html

                                       E-mail   pixie@cottagesoft.com
Online Discussion Group
[http://www.discribe.ca/cgi-bin/net.Thread.pl/message/4/1/58]

## Oldham Genealogical Database
http://www.rootsweb.com/~gumby/genweb/Oldham/Oldham.html

E-mail   joldham@indy.net

### *Outstanding Site*

## Oliver Clan Web Page               http://www.oliverclan.org/

E-mail   noliver@bastion.netlink.co.uk

## O'Reilly Family                     http://www.cavannet.ie/history/families/oreilly.htm

Early Origins
[http://www.cavannet.ie/history/families/oreilly.htm#early]
Peak of O'Reilly Power
[http://www.cavannet.ie/history/families/oreilly.htm#peak]
Plantation of Ulster and After
[http://www.cavannet.ie/history/families/oreilly.htm#plant]

## Pennington Family                   http://users.aol.com/SPRIVETT/pracom.htm

226 Stratford Street                   E-mail   SPrivett@aol.com
Syracuse, NY 13210-3052

Extensive Data and Links
[http://users.aol.com/SPRIVETT/pracom.htm]

## *Outstanding Site*

### Pizzo Family

http://homepage.interaccess.com/~arduinif/

E-mail  arduinif@interaccess.com

Pizzo Collection
[http://www.lib.usf.edu/spccoll/pizzo/pizzo.html]

### Clan Ramsay

http://www.tartans.com/clans/Ramsay/ramsay.html

434 Skinner Boulevard
Dunedin, FL 34698

Online Discussion Group
[http://www.discribe.ca/cgi-bin/net.Thread.pl/message/4/1/59]

## *Outstanding Site*

### Ramsdale Family Register

http://ourworld.compuserve.com/homepages/David_Ramsdale/2homepag.htm

E-mail  100421.3433@compuserve.com

Journal
[http://ourworld.compuserve.com/homepages/David_Ramsdale/2homepag.htm]

### Rathbone Register

http://www-leland.stanford.edu/~dorcas/Rathbone.html

E-mail  ct.doj@forsythe.stanford edu

Links, Rathbone Related
[http://www-leland.stanford.edu/~dorcas/Rathbone.html]

### Richmond Family Association

http://www.lib.usf.edu/spccoll/guide/for/r46for.html

Online Discussion Group
[http://users.aol.com/johnf14246/gen_mail_surnames-qr.html#RICHMOND]

Richmond Castle
[http://www.daelnet.co.uk/local/history/castles.htm#RichmondCastle]

### Robbie Family Ancestry

http://users.aol.com/mrobbie001/index.html

E-mail  MRobbie001@aol.com

Robbie Family Links
[http://users.aol.com/mrobbie001/index.html#Robbie Links]

### Thomas Rogers Society, Inc.

http://members.aol.com/calebj/society_rogers.html

Mrs. George C. Frederick
1208 Maple Avenue
Evanston, IL 60202-1217

Thomas Rogers Data
[http://members.aol.com/calebj/rogers.html]

# Clan Ross Association of the U.S.
http://www.tartans.com/clans/Ross/ross.html
http://www.cyberramp.net/~nathan/ClanRoss/welcome.html

5430 South 5th Street
Arlington, VA 22204

Phone   (703) 671-5210
E-mail   nathan@cyberramp.net

Clan History
[http://www.cyberramp.net/~nathan/ClanRoss/history.html]
Online Discussion Group
[http://www.discribe.ca/cgi-bin/net.Thread.pl/message/4/1/60]

# Scott One-name Study
http://www.mediasoft.net/ScottC/sons.htm

Clan Scott Society
Scott One-name Study
Route 1, Box 15A
Lovettsville, VA 22080-9703

Overview
[http://www.mediasoft.net/ScottC/sons.htm]

# Clan Scott, USA
http://www.tartans.com/clans/Scott/scott.html

P.O. Box 13021
Austin, TX 78711

Phone   (540) 822-5292
Fax     (540) 822-5292
E-mail   willowbend@mediasoft.net

Online Discussion Group
[http://www.discribe.ca/cgi-bin/net.Thread.pl/message/4/1/61]

# Sears Family Association
http://www.genealogy.org/~lrsears/

P.O. Box 865
Duncan, OK 73534

Phone   (405) 252-6049
E-mail   lrsears@halnet.com

Richard Sears, First Eight Generations
[http://www.genealogy.org/~lrsears/richard/index.html]
Richard Sears, Portrait
[http://www.genealogy.org/~lrsears/richard.html]
Sears Family Queries
[http://www.genealogy.org/~lrsears/query.html]

# Sharp Family in America
http://www.cosmos.org/sharp/

940 S.W. 50th Street
Oklahoma City, OK 73109

E-mail   epoole@ionet.net

Biographical Files
[http://www.cosmos.org/sharp/biograph.htm]
Databases
[http://206.153.225.6/HTML/persons.htm]
Online Discussion Group
[http://www.cosmos.org/sharp/maillist.htm]

## Shay Family
http://www.swcp.com/~dhickman/shay.html

Overview
[http://www.swcp.com/~dhickman/shay.html]

## Southworth Family Organization Home Page
http://users.aol.com/sforg/index.html

2656 Cambridge Cross Circle
Riverton, UT 84065

E-mail  kerryms@aol.com

Genealogy
[http://users.aol.com/sforg/index.html]

## Strawn and Allied Families
http://pages.prodigy.com/Strawn/nographs.htm#strawn

E-mail  strawn@prodigy.com

Family Files and Photographs
[http://pages.prodigy.com/Strawn/hstrawn.htm]

## Clan Stuart
http://www.tartans.com/clans/Stuart/stuart.html

111 Masonic Avenue
Monroe, LA 71203

Phone   (318) 343-7305

Online Discussion Group
[http://www.discribe.ca/cgi-bin/net.Thread.pl/message/4/1/62]

## Clan Sutherland
http://www.tartans.com/clans/Sutherland/sutherland.html

3611 Kelway Avenue
Charlotte, NC  28281

Phone   (800) 633-6462
E-mail  janesuth@aol.com

Online Discussion Group
[http://www.discribe.ca/cgi-bin/net.Thread.pl/message/4/1/63]

## Swann Family
http://www.geocities.com/Heartland/7533/

E-mail  swann5@earthlink.net

Overview
[http://www.geocities.com/Heartland/7533/]

## Tennent Genealogy Tree
http://www.wolfenet.com/~dtennent/Tennents.html

E-mail  dtennent@wolfenet.com

Family Records
[http://www.wolfenet.com/~dtennent/Tennents.html]

## Thien Genealogy Home Page
http://www.geocities.com/Tokyo/3998/index.html

E-mail  thien@alfred.med.monash.edu.au

Thien Family Data
[http://www.geocities.com/Tokyo/3998/index.html]

## Clan Urquhart                          http://users.visi.net/~cwt/urq-clan.txt

Family Links
    [http://users.visi.net/~cwt/urq-clan.txt]


## National Association of the Van Valkenburg Family HomePage
    http://haven.ios.com/~wordup/navvf/navvf.html

4925 Bartwood Drive                 E-mail   wordup@haven.ios.com
Route 6                                  WWKD55A@prodigy.com.
Raleigh, NC 27613-7002

Lambert van Valkenburgh
    [http://haven.ios.com/~wordup/navvf/lvvhome.html]


## Clan Wallace                           http://www.clark.net/pub/larrys/wallace/wallace.htm
                                   http://www.tartans.com/clans/Wallace/wallace.html

                                   E-mail   larrys@clark.net
Newsletter
    [http://www.clark.net/pub/larrys/wallace/clanltr.htm]
Online Discussion Group
    [http://www.discribe.ca/cgi-bin/net.Thread.pl/message/4/1/64]


## Washburn Family History Page   http://home.earthlink.net/~cwashburn/history.html

                                   E-mail   cwashburn@earthlink.net
Records
    [http://home.earthlink.net/~cwashburn/history.html]


*Outstanding Site*

## Wibe–A Family from Norway      http://www.accessone.com/~jegge/wibe.htm

P.O. Box 1188                      E-mail   jegge@accessone.com
Woodinville, WA 98072

Norwegian Roots
    [http://www.accessone.com/~jegge/wibe.htm]


## Your Williams Homepage          http://www.cu.soltec.com/~photo/

                                   E-mail   WILLIAMS@MyFamily.org
Family Lines
    [http://www.cu.soltec.com/~photo/]


## Winslow Family Association      http://members.aol.com/calebj/society_winslow.html

P.O. Box 474
Fairview, PA 16415

Edward Winslow Data
    [http://members.aol.com/calebj/ewinslow.html]

## Yoder Family Information      http://www.genealogy.org/~yoder/

E-mail  75757.3371@CompuServe.COM

Online Discussion Group
   [http://www.genealogy.org/~yoder/ylist.html]
Yoder Newsletter, Online
   [http://www.genealogy.org/~yoder/issues.html]

## Zielinski Family Journal      http://www.infi.net/~ajabby/joframe.html

E-mail  ajabby@norfolk.infi.net

Genealogy Charts
   [http://www.infi.net/~ajabby/joframe.html]

ISBN 0-8420-2718-1

90000>